# THE LEATHER BOOK

## Leather Clothes & Furniture
## You Can Make Yourself

# JO LOEB

**PHOTOGRAPHS BY TERRY CLOUGH**

**PRENTICE-HALL, INC.**
Englewood Cliffs, New Jersey

**To my daughter Stephanie**

Design by LINDA HUBER

*The Leather Book: Leather Clothes and Furniture You Can Make Yourself,* by Jo Loeb
Copyright ©1975 by Jo Loeb
All rights reserved. No part of this book may be reproduced in any form or by any means, except for the inclusion of brief quotations in a review, without permission in writing from the publisher.
Printed in the United State of America
Prentice-Hall International, Inc., London
Prentice-Hall of Australia, Pty. Ltd., Sydney
Prentice-Hall of Canada, Ltd., Toronto
Prentice-Hall of India Private Ltd., New Delhi
Prentice-Hall of Japan, Inc., Tokyo

10  9  8  7  6  5  4  3  2  1

Library of Congress Cataloging in Publication Data
Loeb, Jo
   The Leather Book.
   Includes index.
   Leather work.   2. Leather garments.
I.  Title.
TT290-L58   745.53'l   75-8629
ISBN 0-13-527705-1

# CONTENTS

# INTRODUCTION

Today the emphasis is on casual, easy living, and leather fits perfectly with this concept. It is easy to maintain, doesn't collect dust, is easy to work with, and can easily be moved, remodeled, and rearranged.

Leather doesn't have to be used only for a casual western "craftsy" look. No matter what your idea of beautiful clothes and home furnishings, leather can be made to fit in. Traditional, modern, formal, informal — anything you want can be achieved with the clothes and furniture described in this book. A few adjustments, and it's done to your individual design and taste.

The first leather pillows I made were out of two or three large scraps arranged into crazy-quilt patterns. After that I just kept getting into more complicated things. In my living room there are now two sofas (shown in the color section) — one six feet and the other seven feet long. A large floor cushion about three and one-half feet across is used as an addition to the seating area, plus numerous throw cushions of varying sizes. They have been constantly used for years by a very active child, four dogs, and a cat, besides the usual adults. They are easy to care for and the leather (if chosen correctly) seems to grow old gracefully, though I have sprayed them with a silicone spray to retard any spots or stains. Using a lint brush, hair from my pets is easily removed. Any spots that occur are brushed up with a suede brush, and a light going-over with a soft brush keeps the nap raised so that the couches look fresh and new all the time.

These pillows were all made by me; the platforms and table were made by my husband — all inexpensively. Leather just keeps on looking great, and I keep building up my collection of leather items.

"But isn't leather expensive?" people sometimes ask. That depends on what you mean by expensive — go and price furniture of comparable sizes and consider what you would normally pay if you purchased them ready-made. (And these aren't ordinary couches, but unique designs custom-made to fit our needs.) Check the prices in any store and you will know that even with luxurious leather, you are getting away cheaply as long as you make it yourself. Leather looks great and lasts so long that the pillows you make will keep getting better and better with age.

The great versatility of leather lets you create your own style and individuality. It's one of the most exclusive, luxurious, and desirable fashion materials available, and is the only fabric that really lets you change commercial patterns to your own creation. And because leather is a natural fabric, it can get away with a hand homemade look. Therefore, little imperfections don't stand out and can even enhance your garment. What other fabric allows you to punch holes, to fringe, weave, bead weave, stud, and do numerous other things to decorate it simply and easily? Floor pillows to sit on, cushions to soften a hard seat, even throw pillows, can all be works of art as well as utilitarian. Why should beauty be hung on the walls or put on shelves to be looked at? Bring it into your room and use it. You can use plain leather and give it a handmade look by sewing with leather lacings; or you can choose traditional patchwork such as used in Early American quilts, or modern geometric Mondrian-type abstractions. You can even cover a couch or jacket with your own appliqued cartoon animals, studs, zodiac signs, or anything you want.

Ready-made leather garments are extremely expensive, but I don't try to copy leather jackets or coats seen in most stores because they have no real quality that tells me they are special. I like to hand-sew here and there, mix textures and colors, and decorate and finish garments in such a way as to create a fantastic one-of-a-kind. Leather is easy to work with, and as long as you condition it once in a while (as outlined in the section on caring for leather), it will last practically forever. So again, why not make your own leather clothing to fit your own specific needs and wants? You can construct your own for a fraction of what you would normally pay — if you could even buy such exclusive designs.

In this book you will learn not only the actual construction techniques used for making up leather clothes and furniture — either by hand or machine — but also ways of adapting commercial patterns to fit leather's special needs; how to make a muslin; how to make an exact copy of (or rather from) an already-existing garment in your wardrobe; the different types of fasteners and accessories available for use with leather and how to use them; and even how to decorate ready-made garments such as dungarees with leather appliques, rhinestones, and studs.

Keep in mind that no matter how fancifully decorated these illustrated garments may be, each is perfectly fitted. So in making these you will be learning not only how to make a specific garment — such as a jacket, vest, dress, or coat — but also all the possible techniques of construction and variations of decoration. You will, therefore, be able to make any type of outfit you want, from the very tailored and conservative to the extremely flamboyant. It is fun, and what's so wonderful about making your own leather clothes and furniture is that they are exactly what *you* want: individually yours; *your* work of art, *your* creation.

# HOW TO USE THIS BOOK

This book is divided into three parts. Part One covers the basics of working in leather, and I'd advise you to either read this part first, or refer back to these specific sections at the appropriate stages of each project.

Part Two gives full instructions for specific leather furniture projects. You can start working here if you like, but again, I do recommend rereading the basics as a refresher course.

Part Three covers specific projects for leather garments, as well as general basics — such as adjusting commercial patterns, beadwork, and studding — that are particular to clothing alone.

Each section begins with a list of the tools you'll need for that project or procedure, so you can lay your materials out in advance. There are numerous tools for working with leather. Some you really need to work properly; others are superfluous. Preceding each section is a list of the ones I feel are essential for good workmanship.

The manufacturer usually gives directions with each tool. However, you may not know that a competing tool even exists, much less exactly what function it performs, and therefore may never realize there is something that could make your work easier. Moreover, once you know the specific tools and their uses, you are in a better position to judge what projects you want to do. These tools are readily available in local hobby stores, or if you can't find them locally, send to a mail-order supplier listed in the book.

Good luck, but above all, have fun!

PART I THE BASICS OF LEATHER

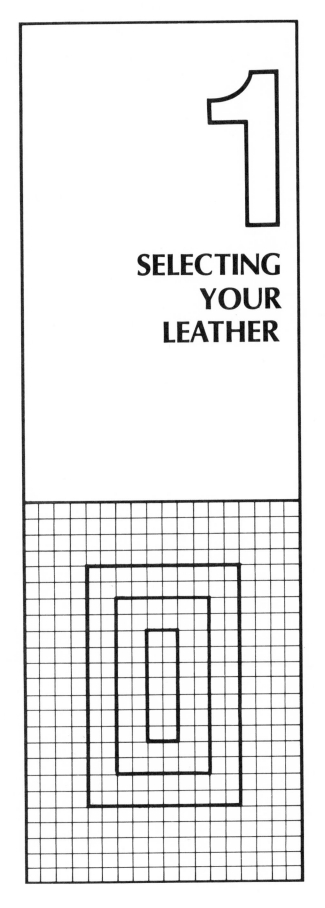

# 1

# SELECTING YOUR LEATHER

An entire volume could be written on the infinitely various types of leather and its qualities, so that "generally speaking" is the only way one can discuss it. But before working with leather, there are a few things you should know about it.

Leather is the skin of an animal. Once the animal is dead, its skin covering is referred to as a *pelt,* which has two sides: the hair (or outer) side and the flesh (or inner) side. After the hair is removed and the skin is cleaned, tanned, and transformed to leather, the hair side becomes the *grain* side. The flesh side, though cleaned, is always called the flesh side.

As soon as a pelt is removed from the carcass, it must be cured immediately or it will deteriorate. If the pelt of an animal is processed properly, it can be used for just about anything. There are two basic curing processes — salt curing and brine curing. In salt curing the pelt is first washed, then salt is generously sprinkled on the inner (flesh) side of the skin. In the brine-curing method, which is much faster and used by most commercial places, the pelt is soaked in huge vats of salt water.

Curing preserves the pelt by neutralizing all protein-destroying organisms, thus stopping any decomposition which naturally occurs after an animal is dead. The most common material used for curing is salt, which preserves the pelt in the same way that salt, when used in food, prevents it from rotting or going bad. This curing process is done in the slaughterhouse; the pelt is then transported to a tannery to be turned into leather.

When the pelt reaches the tannery it is soaked in vats of water and chemicals to restore moisture, disinfect it, and get rid of any unpleasant odors. Any flesh still remaining on the flesh side is then removed by scraping, either by hand or machine. The grain side of the pelt is then de-haired by soaking in depilatory agents — usually a lime solution — and also by a mechanical scraping process. The characteristic pores of grain leather are the former sites of hair follicles.

The pelt then goes through a process generally called *bating,* which involves three steps: washing in a de-liming solution to remove the hair; washing in a chemical alkaline solution (formerly manure) to soften the hide and prevent any further deterioration; and a final washing to rid it of all chemicals used in the two previous steps. The pelt is then "pickled" by being soaked in sulfuric acid and salts to make sure that it is in the right stage of preservation and to be tanned properly.

Actual tanning is the process of converting the pelt into leather. There are several different types of tanning processes. In *vegetable* (or bark) tanning, the pelt is soaked in a large revolving drum filled with materials derived from certain woods and plants. In *mineral* tanning, it is soaked in salts of either chromium (the most common, often referred to as chrome tanning) or aluminum. In *oil* tanning, pelts such as chamois are soaked in certain fish oils which tend to produce soft, pliable leather. Most washable leathers come from this process and usually have a yellowish-beige color. No matter what process is used, the purpose of tanning is to turn the pelt to leather.

Once tanned, the leather is then wringed or rolled to get out the moisture, and fed into a machine that looks like a horizontal band saw. Depending on the pelt's original thickness and what it is to be used for, it is split into layers — usually two. The bottom layers are called *splits*. Since there are no fibers (slender, threadlike structures interwoven as in a knitted sweater to form the structure of skin) to hold them together, they have no natural grainy texture and are far less strong than top grain. The Federal Trade Commission does not allow splits to be called genuine leather.

The leather is then shaved to make it a uniform thickness throughout, then it is dyed or stained. Oil and fatty substances are added to lubricate and give softness to the leather. It is then redried and, to avoid brittleness, conditioned in such a way as to raise the water content to about 10 to 12 percent when dry. It is then mechanically pulled and rolled to make the skin pliable.

When leather is put on a buffing machine to clean up surface blemishes, it is changed to suede. Skins used for making suede are usually ones with the grain side in bad condition in the first place. The flesh side of the skin is buffed on a machine with rollers working in all different directions until the nap is of a velvety texture. (Splits are generally sueded on both sides.) A huge exhaust machine sucks all the excess nap or *crocking* away. This does not always work, however, so some of this crocking remains as the dust that always seems to brush off suede.

Unbuffed leather is called full-grain leather, but still must have a finish put on it. This is done by applying a thin layer or layers of film to the grain to enhance the color and increase resistance to staining and abrasion. There are an infinite number of finishes, from shiny to dull and all variations in between.

Today leather is made out of every skinnable creature imaginable — even frogs. However, I use only the skins of animals normally killed for food. I don't believe in the use of furs, or the leather from any animals killed just for their pelts. That is pure waste. Why not be content with what we have — especially since these skins are the best to use anyway? Some people love to work with exotic skins, but you can get food-animal skins with the exact same properties, since different tanning and finishing processes change the entire character of leather. Processed one way, for instance, cowhide is soft and usable for garments; another tanning process renders it thick and stiff, more useful for shoes, belts, or novelty items.

The only available charts on leather are made by the companies advertising their specific product, and no one company has all of the numerous varieties. The best way to learn about leather is to feel, look, and ask merchants about the different textures and types.

Since we eat mostly mutton and beef as food, sheep and cows are the most common sources for leather in the U.S. You can buy cowhide or sheepskin embossed to simulate lizard, snake, or alligator. They are cheaper than reptile skins, of course, and also far more convenient than the skins they emulate. They don't scale, aren't as fragile, have a much larger working surface, are easily cleanable and more pliable — and therefore easier to work with. But there are other soft leathers, and those in the following list have finishes suitable for use on garments or furniture.

*Buckskin* is soft but strong yellowish-grey leather originally made from deerskin, but now made chiefly from sheepskin. The outer grain is removed and the pelt is tanned with fish oil. It is hand-washable, and can be used for just about anything. It is especially attractive for hand-laced articles.

4

*Cabretta* is soft, fine leather originally made from an Iranian sheep-goat, but now made mostly from a Brazilian hair-type rather than wool-type sheep. It has a shiny finish on the grain side and tends to stretch, which is why it should be lined. But it cleans beautifully with saddle soap and water. Use it for any article of clothing, as long as you can line it. It is fine for patchwork overlay on director's chairs, and for all appliqués, but it's a good idea to use muslin backing if you use it for cushions or any spot that comes under pressure.

*Capeskin* is leather with a silky-smooth texture made from South African sheep. It is generally used for making coats and jackets, but you can also use it for patchwork.

*Chamois* is soft yellow-beige "suede" — actually a split, as it is the underside of various kinds of leather, but much stronger because it is tanned with fish oil, thus making it more flexible and resilient. It used to be prepared from the skin of a chamois (a small goatlike antelope), but now it is usually made from sheep or lambskin, so the skins are smallish. It washes beautifully by machine or hand, makes beautiful, soft clothing (including shirts), and feels fantastic next to the skin. Because of its softness, it is excellent for using a machined zigzag stitch, but looks equally beautiful if hand-laced. Use it for anything. This is the one leather that comes by the yard in a prefabricated machine-patchworked design.

*Deerskin* is the term applied to elk and deerskin with the grain left intact. It is soft but strong, with a yellowish-beige tint. It is tanned in fish-oil and therefore washable by hand or machine. This leather is useful for almost anything.

*Garment cowhide (cattle hide)* is a soft leather with suede on one side and a smooth, full-grain leather on the other.

I'm rather partial to cowhide, as it usually comes as a very large skin and is dyed all the way through, so you can use either side and thus have two different textures from the same purchase (the suede should be cleaned with a brush and a suede cleaner, the leather with saddle soap). It comes in a variety of colors and is one of my favorites — it's soft yet strong, very easy to work with, extremely durable, and can be used for anything.

*Goatskin* is the skin from a mature goat, usually sueded and good for everything. It is very soft and easy to work with.

*Kidskin* is the skin from a young goat. It is soft and pliable and often — but not always — sueded.

*Lambskin* is a very fine suede made from young sheep or lambs. Best for garments, but should be professionally cleaned.

*Pigskin* is soft, yet firm, waterproof leather. It is easily recognizable by the little holes all over it — follicles from which the hair has been removed. It doesn't stretch much, but is pliable and can be used for anything you want. It is especially good for rough wear (hence its use in turn-of-the-century footballs) and is now generally used to make soft pigskin gloves.

*Sheepskin* is the skin from a mature sheep. It can be either sueded or have the grain left intact. The under-layer is used to make chamois.

*Sueded split* is the extra layer created when a thick skin is divided layerwise to form two or more sheets. It is characterized by being sueded on both sides, and is of a rather rough texture. It is inexpensive, and can be used for beginning projects. But since it has no fibers to hold it together, I use it for patchwork only after gluing muslin to the back to compensate for the missing fibers. Since perspiration will make splits rot, they are better for bags and garments that do not touch the skin. Clean them with a brush and suede cleaner.

People often use reasonably priced suede splits for making their first projects. They are very easy to sew, but I don't really like them and find them treacherous to work with. The real problem comes when you try to *use* the pillow or garment. Suede splits have no fibers to hold them together, so they will suddenly fall apart for no apparent reason. There is nothing worse than making an intricate design and having the center piece rip — and, believe me, it can happen with splits. So if you do plan to use them, be sure to feel them very carefully. Pull on the edges as if you were going to tear a piece of paper. Even if they don't tear, glue muslin to the back of them before sewing; this will — hopefully — hold them together. (Use a glue that dries to a soft, flexible texture, not one that dries hard as a board — Sobo or rubber cement are good bets.)

**5**

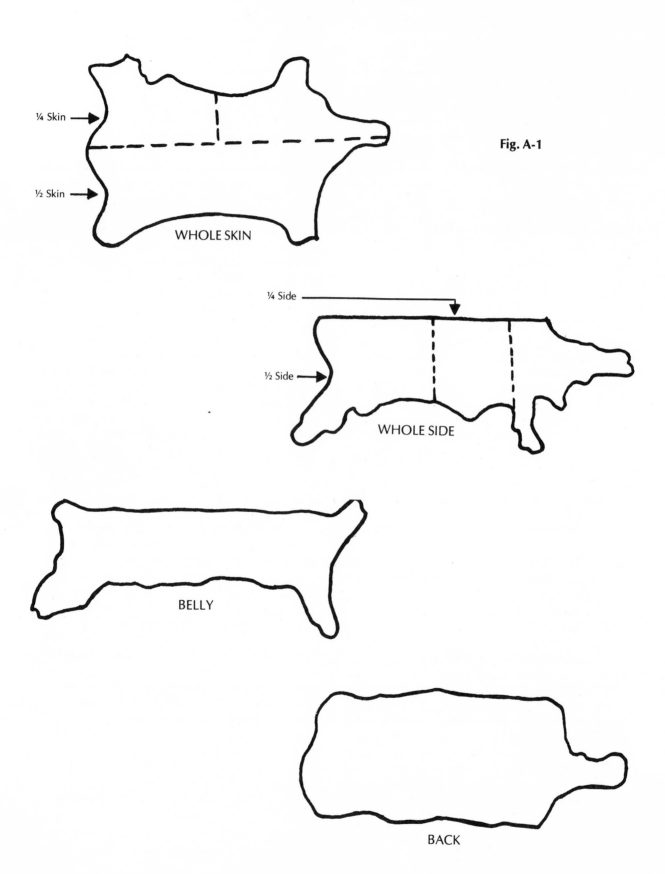

¼ Skin

½ Skin

WHOLE SKIN

Fig. A-1

¼ Side

½ Side

WHOLE SIDE

BELLY

BACK

In fact, the muslin trick is good for weak spots on any type of leather.

Again, the easiest and most important things to remember are that:

- Suede — which has a velvety texture — is the flesh side or inside of the skin after it has been buffed.
- Smooth leather is the outside of the skin, with the hair removed.
- A split is the second layer from a heavy skin, split off and thus sueded on both sides; it has no fibers to hold it together properly and is not genuine leather.

You can buy leather at hobby stores, department stores, fabric stores, tanneries, and special leather retailers.

When you go in, you will find leather usually comes in its natural shape, with an irregular outline and ragged edges. This shape corresponds to the shape of the animal skin slit down the belly from neck to tail, with extremities such as the head and feet removed (see Fig. A-1). The ragged edges and flaws are there because that is the way the animal was shaped and scarred.

These skins will come in various sizes and finishes, depending on what size animal they came from and how they were tanned and finished. The very large skins are called *hides*, the next size smaller is a *kip*, and the very small a *skin*.

Sheepskins usually measure 5 to 7 square feet and are generally sold as whole skins. Cow and calfskins run 20 to 60 square feet and are most commonly sold as a whole skin. If the skin is cut, it is usually cut to a side (or half), or a quarter. Whole skins are bought in their natural or regular shape; sides (half skins) are cut straight down the center of the backbone from head to tail; quarter skins are half skins cut across the center from the backbone to the belly as if around the "belt line." Backs are not usually sold separately, since they are the best and most expensive parts of the skin; and the belly is really not worth much, as it is the irregular part of the underbelly and doesn't have much strength (see Fig. A-1).

Leather is sold by the square foot, but not perfect square feet because of the irregular shape of skins.

After tanning, a skin is stamped with numbers indicating its area in square feet. In this system of marking, the large first number is the full square footage, and the small or last number is the remaining percentage of a square foot expressed in quarters. For example, $7^2$ would mean seven and two-quarters — or 7½—sq. ft. $0^1$ means one-quarter square foot; $0^2$ is half a square foot; $0^3$ is three-quarters of a square foot; and so forth.

Still, how much leather to buy can be a chore to figure out. If you are using scraps, it's no problem; but if you want a specific area, you must know the conversion table — basically 13 square feet to 1 yard of 54-inch fabric, and 9 square feet to 1 yard of 36-inch fabric. In addition you must allow for waste, which depends on the condition of the skins purchased, but which is usually 15 percent for large skins and 20 percent for small skins.

You therefore multiply the number of fabric yards needed by the appropriate conversion number (13 for 54-inch and 9 for 36-inch) and then add 15 or 20 percent of the total number of square feet arrived at, and you have the total number of square feet of leather that you need. For example:

If yardage requirement is 2 yards of 36-inch fabric:

**Large Skins**

$2 \times 9 = 18$
$18 \times 0.15 = 2.7$
$18 + 2.70 = 20.7$

You need: 20.7 sq. ft. of leather

**Small Skins**

$2 \times 9 = 18$
$18 \times 0.20 = 3.6$
$18 + 3.6 = 21.6$

You need: 21.60 sq. ft. of leather

If yardage requirement is 2 yards of 54-inch fabric:

**Large Skins**

2 x 13 = 26
26 x 0.15 = 3.9
26 + 3.9 = 29.9

You need: 29.9 sq. ft. of leather.

**Small Skins**

2 x 13 = 26
26 x 0.20 = 5.2
26 + 5.20 = 31.2

You need: 31.2 sq. ft. of leather.

I find that the easiest way to do it, however, is to say that for every yard of fabric, I need so many square feet of leather.

**Large Skins**

1 yard of 54″ fabric = 14.95 (15) sq. ft.
1 yard of 36″ fabric = 10.35 (10¼) sq. ft.

**Small Skins**

1 yard of 54″ fabric = 15.6 (15½) sq. ft.
1 yard of 36″ fabric = 10.8 (11) sq. ft.

Now multiply by the yardage required, and it's done:

14.95 x 2 yds. = 29.9 (30) sq. ft.
10.35 x 2 yds. = 20.70 sq. ft.

15.60 x 2 yds. = 31.20 (31) sq. ft.
10.80 x 2 yds. = 21.60 sq. ft.

Another important thing to keep in mind is the grain factor — not grain in the sense of full-grain (unbuffed) leather, but rather grain in the way it is applied to fabric. The grain in leather has to do with the growth and stretch of the animal. The grain of all your major pattern pieces should — ideally — run parallel to the backbone of the animal, so plan accordingly. Pull on the leather. See where it stretches most, and if it stretches too much. Perhaps the stretch is going the wrong way for the way you planned your skin, if so, take another skin and try it (see Section 2 for complete details). Also check the skins for scabbling (uneven dyeing).

The *grading* of leather refers to how much of the skin is usable, which depends on the number of holes, scars, and the like found on the skin. This grading is either A, B, C, D, or 1, 2, 3, 4.

Remember that the skin is graded by the *workably* good area of the skin. Grade A or 1 has the highest percentage of usable skin, B or 2 is the second, and so on down the line. Grade A or B skin means that a high percentage of the skin is free from holes, scars, and uneven tanning (scabbling). But no matter what the grading, always check for any discoloration, scars, and holes. It only takes a few minutes to look and you may save yourself a lot of time and trouble later.

Examine the skins by touch as well, so that you can find thinness and weak spots that cannot be seen by the eye. These thin spots may be caused by uneven shaving or may be simply thin areas found naturally on animal skins, but they are difficult to see. The center of the skin is the most useful area, and so thin spots any distance from the side are a special problem. Thinness in the skin makes it subject to tearing, and thin leather should never be purchased for heavy use. In addition to working out the amount you need, it's always a good idea to lay your pattern out on the leather before buying just to be sure you will have enough. Laying out your pattern also allows you to check where the flaws fall.

Don't be nervous; just remember to choose the right leather for your project. Think of what you are making, of what you'll want from the finished product. Make sure the leather you buy has all the characteristics you'll want later. Above all, try to buy leathers that will grow old gracefully and won't be bothered by a little bit of dirt. You should have some trust in whomever you buy from. Ask questions! Tell him what you have in mind and what qualities you are looking for. Feel the thickness and surface characteristics. See if you think it would suit your project as well as your taste.

If you are planning garments or articles that require small amounts of leather pieced together, you can buy lower quality leather and work around the flaws — as long as the type of leather you buy is the right type for the project. And if you find small flaws on a skin that you thought was perfect, try gluing a patch of leather or muslin to the wrong side of the leather over the flaw or weak point.

Buying in person is the best way to buy leather, of course, but if you can't find any leather outlet nearby, there are mail-order houses where you can buy leather and supplies listed in the appendix. They value your business and are generally very reliable. Some suppliers will send catalogs or charts of the types of leathers they offer, and for a small fee, some will also send leather swatches as samples. (If so, get them.)

If ordering by mail, always send converted square footage and a traced copy of your pattern, or exact measurements of whatever you're planning to make. Along with your order, write a note telling exactly what you are making and what characteristics you expect from the leather. Also specify what grade you want (I usually take top quality unless I can get a real bargain), and where you *don't* want any flaws (especially the center, unless you are using small pieces). If you have swatches, you'll of course be able to judge for yourself to a great degree, but it is still a good idea to ask for help and advice, but make it clear that you expect to receive the correct type and quality of leather for the articles you enumerate.

## TOOLS NEEDED

HEAVY BROWN PAPER
CLEAR DRESSMAKER'S RULER
MASKING TAPE
WATERPROOF FELT-TIPPED PEN
DRESSMAKER'S TRACING WHEEL
DRESSMAKER'S TRACING PAPER
SHEARS, X-ACTO KNIFE, OR RAZOR
SMALL SCISSORS
RUBBER OR LEATHER CEMENT AND
   BRUSHES

OPTIONAL

RUFFER OR SANDPAPER

# 2

# PREPARING THE LEATHER FOR SEWING — MARKING AND CUTTING

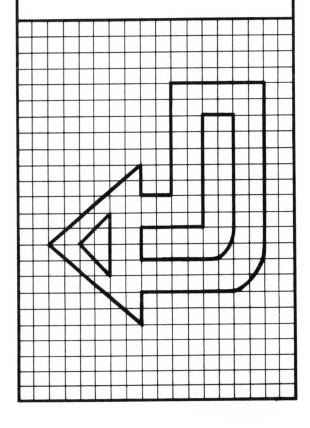

After deciding on your project, the first thing you should do is prepare a pattern for whatever you wish to make.

*Heavy brown paper,* wrapping, or "butcher" paper (or even a brown paper bag) is what I advise for making new patterns or for adding to and adjusting commercial patterns because a grade of stiff paper is needed; in general, you'll be tracing around the edges of any pattern and a very soft paper is difficult to hold flat. Its edges are easily destroyed, thus making the pattern useless.

*A transparent dressmaker's ruler* is an indispensable tool for leatherwork, useful not only for adding seam allowances or any other needed adjustments, and drawing perfectly straight lines, but also for measuring the hole-punching patterns and spacing with complete accuracy. This is a clear ruler with lines running through it clearly indicating inches, half-inches, quarter-, eighth-, and even sixteenth-inches, both vertically and horizontally (see Fig. B-1).

For specifics on pattern-making and adjusting, see Section 15 and also the individual projects discussed in parts two and three. In Section 15 you will find information on the various seams suitable for leather (see Fig. O-2), and also the methods used for adjusting commercial patterns to fit leather's special needs. In each of the other sections, full instructions are given for the making of the patterns necessary for the particular projects covered in that section.

Even grade A leather usually has a certain number of scars caused by cuts or whatever when the animal was alive, and maybe a small amount of scabbling (uneven tanning). These flaws are fine if you are making a rugged-looking piece, but for fine articles try to avoid surface marks, or at least place them in inconspicuous areas. Before you start working on the leather, turn it wrong side up and mark around all the flaws so that you can avoid them when cutting.

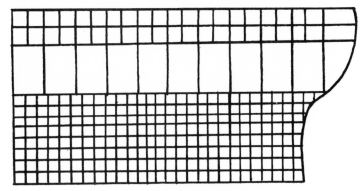

**Fig. B-1**
TRANSPARENT
DRESSMAKER'S RULER

If the flaws are minimal and do not cause major weakness in the leather, the pattern can be arranged so they occur in non-stress areas. If you want to strengthen small areas and make them more versatile, glue a piece of leather or muslin over the weak area on the wrong side of the leather.

If possible, lay all pattern pieces out at the same time so you can move them around and see which way they fit closest — thus saving you leather.

Place all major or large pattern pieces on the lengthwise grain of the skin parallel to the animal's backbone. If you can't tell where the backbone of the animal is, then test for the direction of the stretch (or cross grain). Pull gently on the leather so that you can see where the stretch is. Now and again a skin will have several stretchpoints, some natural and others the result of tanning. Usually, however, the most stretch is around the animal, so lay out your pattern according to where you want the most stretch to go. In general, the stretch on a garment should go around the human body, just as it did on the animal.

Grain doesn't affect small areas, which can be cut on the cross grain or whichever way you want. But when working with patchwork, I prefer not to cut on the diagonal grain since this tends to make the leather pucker when sewn. If you are going to sew two patches together, one of which has been cut on the cross grain and the other on the grain, be sure to ease the cross grain with its stretch into the grain piece. If you don't, the two seams will not fit together perfectly and with patchwork, all seams must fit exactly.

When laying out pattern pieces, you should also work the nap areas. In patchwork, nap going in different directions can often add interest. To test the direction of the nap, run your hand over the suede. It will raise up when you brush in one direction, and flatten when you brush in the other. Rough suedes and sueded splits tend to have little or no nap, so there is no need to bother about testing the nap with these leathers.

Once your pattern is in place, tape it down with masking tape placed every 6 inches or so around the edges. If your pattern is made out of a heavier material such as heavy brown paper, cardboard, or sandpaper, you needn't bother to use tape, especially if it is a small pattern piece. You can either place a weight on this type of pattern to keep it in place or just press your hand on it to keep it steady. Trace around patterns (on the wrong side of the leather, of course) with a waterproof felt-tipped pen, and then remove the pattern before cutting.

For leather a *felt-tipped pen* is the best marker you can use. In different colors, these pens are also great for drawing on leathers. Test them out on scraps first to see the color effects you get from the type and color of leather you are using.

A *dressmaker's tracing wheel* is then used to transfer any markings from the pattern to the wrong side of the leather. Use it while the pattern pieces are still laid out on the leather. Simply run the tracing wheel firmly over the markings on the pattern. This will make little indentations in the leather which you will be able to see quite readily. If the wrong side of the leather is sueded or rough, however, you will need to use dressmaker's tracing paper along with the wheel, as the nap or roughness will camouflage any perforations the wheel leaves behind. Place the tracing paper, color side facing the leather, between the pattern and the leather. Run the tracing wheel over the markings to transfer markings to the leather (see Fig. B-2).

After all the pattern pieces are traced around and the markings transferred, you are ready to cut the pieces out. Always be sure to cut your leather so that the line marked around them when tracing is left on the scraps, not on the pattern piece. If you don't cut exactly on the inside of that line, it looks messy, and the piece you cut will be a little larger than anticipated. This may sound petty, but it's not, especially with lots of seams.

*Sharp dressmaker's shears* (see Fig. B-3) are used for the basic cutting of pliable leathers. Cut with smooth strokes, never quite closing the blades, to give the smooth edges essential for good work. I prefer these sharp fabric shears because I feel I have more control and don't need any special surface for cutting. Of course if the leather is very thick, such as the kind used for

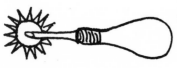

**Fig. B-2**
DRESSMAKER'S TRACING WHEEL

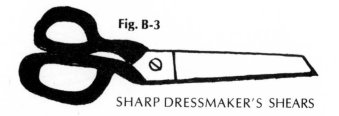

**Fig. B-3**

SHARP DRESSMAKER'S SHEARS

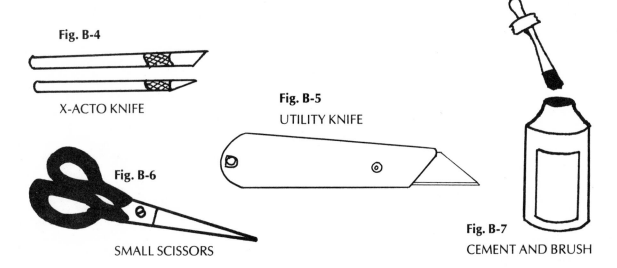

Fig. B-4
X-ACTO KNIFE

Fig. B-5
UTILITY KNIFE

Fig. B-6
SMALL SCISSORS

Fig. B-7
CEMENT AND BRUSH

belts, use an X-Acto knife or utility knife (see Figs. B-4 and B-5), both of which are good on heavyweight leathers, such as belting leather. To cut a straight edge, align the blade with the edge of a ruler or draw a line. Then, keeping the leather steady with one hand, cut the leather with long smooth strokes. Cut on a hardwood or marble base and keep the edge as smooth as possible.

You will also need *small, sharp scissors* (see Fig. B-6) for cutting leather lacing, for small cut-outs, and appliqué pieces. In fact small scissors are a must for all small areas where you need to have good control, and where large shears would not fit properly.

Always work leather in a single layer, with the wrong side up, and be sure you are working on a clean surface. This can be a clean floor, table, or any other flat surface. Again, if you are cutting with an X-Acto knife or a razor blade, you will need to cut on a heavy hardwood or marble surface.

After I have cut out my leather, I like to put in additional seam allowance markings as a guideline for assembling the seams to give me complete accuracy. Use a clear dressmaker's ruler and a waterproof felt-tipped pen. Place the appropriate line in the ruler over the raw edge and draw in a line indicating where the edge of the ruler reaches inside the pattern piece. On commercial patterns, the allowance for concealed seams is ⅝ inch, but on my original patterns I leave only a ½ inch seam allowance. Overlapping seam allowances vary according to the type you are using. For lapped seams it is easiest to mark only the wrong side of the overlapping edge, either ⅝ or ¾ inch. To construct the seam later, just line up the edge of the underlapping piece with this line, glue it down, and it's done. If you use a 1-inch strip for backing, (see Fig. 0-2) mark a ½ inch allowance on the wrong side of either edge. Glue the strip down along these lines, and you will get a perfect seam.

*Glue and brushes* (see Fig. B-7) are used for overlapping seams, facings, hems, or holding any two pieces of leather together. You need a glue that holds fast and yet is flexible. Use either rubber cement, Jiffy Sew, Sobo, or a good leather cement such as Tandy Leather Company's. These can be pulled apart and reglued quite easily.

For permanent fastenings, a permanent cement such as Barge's All Purpose is good. If you are hand sewing, you will find that you have to pull two layers of leather apart in order to neatly join, begin, and end edge-stitching. I find that rubber cement is the type I use most frequently. However, in places that need a good permanent bond you can also use Sobo or the Tandy Leather glue if you will be sewing over it. If you are not planning on sewing at all, then use the Barge's All Purpose. Always use a brush to apply the cement as it gives you control. Apply it evenly, and only in the areas where needed.

A *ruffer* or *sandpaper* (see Fig. B-8) is used on very smooth leathers on areas to be glued together. It raises a rough surface to which the glue can adhere and penetrate. Be careful to rub it over only the areas you wish to glue, or you will ruin the finish of your leather.

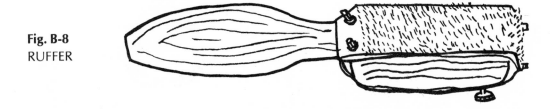

Fig. B-8
RUFFER

## TOOLS NEEDED

**GLOVER'S MACHINE NEEDLES
EVEN-FEED OR WALKING FOOT
   (OPTIONAL BUT HIGHLY
   RECOMMENDED)
HEAVY MERCERIZED THREAD
RAWHIDE MALLET
RUBBER OR LEATHER CEMENT AND
   BRUSHES
CLEAR DRESSMAKER'S RULER
SHEARS AND SMALL SCISSORS
WATERPROOF FELT-TIPPED PEN**

**OPTIONAL**
_____

**TISSUE PAPER
MASKING TAPE
RUFFER OR SANDPAPER
SILICONE SPRAY**

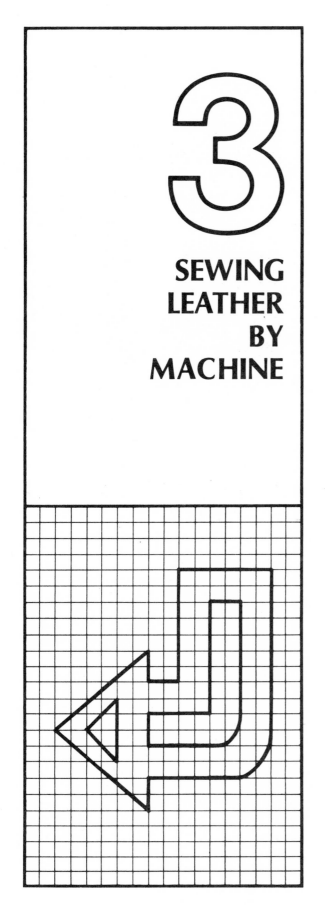

# 3
# SEWING LEATHER BY MACHINE

There are basically two different ways to sew leather — by hand and by machine. Some people believe that leather should be treated in a way that fits with its natural rugged quality, and should be hand-crafted only, with punched holes and leather lacing. Others feel that leather belongs in the modern world, and looks more sophisticated and polished when sewn with a machine.

I feel each method has its advantages and disadvantages. There are so many different types of leather and leather finishes — some require hand sewing, others machine sewing. I like to work both ways and combine the two techniques to achieve the specific look I want as well as strength and utility in construction.

If you are planning to do a lot of sewing with leather, I suggest an industrial sewing machine. However, a regular home machine should readily do the job — if you use a glover's needle, an even-feed foot, good strong thread, and if you sew carefully at a slow, steady speed so as not to break the thread.

Don't even attempt to sew leather without a *glover's needle* (see Fig. C-1). Leather can be sewn with ordinary needles, but until you use a glover's needle you won't know how simple it really is. These needles have a three-sided, wedge-shaped point especially designed to make it go through leather easily. Special glover's nee-

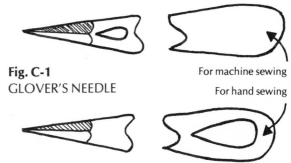

**Fig. C-1**
GLOVER'S NEEDLE

For machine sewing

For hand sewing

**Fig. C-2**
EVEN-FEED OR WALKING FOOT

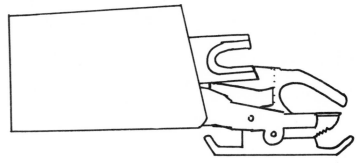

dles are available for machine and for hand sewing. Use size 11 (fine) or 14 (medium) for regular sewing, and size 16 (heavy) for topstitching or stitching through many layers of leather. For any hand stitching you may have to do in conjunction with machine sewing, get glover's needles for regular sewing — sizes 6 to 9.

An *even-feed foot* or *walking foot* (see Fig. C-2) is a special sewing foot which acts like the walking foot found on the huge industrial leather machines. It feeds leather through the machine smoothly by pushing it through bit by bit according to the size stitch being used. The teeth, which move back and forth on the foot to push the leather through, are made of plastic and cannot damage the leather.

For regular stitching with a machine, use *heavy-duty mercerized* or *cotton-wrapped polyester thread* — size 40 or 50. For topstitching on heavy leather, use buttonhole-twist or heavy-duty mercerized cotton — size 40.

Before actually overlapping and topstitching delicate leathers, it is sometimes advisable to reinforce the seams. First sew the seam allowances together as you would if you were making regular concealed seams. Then make an "over lapping" seam by folding both seam allowances to one side and gluing and hammering them flat. For reinforced abutted seams, sew the seams together, open the seams to both sides, glue, and hammer flat. Then carefully glue a strip of leather 1 or 1½ inches wide on the inside along the seam line so that the stitching is centered. Topstitch as with a regular abutted seam.

A *rawhide mallet* (see Fig. C-3) is best for hammering seams flat after they have been glued. If you prefer, you can use a hammer padded with layers of fabric. An ordinary hammer will make marks on the leather when you hammer the seams, and may even cut through the leather.

If you are using overlapping seams, "baste" them together with glue, allow to dry, and then sew. To glue overlapping seams together, use either a rubber cement or leather cement. If you use rubber cement, apply to both overlap and underlap part of the leather (only where the leather will cover), allow to dry partially, then press together. Leather cement needs to be applied to one side only, but it is permanent and you cannot change your mind as you can with rubber cement.

ing by holding the seams or abutted raw edges together on the wrong side of the leather until you sew, (see Fig. C-4), and can also be used as a stitching guide. Make sure the tape is not very sticky and that you don't press down too hard; otherwise it can damage the leather, especially if you use it on the grain side. I recommend that you use it on the wrong side only.

Before sewing, clean oil and lint from the machine, since an excess of oil can stain leather permanently. An easy way to remove excess oil is to stitch — without thread — through scrap materials or paper towels.

Next, make sure the machine is adjusted properly and working correctly by sewing through the appropriate layers of scrap leather from your project. At this time you can adjust the tension of the stitch — if too loose, it will show in open seams; if too tight, the thread may pucker and cut the leather. You can also judge to see if the machine is sewing the leather easily.

When the machine appears to be sewing

**Fig. C-3**
RAWHIDE MALLET

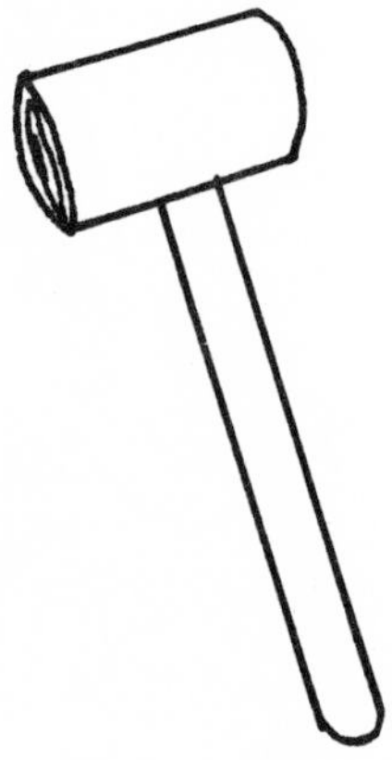

**Fig. C-4**

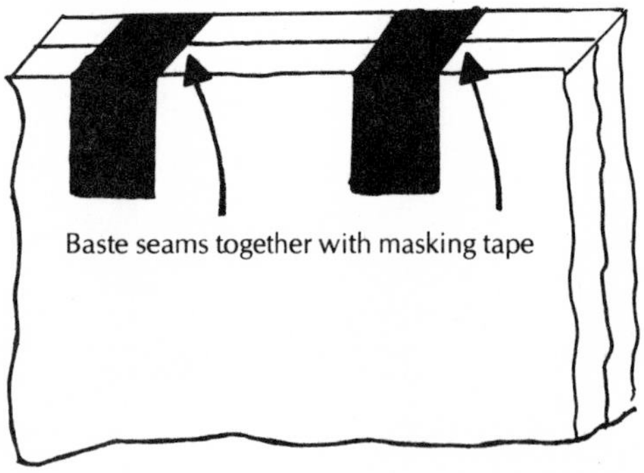

Baste seams together with masking tape

**Fig. C-5**

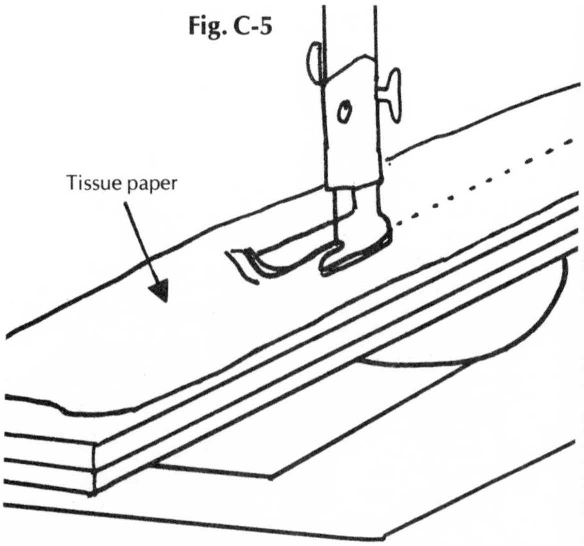

Tissue paper

through the scraps correctly, then you can start stitching the actual project. But make sure you have prepared everything properly. Are all directions marked on the wrong side of the leather?

When finishing off a seam, either tie off the ends or backstitch directly into the holes made by the existing stitches. But be careful, because too many holes — besides looking messy — can weaken leather by perforating the skin and perhaps causing it to rip.

If you find that your machine slips a little on the leather, put *tissue paper* between the leather and the sewing foot (see Fig. C-5) and/or between the leather and the throat plate of the machine.

You may also need to place tissue paper between shiny leather and a sewing machine to prevent the shiny surface from sticking to the metal. At the same time, the paper keeps the machine's foot or throat-plate teeth from damaging the grain finish. This is especially important for topstitching, where any damage would be disastrous, since the machine touches the outer surface of the leather. Tear the tissue off later after the stitching is complete. Masking tape can be used for the same purpose, but only on the wrong side of the leather.

If I am working on a very slippery surface, however, and find I can't get a grip on the leather (and tissue slipped under the foot makes visibility difficult), the special walking foot, or even-feed foot, as it is called, should really help solve the problem. Again, this foot pushes the leather through after each stitch and there is no, or very little, slippage; and it can't damage the outer surface of the leather since its gripping teeth are made of plastic. It is a gadget I recommend if you are doing a lot of topstitching or any kind of sewing with leather.

If the leather seems a little heavy, put in a larger needle and adjust the stitch size so that it runs smoothly. (But don't make stitches any smaller than seven to an inch.) If the thread seems to be pulling, spray it with a silicone spray to make it run smoothly through the machine. If you have overlapping seams, you can use a zig-zag stitch with the same color or contrasting thread. The zigzag stitch is especially effective on soft leathers and suedes, and will help prevent slipping on very shiny leathers such as cabretta or any leather with a glazed finish.

When finishing off a seam, either tie off the ends or backstitch directly into the holes made by the existing stitches. But be careful, because too many holes — besides looking messy — can weaken leather by perforating the skin and perhaps causing it to rip.

Always remember that stitching punctures leather, leaving holes that show, so be sure you follow your markings carefully. You might be able to get away with a few mistakes with suede, since the nap tends to smooth over the holes, but not with full-grain leather. This is why the preparatory steps are so important. If you have cut and marked everything properly, there should be no problem.

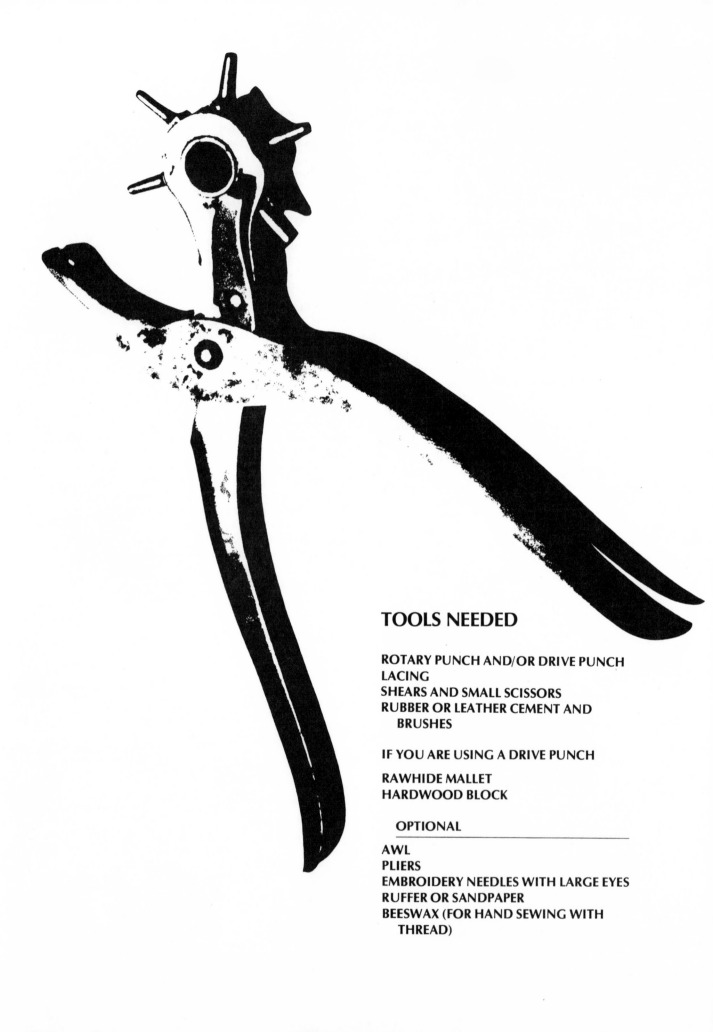

## TOOLS NEEDED

ROTARY PUNCH AND/OR DRIVE PUNCH
LACING
SHEARS AND SMALL SCISSORS
RUBBER OR LEATHER CEMENT AND
   BRUSHES

IF YOU ARE USING A DRIVE PUNCH

RAWHIDE MALLET
HARDWOOD BLOCK

   OPTIONAL

AWL
PLIERS
EMBROIDERY NEEDLES WITH LARGE EYES
RUFFER OR SANDPAPER
BEESWAX (FOR HAND SEWING WITH
   THREAD)

# 4
# HAND SEWING, PUNCHING, AND LACING

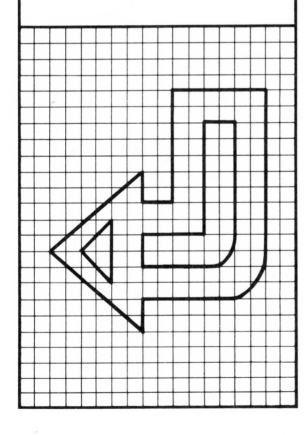

Sewing leather by hand requires different techniques and tools from machine sewing. It is no harder or easier than machine sewing, just different.

In machine sewing, it's the machine that punches holes through the leather. In hand sewing, it's you — and there are two tools which will punch perfect holes for you: the rotary punch and drive punch.

A *rotary punch* (see Fig. D-1) can be used for making holes in most leather articles and is a good tool to have. You will probably use it quite a bit, so don't try to get a bargain. Buy a good rotary punch — it will last a long time and be easier to work with than a poor quality one.

Before punching out any holes, be sure that the right size puncher is in position. Twist the wheel forward till the correct-size punching barrel clicks into place. Then place the punching barrel over the mark on the leather where you want the hole to be. Make sure the punching tube is on top and the anvil on the bottom. Now press the handles together, removing a round core of leather.

Since the rotary punch cannot reach too far, glue only 5 or 6 inches of seaming down at a time, then punch the holes. If the leather is soft and folds easily, it will punch easily; but if it's heavy, you might have some difficulty. Edge holes are no problem, but with seams, work toward yourself and ease out the seam after punching. Make sure the leather doesn't accidently double, or you might end up with an extra hole through more layers than you want. A *drive punch* does the same job as the rotary, but it gets into places where a rotary punch can't fit.

Drive punches come in various shapes — round, oval, and oblong — but I feel that the rounds

**Fig. D-1**
ROTARY PUNCH

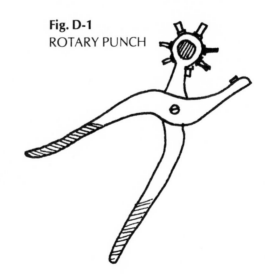

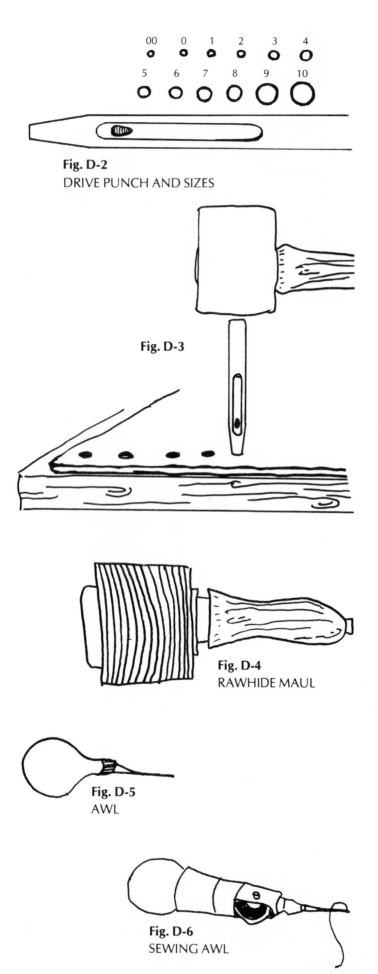

**Fig. D-2**
DRIVE PUNCH AND SIZES

**Fig. D-3**

**Fig. D-4**
RAWHIDE MAUL

**Fig. D-5**
AWL

**Fig. D-6**
SEWING AWL

are sufficient and can be used for anything. They come in sizes that correspond with a rotary punch's barrels, as well as additional sizes (see Fig. D-2). To use a drive punch, you need a mallet and a clean piece of hardwood. The hardwood must be placed under the leather when you are using a drive punch; it prevents any damage to your table or working surface, and protects the punch blade. Make sure this wood is clean, especially if you are going to put the outer surface of the leather on it when punching your holes. You can also use a hardwood stump or even a hardwood block table if you have lots of room and are planning to do a lot of punching.

Place the leather over the hardwood, then place the drive punch over the spot marked for a hole. Hit it with a rawhide mallet or maul, just as if you were driving a nail, removing a small hole from the leather (see Fig. D-3). For very heavy leathers, you may have to hit several times; be careful not to let the punch slip between blows.

I work mostly with a drive punch, since it can be so easily maneuvered. It doesn't hurt my hands and is faster and surer than a rotary punch.

A rawhide mallet is best, since a regular hammer may damage your punches by flattening the top after much hammering; in addition a regular hammer makes a lot of noise when the metal head hits against the metal of the drive punch. A *rawhide maul* (optional) is also used to punch holes, but usually in heavier leather. If you get one at all, the lighter one — 2½ pounds — is usually sufficient for the average person (see Fig. D-4).

You can also use a sewing machine to punch holes in rather heavy leather, or if you are sewing by hand with a heavy thread such as a buttonhole twist or a waxed thread. Simply remove the thread from the machine and sew. This will punch evenly spaced holes into which you can sew later by hand.

Most people already have an *awl* in the house. This tool (see Fig. D-5) is used to widen holes that are too small and pierce leather so that you can sew easily with heavy thread or cord. Place the leather over a hardwood base and press down on it with the awl or hit with a mallet. Do not try to stab the leather, or you might slip and gash yourself.

A *sewing awl* (optional) (see Fig. D-6) guides a heavy wax thread and gives the same effect as a lock stitch on a sewing machine. It is good for finishing off machine-sewn articles or for sewing heavy, rugged-looking articles without having to punch holes and then lace them. I don't use an awl too often, but it is inexpensive and a handy tool to have.

When you are making a hand-sewn article, all seams are overlapping, and as such must be glued. Most edge facings are raw. The rest are self facings, such as on hems or cuffs, and must be glued (together). Don't use a permanent glue for hand stitching, since you may have to pull seams and facings apart. Use rubber cement, apply it lightly and to only one surface; it will hold, but will also allow you to pull the two surfaces apart if necessary.

Before I start making any holes in the leather, I try to judge how to get around corners and see the overall picture. When doing a complicated piece of punching, such as for weaving or beading, I mark the entire hole punch design before starting to punch. Of course, if you have a good eye, after making a few things you will probably be able to make pretty accurate punch holes without measuring. If I am making a rugged-looking article, I use my judgment as to where to punch the holes. But in general — and especially with anything that needs to have a really polished look — I measure. It's really so easy and fast, it's almost foolish not to.

When measuring and marking the spots where the holes are to be punched, use a clear dressmaker's ruler and a pencil or felt-tipped pen. If possible, turn the leather wrong-side up and mark — this method assures that you won't damage the front if you make any mistakes, and allows you to correct any you might make. If you must mark on the right side, do so very lightly. After I have marked the article completely, I lay it out flat on a board, take my puncher and mallet, and punch away.

The size of the hole you want punched can vary according to how tight or how loose you want the stitching, how close you want it together, what lacing you are using, and the type of leather you are sewing. A softer leather has enough give so that you may need only a small hole, but heavy leather holds its shape and may need a larger hole. Punch a few test holes through scraps, then stitch with your intended lacing to see which is the best sized hole.

If you are not using thread, you will need leather *lacing* to sew with. You can buy precut lacing or cut your own from scraps. Select a scrap of leather of fairly uniform thickness throughout, of not too heavy a texture, and without too much stretch. With a pair of scissors, cut the scrap into a circle — it doesn't have to be exact, but get rid of any sharp edges. Now cut a spiral of lacing (see Fig. D-7). Lacing should generally be from ⅛ to ¼ inch wide, depending on the effect desired, but try to keep the lacing a uniform width as you cut.

*Tapestry or embroidery needles with large eyes* can be a great help with hand stitching. Thread your lacing into the needle's large eye and stitch into the punched holes with ease. Or cut the lacing end obliquely, forming a point, so that it threads easily through the holes (see Fig. D-8).

If you are sewing by hand with thread, coating it with *beeswax* (see Fig. D-9) will prevent tangling and will make the thread stiffer and stronger.

*Pliers* in leatherwork are commonly called lacing pliers (see Fig. D-10), but you could use any good pliers you already have in the house. They are

**Fig. D-7**
STEPS FOR CUTTING LACING

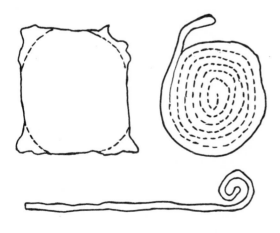

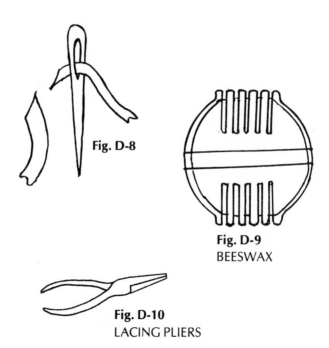

**Fig. D-8**

**Fig. D-9**
BEESWAX

**Fig. D-10**
LACING PLIERS

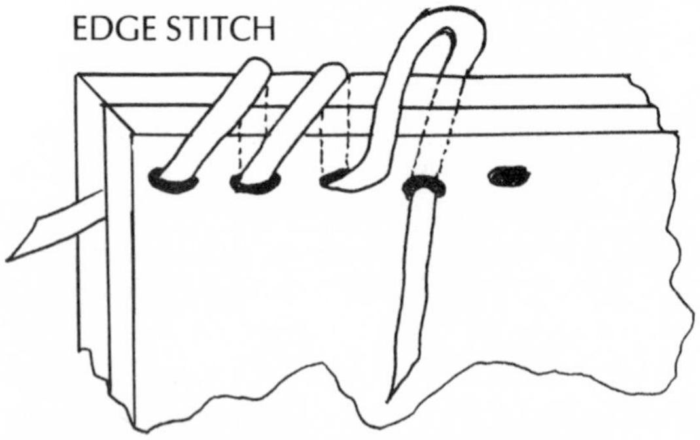

**Fig. D-11**
WHIPSTITCH OR SINGLE-
EDGE STITCH

**Fig. D-12**
THE CROSS WHIPSTITCH
OR CROSS-EDGE STITCH

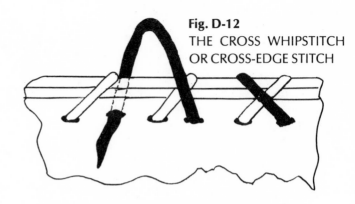

used to pull tight-fitting lacing through holes. Simply bring the tip of the lacing through the hole, grasp it with the pliers, and pull. It saves a lot of wear and tear on your hands if you are working with rough leathers.

There are many different types of lacing stitches. They are generally based on decorative embroidery stitches, but instead of simply using a needle and thread here, you punch and stitch with lacing. However, there are only a few stitches you really need to know. These will let you stitch anything with leather lacing strongly and beautifully.

*The whip or single-edge stitch* (see Fig. D-11) — For ¼ inch lacing, punch a row of holes approximately ¼ inch from the edge and approximately ¼ inch apart; and for the ⅛ inch lacing, punch ⅛ to ¼ inch from the edge and ¼ inch apart. Now simply insert the lacing into the first hole from inside the two layers of leather (if it is a single layer, simply insert from the wrong side), and emerge on the right side. Then whip the lace over the edge of the leather and insert the leather into the next hole from the underside.

*The cross-edge stitch* (see Fig. D-12) — Punch holes in the same way as you did for the whip stitch. Starting as you did with the whip stitch, first whip the lacing into every other hole. When you have finished lacing that way, then turn and repeat going in the opposite direction. Glue the ends between the leathers.

*The double cross edge stitch* (see Fig. D-13) — For edge-stitching, the heavier cross-stitch is a good idea if you want to give your edges a rolled look. Punch your holes the same way as for whip or cross edge stitch. Bring your first stitch from the right side to the wrong side (see Step 1). Take the loose end on the right side and flip it over the edge to the wrong side — not sewn, just over. Now glue this tab between the first and second holes so that the end is secured on the wrong side (see Step 2).

Now take your long lacing and whip it from the wrong side over the edge into the next (second) hole. Then bring the lacing back over the edge to the right side and stitch once again into the first hole (see Step 3), bringing the lacing back to the wrong side. Bring the lacing over the edge to the right side and stitch it into the next empty hole (third hole), bringing it through to the wrong side (see Step 4). Keep repeating this sequence until the edge is sewn (see Step 5). Join the lacings by either stitching the lacings together or gluing them tightly together, or backstitch into a few holes. This is a very heavy stitch and not easy to do.

*The running stitch* (see Fig. D-14) — Punch a single row of stitching the same as for the whipstitch. This stitch can be used for either an edge or for an overlapping seam. For overlapping seams punch holes through the double thickness of the seam. For ¼ inch lacing, punch a single row of holes about ¼ inch in from the raw seam edge and about ¼ to ½ inch apart. For ⅛ inch lacing punch ⅛ to ¼ inch from the raw seam edge and about ⅛ to ¼ inch apart. It is a simple in-and-out stitch. Start stitching from the wrong side and pull the lacing through the first hole to the right side, leaving a 1 inch tail on the inside. Now simply weave the lacing in and out of each consecutive hole.

This is not really a very strong stitch, but good around a turned-under edge for overlapping seams that do not get much wear, and for decoration. You can use a single row on a lapped seam or a double row on a slot.

*Backstitch or saddle stitch* (see Fig. D-15) — This is similar to a running stitch, but much stronger. Punch holes the same way as for the running stitch. Start stitching by bringing the lacing up through the second hole (a), then lace it back into the first hole (b), then pull it through the third hole (c). This stitch is therefore accomplished by stitching the lacing back into its starting point and then pulling it

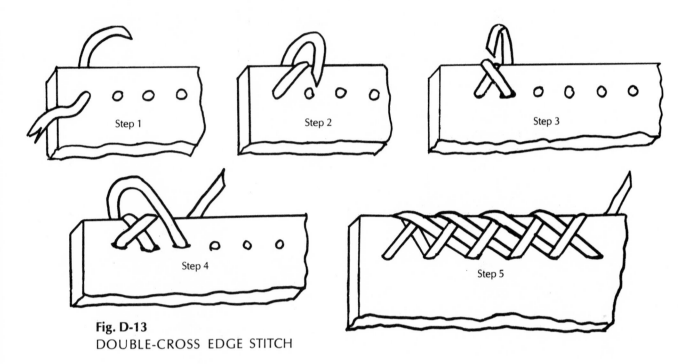

Step 1

Step 2

Step 3

Step 4

Step 5

**Fig. D-13**
DOUBLE-CROSS EDGE STITCH

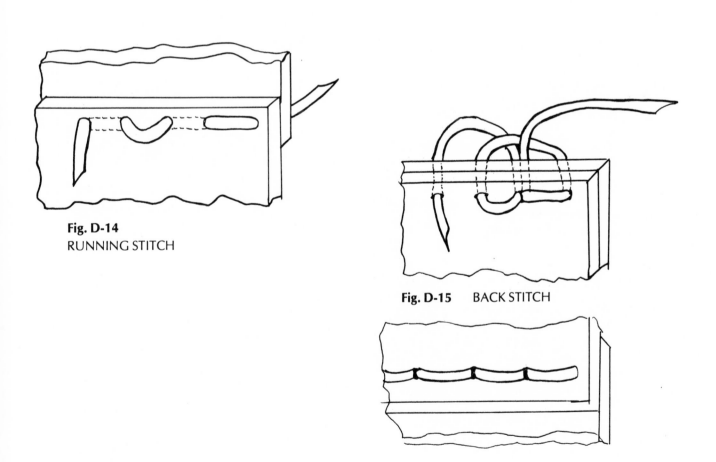

**Fig. D-14**
RUNNING STITCH

**Fig. D-15**   BACK STITCH

through the next empty hole. Join and begin and lace as described.

*The diagonal stitch* (see Fig. D-16) — This is basically just a variation of the whip and running stitches. It is excellent for all overlapped seams. According to the width of lacing you are using, make two rows of punched holes, but with only one hole punched at the beginning of one seam and one hole punched at the end of the other seam. The distance between the two rows should vary from between ¼ to ½ inch depending on the type of lacing being used and the width of the underlap. I usually make my rows ⅜ inch apart. The holes in each row should also be from ¼ to ½ inch, again depending on the size of the lacing and how much spacing you want between stitches.

For overlapped seams, there are two ways of punching the holes. If you want the stitching to lap over the raw edge of the seam, then punch one row of holes on one side of the edge and one on the other. If you want the stitching all to go through the double thickness of the seam overlap, then punch both rows to the side of the raw edge that has the double overlap.

For an abutted seam, punch a row of holes on either side of the abutted edges. Be sure that all the holes go through both the surface leather and the strip glued beneath it.

To sew the diagonal stitch, bring the lacing from the wrong side through the first hole (on the row with the single hole) at the beginning. Now insert the lacing diagonally into the first hole of the next row. Bring it straight across on the wrong side to the adjacent hole, and bring it back up through to the right side. Continue this way.

*The flat cross-stitch — both connected and spaced* (see Figs. D-17 and D-18) — This stitch is excellent for all overlapping and abutted seams. According to the width of the lacing you are using, make two rows of punched holes. The distance between the two rows should be from ¼ to ½ inch depending on the lacing being used. Mine are usually ⅜ inch apart. If you want the stitching to overlap the raw edges of the seam, then punch one row of holes on one side of the edge, and one on the other. If you want the stitching to go through the double thickness of the seam overlap, then punch both rows to the side of the raw edge that has the double overlap. For the abutted seam, make a row of

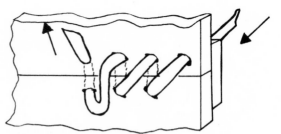

**Fig. D-16**
DIAGONAL STITCH

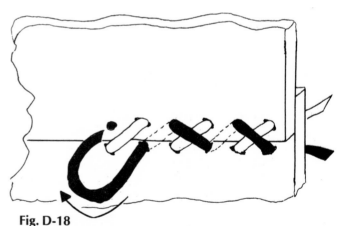

**Fig. D-17**
CONNECTING FLAT CROSS-STITCH

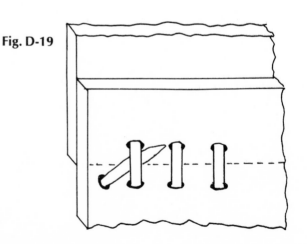

**Fig. D-18**
SPACED FLAT CROSS-STITCH

**Fig. D-19**

24

holes on either side of the abutted edges. Be sure all the holes go through both surface leather and the strip glued beneath it.

To do the connected cross, first stitch the seam as if you were doing a diagonal stitch, and then turn around and sew back, filling in the empty spaces to form crosses.

The spaced flat cross is done by bringing the lacing from the wrong side through the first hole. Then insert the lacing diagonally into the second hole of the other row. Then on the wrong side, bring it across diagonally through the third hole of the first row. In a sense, you are doing a diagonal stitch, only sewing into every other hole. When you reach the end, turn around and do the same thing in the opposite direction.

The length of the lacing is basically up to you. Some people like to use long lacings, while others like shorter ones. I use rather long lacing — but not long enough for it to tangle — to avoid having to make too many joins in it. What joins I have to make are as invisible as possible, so the lacing looks like one continuous strip.

Do not join lacing by tying knots in leather unless absolutely essential — and then add a drop of glue and hammer the knot flat.

When sewing seams, always begin and end stitching on the wrong side of the leather. Leave an inch of extra lacing at the beginning and end of each strip — on the inside, of course. Then when you have finished lacing the seam, go back and work the tabs at each end under the first and last stitch, respectively, and glue them down (see Fig. D-19). Unless there will be leather glued over it (as in a hem or facing), glue a small piece of leather or muslin over the tab to make it secure. If there are loose tabs in the middle of the seam, trim the tabs to ½ inch, overlap them, and glue them tightly together (see Fig. D-20). (If the lacing is made of soft, pliable leather, then hand-sew the end tabs together). Now glue a small piece of muslin or leather over the join.

When edge-stitching (see Fig. D-21), you will usually be working with two pieces of leather lightly glued together. In this case, begin stitching by passing the lacing through the first hole from between the two layers of leather — so that you stitch through the hole on only one of the layers — and leave a 1 inch tail between the two layers, which you should glue down immediately. Each time you run short of lacing, gently pull the two layers apart and pass the lacing through the next hole, but only through one thickness of leather. After pulling the stitches taut, cut the lacing so as to leave a 1 inch tail which, again, should be glued between the two layers. Then starting from between the two layers of leather, pull the new lacing through the hole in the other layer of leather opposite the one through which you ended the last lacing. Leave a 1 inch tail from this piece of lacing, glue it down flat as you did with the first lacing, and then glue the two layers back together and continue lacing.

To end edge-lacing, stitch into the hole opposite the one you started from, pull the stitch taut, cut the lacing so there is a 1 inch tail, and glue the two layers of leather together, making sure the tail is inside.

If you are working an edge that has a self facing, you use almost the same procedure. To start stitching, pull open the facing where you want to start your sewing and begin lacing from inside the two layers, gluing the tail flat inside the facing. Stitch through the rest of the holes until the end; then go through the side opposite to the beginning hole. Glue the tail flat and glue the facing down thoroughly, catching the tails inside. To join lacing, do the same as with separate facing.

With a single thickness, to join lacing you simply overlap the laces, glue thoroughly together, and continue to stitch — being sure that both parts of the lacing go through the punched holes. Put a few drops of clear glue carefully on the inside of these stitches to help hold. Or you can sew the laces together by machine or hand. To end, merely stitch over three or so of the beginning stitches (like back-stitching), pull both lacing ends taut, and trim the ends. If you want, of course, you can use this method for all of your edge-stitching.

**Fig. D-20**

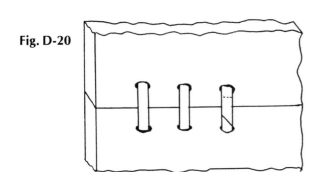

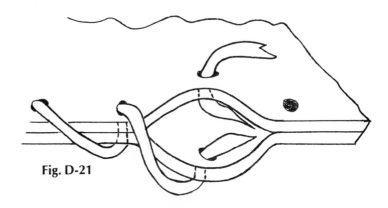

**Fig. D-21**

# STUFFING
# AND FORMS
# FOR PILLOWS
# AND
# CUSHIONS

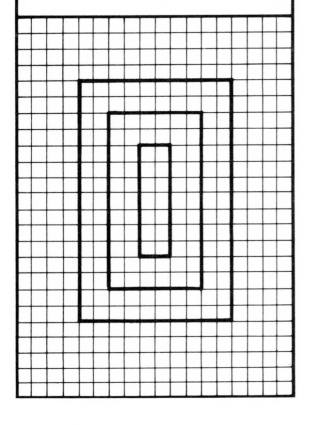

For a loose stuffing I prefer polyester or polyester Poly-fil, and for solid stuffings — especially for large cushions — foam rubber wrapped with polyester batting. But different people prefer different types. Think about the texture and weight of the leather used for the pillow, and think of its size and use (couch? throw pillow?), and how much wear it will receive. Then check the qualities of the different stuffings, and choose the one that best fits your purpose.

*Cotton* is hard to find as a loose stuffing and usually comes in rolls as cotton batting. You can cut and stack these rolls, or wrap foam with it, or pull it apart as loose stuffing. I like to pull it apart for use in smaller cushions, especially little ones. And I put a potpourri in the center of them: cotton lets it really breathe. However, cotton has a tendency to mat and is therefore impractical for larger cushions. In addition, it doesn't wash, can lump, and is heavy.

*Down* is the soft, fluffy feathers from ducks, geese, and other water fowl. It is extremely expensive, but luxuriously soft, long wearing, and fabulous for smaller pillows made with really soft suede or leather.

The best way to buy down is in a prestuffed form, but you can also get it from an old bed pillow or buy one on sale. Then transfer the feathers to a muslin form. To keep the down under control while transferring it, place the pillow and the muslin form cover in a large clear plastic bag. For knife-edge pillows, you can simply use the existing cover as your form. Decide on the size of your pillow and mark where you want to cut it. Make two parallel lines of stitching straight across the pillow, one on the mark and one about ½ inch on the outside of it. Now cut between the two lines, leaving a ¼ inch seam on either side, and you have a form.

*Foam rubber* is made of natural latex and is extremely comfortable and luxurious in feeling. It comes in preshaped forms for knife-edge pillows. Foam comes in slabs of different thicknesses, but many stores (look in the phone book under foam rubber) can cut these slabs to any shape or length you want.

To make foam rubber thicker, you simply stack layer upon layer, then hold them together with special foam rubber cement or double-faced masking tape. If you can't get it cut to size in the store, you can cut foam rubber yourself, using a serrated knife.

Foam can be very practical, but there are a few tricks that can help you along. If you are using a box-edge form with corners, for instance, it is a good idea to cut a fraction off the extreme corners so that they fit better into the cover. If you don't want a cushion with an extremely boxy look, trim off the sharp edges and round them slightly. Generally, the foam should be slightly larger than the cover so that it fits snugly and looks tailored rather than square — about ½ inch longer, wider, and higher than the cover is about right. If the foam is too small, you will get wrinkles on the top; if it is too large it will pull the leather and cause the edges to curve up.

*Foam rubber covered with polyester batting* is extremely good for stuffing large cushions — either box- or knife-edge floor cushions. This combines firmness, softness, and durability for cushions that will be sat on a lot.

For this stuffing, you should have a slab of foam the length of the pillow and about 2 or 3 inches narrower than the width, and 1 or 1½ inches narrower than the height. Then wrap batting around this slab so that it becomes the right size for the pillow. If the pillow is longer than the normal 16 inch width of the polyester batting, simply wrap it as you would a bandage around your finger, or else wrap it in sections. For a very flat bottomed pillow, use a slab of foam the *exact* size of the cushion and lay batting top so it overlaps the sides.

*Kapok* usually comes in prestuffed standard-sized forms, and is rarely sold as loose stuffing. It makes a very dense pillow but tends to mat and harden, and doesn't really wash. In addition, it is very hard to work with, since it is made up of very fine particles which tend to waft all over — including into your lungs. So if you use it, do so with your work inside a large cotton pillowcase — or even better, a clear plastic bag — to contain the stuff. Otherwise you will probably need to wear a mask so you don't breathe it in and choke. Often you will find kapok mixed with foam rubber, and this mixture has much more bounce than kapok alone. It takes a lot to stuff a pillow and tends to be heavy.

*Polyester* comes either as batting or shredded. Polyester batting is usually sold in a roll about 16 inches wide and 1 inch thick. It can be cut and stacked or wrapped around itself or around foam for larger cushions. For stuffing smaller cushions you can shred it by hand. Shredded polyester is the same material, only ready-shredded for use in cushions.

Polyester is a highly desirable filling, as it keeps its fluffy quality, has little tendency to mat, is washable (if desired), and doesn't deteriorate. It also comes in prestuffed forms of standard sizes.

*Poly-fil (polyester Poly-fil)* is an "exploded" polyester. It is sold in prestuffed forms, in 1 pound bags of loose stuffing, or in rolls like the polyester about 16 inches wide and 1 inch thick. It is an excellent-quality product to use for stuffing. It is more resilient than plain polyester, is less expensive, and less of it is needed to stuff a pillow. However, it has the same basic qualities: it has little tendency to mat, is washable, and doesn't deteriorate.

*Shredded foam* comes in prestuffed forms or as loose stuffing. It is reasonably easy to work with, but works best when you transfer the stuffing inside a large clear plastic bag, since part of the foam tends to pulverize and can get all over the place. I have used it with smaller cushions when I was recycling shredded foam stuffing from older cushions. It is fine for larger throw cushions, but do put in a little extra, since after awhile it tends to flatten and lump together (and therefore gives a flatter, firmer pillow). In addition, it tends to dry out and disintegrate to powder with age.

*Styrofoam pellets* are used to stuff larger cushions. I'm not really crazy about them, but they are used in bean bag chairs. If not stuffed too tightly, they give a soft pillow you can sink into.

There are no hard and fast rules for the amount of stuffing to use in pillows. However, I have worked out a basic formula which seems to give a fairly good idea of how much stuffing is needed for any size pillow: Simply multiply the width by the length in inches. For every 100 in the answer, use the following amount for each type of stuffing listed. (If the answer falls in between hundreds, always round off to the higher figure. For example, if your answer is 535, assume it's 600). For box-edge pillows, add an extra 100 or 200 to the answer depending on the size. The amounts are not exact, of course, and you will probably want to add or deduct to fit your own tastes.

| | 10"-100 | 20"-400 | 40"-1600 |
|---|---|---|---|
| **Cotton** | 12 oz. | 2 lbs. 12 oz. | 12 lbs. |
| **Chopped Foam** | 12 oz. | 2 lbs. 12 oz. | 12 lbs. |
| **Down** | 7 oz. | 1 lb. 12 oz. | 7 lbs. |
| **Kapok** | 8 oz. | 2 lbs. | 8 lbs. |
| **Polyester** | 7 oz. | 1 lb. 12 oz. | 7 lbs. |
| **Poly-fil** | 5-6 oz. | 1 lb. 4 oz.— 1 lb. 8 oz. | 5-6 lbs. |

You might think that a 40 by 40 inch pillow would take twice as much stuffing as a 20 by 20 inch one, but as you see, that is really not the case. In addition, each type of stuffing requires that you use different amounts. Therefore, put in the amount recommended and see if the pillow feels really full. Any stuffing will eventually flatten a bit, so always put in more than necessary.

# 6

# CARING FOR LEATHER

Leather is a strong durable material and does not really need special care. However, you don't clean and care for leather the same way you would for cotton and wool.

Mild soap and water will clean off occasional spots, but saddle soap and other leather conditioners are the best, since they soften and condition smooth full-grain leather. When using saddle soap, really work up a lather, not using too much water. Then rub a clean wet rag or sponge over it to remove excess. This will leave a protective coating that helps prevent soiling.

If you want you can also add a conditioner. Leather is able to absorb moisture, but it needs conditioning once in a while to keep it soft and pliable. With patchwork, work each patch separately. Chamois, deerhide, buckskin, or any leather tanned and prepared like either of the last two can be washed in mild soap and water. They may even be machine-washed if removed before the spin cycle so no wrinkles get into them.

Suede and sueded splits can be cleaned with a hard bristle brush or fine sandpaper for spots. The metal suede brushes are rather harsh, but can be used for heavy suede and very dirty splits. If it is just a spot, brush it till clean and the nap is raised. If it is a stubborn spot, a fine sandpaper rubbed on it will do the job. You can damp-clean the spot if you want; when dry, gently brush up the nap. For cleaning an entire article, you can use one of the spray suede cleaners on the market. Before using any cleaner, however, test it on a scrap of that particular type of suede to see how it works. If you're satisfied, go ahead and use it.

I use a silicone spray or suede cleaner on all articles that will accept it right after I make them. These sprays may darken leather slightly, so be sure to test first. I feel a little darkening is worth it for the assurance that I can give my things a lot of wear without worrying about them. (I keep this darkening in mind when buying leather — but remember it is very slight, so don't buy leather three shades lighter than you want it.)

Really major cleanings (which should occur infrequently — especially if you have chosen leathers that grow dirty gracefully) should be done by a professional leather cleaner. Tell the cleaner to test the leather first to make sure it will be all right — especially on multicolored things. Make sure it is an expert cleaner; otherwise it is best to do the cleaning yourself at home.

If leather gets wet, shake it out and hang it up in a cool, dry place, making sure to smooth out wrinkles. If it is full-grain leather, wipe it off with a dry cloth. Let suede dry first, then brush up the nap.

In general, keep suedes and leathers in a cool, not-too-dry place. If you keep them warm, they may become stiff and brittle. Excess moisture may cause mildew. Leather needs to breathe, so don't put it in a plastic bag. Too much heat or light may discolor it. Of course I am talking about excesses; a normal amount of heat, humidity, or light will do no damage whatever. In general, leather stands up very well under all conditions, but should be conditioned in the appropriate manner once in a while to maintain its softness and pliability.

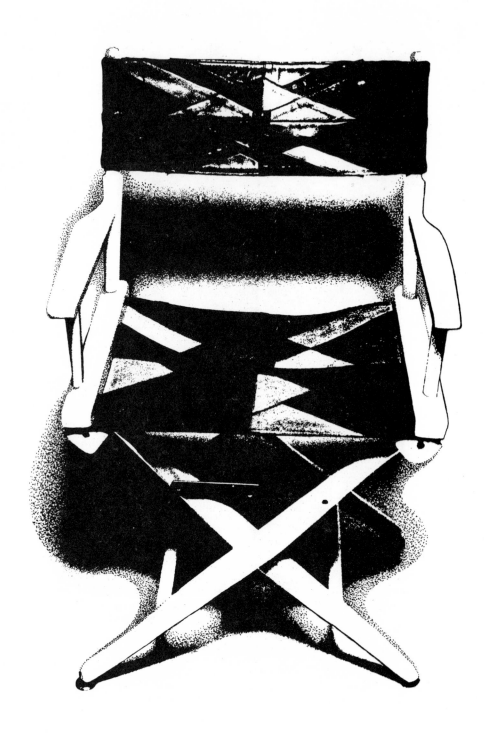

PART II LEATHER FURNITURE

## TOOLS NEEDED

HEAVY BROWN PAPER
CLEAR DRESSMAKER'S RULER
WATERPROOF FELT-TIPPED PEN
SHEARS AND SMALL SHARP SCISSORS
RUBBER OR LEATHER CEMENT AND
  BRUSHES
MASKING TAPE (OPTIONAL)

- MACHINE SEWING

EVEN-FEED OR WALKING FOOT
  (OPTIONAL BUT HIGHLY
  RECOMMENDED)
GLOVER'S NEEDLE FOR BOTH MACHINE
  AND HAND SEWING
HEAVY MERCERIZED THREAD

### OPTIONAL

TISSUE PAPER
SILICONE SPRAY

- HAND SEWING

DRIVE PUNCH
LACING
HARDWOOD BOARD

### OPTIONAL

LACING PLIERS
LARGE-EYED EMBROIDERY NEEDLE
AWL
ROTARY PUNCH

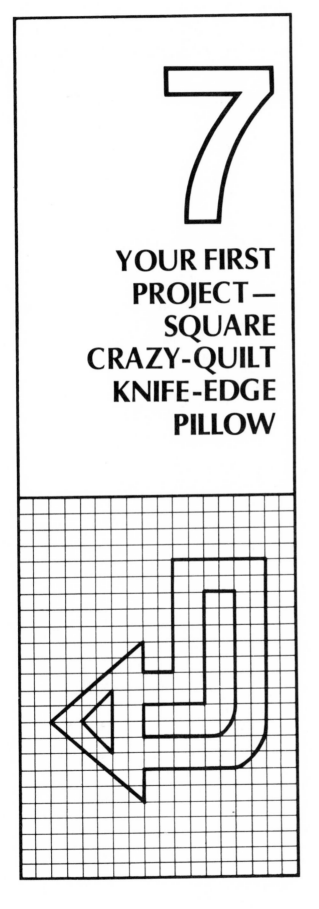

# 7

# YOUR FIRST PROJECT— SQUARE CRAZY-QUILT KNIFE-EDGE PILLOW

People sometimes don't keep their first projects around because they feel these trial balloons don't quite live up to their expectations. But I don't believe there's any point in waste. You should be able to use every thing you make. Eventually, of course, you will be getting into much more intricate designs, but I still use the first leather pillow I ever sewed, years after having made it. The square, crazy-quilt knife-edge pillow is the one project anyone can start with — even if you already have plenty of throw pillows. It will give you practice in working with leather without having to buy a lot of tools and materials. Here you will learn how your sewing machine works — or, if you are sewing by hand, the basics of punching and stitching. I'd like you to learn as much as possible from the very beginning, and experience the joy of creativity from your very first try.

Although you'll probably look on this pillow as an experiment, it is something of real utilitarian value. A pillow is probably the most versatile furnishing you can own. It can be made small enough for a head rest, or large enough to replace your couch. In fact, a pillow can be formed in any shape, becoming a beautiful and practical piece of soft sculpture. Depending on the type you make and the way it is stuffed, a pillow can be put on a platform, into a frame, or just thrown on the floor — according to your taste — and replace much of the large seating furniture in your home. Different types and sizes of pillows, along with director's chairs, are all you will ever need in the way of seating furniture.

No matter what the shape of a pillow, there are only two basic pillow types: the knife-edge and the box-edge. The box-edge pillow has an equal thickness throughout; the square knife-edge is the simplest type of pillow you can make — rounded at the center and tapering to a sharp edge. In making a knife-edge pillow, you will learn the basic construction of leather furniture. And once you have mastered the techniques of constructing the box-edge pillow as well, the whole world of leather furniture making is open to you.

You can make a knife-edge pillow simply by sewing two pieces of leather of equal size together to form the cover for stuffing. However, I suggest crazy-quilt patchwork because any mistakes don't really show up too much; people think they are an intentional part of the design.

I work with patchwork for most furniture, as I love its look, but one additional advantage is that leather seems to be stronger when the "give" is distributed among small patchwork pieces which are joined together. A good example of this is the "pigskin," or football, which is constructed from many pieces put together to form a perfectly balanced, super-strong article.

The idea of patchwork dates back to early Colonial days when cloth was scarce. Women saved little scraps and pragmatically pieced them together, rather than appliquéing them to a background. After a while this procedure refined itself, and classic patchwork quilts were made in more elaborate designs. Common motifs were taken from everyday life and were abstracted into geometric design forms such as Cabin Steps and Le Moyne Star.

I also have leather scraps I don't want to waste, but I don't limit myself to the traditional designs. Just as an artist uses paints to interpret forms and colors in his own way, I use leather, either piecing or appliquéing by machine or by hand, depending on my intentions.

The pillow described here will measure 20 inches by 20 inches. To make this crazy-quilt patchwork throw pillow, you will need two squares of equal size, one for the front and one for the back. The front will be a crazy-quilt assemblage of variously colored leather scraps, and the back will be a solid piece of leather.

## PATTERNS

It is always advisable to make a pattern for a pillow to avoid mistakes when cutting. Accuracy is important. Even though most pillows are square or rectangular, they don't have to be. They can be any shape you want, but if you want an unusual shape your cutting must be accurate. In addition, leather doesn't come in a regular shape, but follows the shape of the animal after it has been slit down the center of the belly. It is therefore hard to draw and cut perfect right angles for corners, to say nothing of straight lines. However, brown butcher paper or even a brown paper shopping bag from the supermarket has definite straight edges, making it much easier to cut accurate patterns that can be transferred to leather.

Cut out a piece of brown paper, the exact size of the pillow bottom — in this case, 20 inches by 20 inches — plus an additional inch in both dimensions to allow for a ½ inch seam al-

lowance all around; if you want a back zipper, add an extra inch on the length. Now fold 1 inch of the pattern length under so that you have a 1 inch flap. By adding this final inch, you will have a pattern that is ready for any contingency (i.e., you can decide later whether to put in a zipper — see section 9 for instructions on zipper insertion).

The pattern for a 20 by 20 inch pillow, therefore, should measure 21 by 22 inches, with a 1 inch flap on the 22 inch side.

You don't have to worry about purchasing large quantities of leather for this first project, but you should still take care when selecting your leather. Lightweight suede or leather — soft but not paper-thin — will be really easy to sew for your first try. When you check your local Yellow Pages for leather suppliers in your area, call them first to see if they sell small quantities. An occasional tannery will sell small amounts; or if a manufacturer of leather articles uses the kind of leather you want, buy his scraps. (Tanneries usually have scraps too, but of a rougher complexion.) Try to find a store that offers leather scraps and buy a bundle of these. The pillow top can be any combination of colors you want. You can mix many different types and textures for effect, but try to have some similarities between them. Make sure the scraps aren't too small, or they will be hard to work with, especially for a first project.

Now ask the leather man for help. Don't use a leather whose dye tends to bleed with one that doesn't. Try to use leathers of about equal strength, and use hides that can be cleaned with the same technique. If you can't find scraps, then buy three small skins of different colors.

For the pillow back, buy one small skin (an animal skin of under 15 square feet). It should be a neutral-colored leather such as brown, black, navy, or beige; or one that picks up the background color of the pattern without clashing or so vibrant as to draw attention from your design.

Mark the back of your cushion first so that you know exactly how many scraps you will have left for use on the top. Lay the pattern flat (with the 1 inch flap turned under if you are not using a zipper in the back) on the wrong side of the leather. Be sure that a straight seam line is always lined with the stretch, so that the straight edges do *not* run diagonally across the grain of the leather. If you cut on the diagonal the leather may not sew properly; worse, you may throw the seams off so that the leather pulls in a diagonal direction, thus making the pillow look as if it is twisting. So fit your pattern's sides parallel to the animal's spine (the straight grain of the leather).

To make the crazy-quilt front — for either hand or machine sewing — take your scraps and sort them according to size. Discard any that are really small and irregular in shape. Trim the larger ones so that they are fairly regular shapes, and lay them over each other in a design you like. If you purchased whole skins, they should be cut into fairly large pieces one by one as needed, and combined with the scraps left after the back piece is cut. Make sure the scraps overlap one another by at least ½ inch. Now trim the excess from the edges, leaving only the ½ to ¾ inch required underlap. Using a brush, glue the pieces together carefully with rubber cement.

If the glue gets on shiny leather, just rub it off when dry. If it falls on suede, let dry and scrape it off gently with a razor, fine sandpaper, or a brush. But try not to be too messy. Rubber cement can become much like used chewing gum sticking to your fingers on a hot day.

When you have glued together enough scraps to cover an area larger than the required amount for the pillow, take your brown paper pattern — with the flap invariably folded under (21 by 21 inches), and place it on the wrong side of the leather. Tape it down or hold it in place with weights. Trace around it with a felt-tipped pen, then cut out the pillow top. If the leather is really thin (or if you are using splits), glue a piece of unbleached muslin or similar fabric very lightly to the back with rubber cement or with leather cement such as Sobo, which remains pliable when dry. Apply the glue very evenly with a brush, and smooth down the backing by running the edge of your ruler over it. This eliminates any air bubbles or lumps of glue that could later form a bump in the cushion.

Any pieces of leather remaining after the pillow is made should be put away for future use. In fact, now is the time to set aside a scrap box or bag into which all scraps and patterns left over from your projects should go. These are very useful for patchwork, appliqué, lacing, and adaptation for future projects.

Give the glue a few minutes to dry. If you sew through wet glue, the needle can become stuck and pull out of the machine, or become dull so it doesn't sew properly. The thread itself may stick in the needle and pull so the leather puckers and, perhaps rips. If you are hand sewing, wet glue will ooze right through onto the right side of the leather when you punch the holes; and the little punched-out circles of leather can become stuck in the barrel of the puncher.

## TOPSTITCHING BY MACHINE

Before starting with the machine, check it over. Put in the appropriate size 14 to 16 glover's needle and, if possible, an even-feed or walking foot. Unless you are using overlap seams with a zigzag stitch, make sure you are using a straight-stitch throatplate (one with a small hole) to prevent the leather from catching in the needle hole — this is especially important for lightweight leathers. Adjust the stitch length to 7 to 10 per inch (for topstitching, 6 to 8 per inch). Any shorter stitch will perforate the leather excessively, causing it to weaken and tear at the seams. (If you do accidentally perforate the seams, make the seam ¼ inch wider, thus avoiding the rip, and glue a tiny strip of muslin over it.)

To sew the top, stitch a row of basting stitches (long stitches) ⅜ inch from the edge around the entire square so that the leather doesn't stretch out of shape with all the pulling when working on it. (This is especially important if you did not back the leather after overlapping). Now the leather top will stay the exact size you planned, and it will fit correctly against the cushion's single-piece back. Then topstitch ⅛ inch in from the edge of each and every piece of the crazy-quilt patchwork pattern (see Fig. G-1).

You can use different types of stitches to sew each piece of the patchwork. You can use a zigzag, a single topstitch, and/or a double row

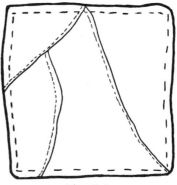

**Fig. G-1**

of topstitching to form a type of double saddle stitch. (When topstitching with my machine, I use a lot of the double saddle-type stitching — not so much with patchwork pillows and things, but a lot with clothing. You might want to practice it here for later use.) I like my topstitching to stand out, so I use thread of a contrasting color — such as red against yellow — which really adds an extra touch. A double row of topstitching gives added strength to places that might need it, but generally I use it as a purely decorative form. (For crazy-quilt pillows, I recommend a single row of topstitching 1/8 inch in from the edge.) You can use different decorative stitches on your machine if you like, but don't make the stitches too close together. Zigzag stitching is best for places that don't get too much wear, because if the stitches are too close together, the leather may rip; and if you put the stitches too far apart, they can snag and break, causing the entire seam to come apart. Keep them at a medium distance — enough for show and strength but not too close or tight to rip and not loose enough to snap.

For topstitching, use a heavy-duty mercerized cotton or industrial three-strand thread if your machine will take it (it should if you are using a heavy glover's needle). Keep the machine going at a slow, steady pace, since sudden stops and starts and too fast a pace can snap the thread. Hold the leather taut both in front of and behind the needle to keep the leather feeding through properly and the stitches even. If the stitches or thread seem to be pulling, use a silicone spray on the spool and bobbin, and perhaps lightly on the leather itself.

Don't worrry if the stitching wobbles a little. Mine does too, but I don't let it bother me unless it's extreme. You can't use the seam guide on your machine here because you will be working in the center of the cushion, so I use a little trick to topstitch leather — I put the zipper foot on the machine. This way I can easily see where the edge of the leather is and am able to judge the 1/8 inch distance. I then stitch around the edges of all the patches, following the corners and curves, being careful to keep as even a seam as possible. It's a snap to do it this way, and I am able to get a row of stitching very close to the edge.

You can't line up a walking foot with the edge as easily as a zipper foot, but it can be done. This even-feed foot has large hole through which the needle passes (like a zigzag foot), so if you sew at a slow, steady pace (as you always should when sewing leather) you can sight through the hole to keep an even 1/8 inch distance from the edge. (You can also use this method with an ordinary zigzag foot in place of the zipper foot.)

If you want a double row of stitching, just line up the edge of the foot 1/4 or 3/8 inch from the raw edge of the leather. Then, using your first row as a guide, sew a second seam line, being sure that the raw edge of the leather and the edge of the foot are always aligned. (For further information on machine sewing refer to Section 3.)

## TOPSTITCHING BY HAND

Either the diagonal stitch (see Fig. D-16) or the flat cross-stitch (see Fig. D-18) — or even a combination of the two — is excellent for use with overlapping seams such as those on the pillow top. Each of these stitches calls for two rows of punched holes, evenly spaced, one on either side of the raw overlapped edges around each patch. For the diagonal stitch, punch a hole in only one row at the beginning of a seam and one in the other row at the end.

Use contrasting lacings or perhaps lacing made from the same color as the back to sew the patches together. The width of the lacing you use can vary according to the effect you want and how detailed the stitching will be — the finer the lacing, the more detailed and closer the stitching. Lacing should be anywhere from 1/8 to 1/4 inch depending on the effect you want.

Again, the size of your lacing and how widely spaced you want the stitches determines the distance between the rows and the punched holes within each row.

Use your clear dressmaker's ruler with its easily readable markings to measure the distance between the punched holes. Mark the places to be punched very lightly with chalk or a lead pencil. You can't be absolutely accurate here, as the patches will all be odd-shaped. Try to judge how to get around corners and curves, and envision the overall picture before you start making

*Left:*
**Author's dining room decorated with leather patchwork director's chairs made from assorted leather scraps (Section 8).**

*Below Left:*
**Close-up of the bulls-eye pattern patchwork director's chair shown in the picture of my dining room — only here on a contemporary high-gloss white enamel frame (Section 8).**

*Below Right:*
**The diamond pattern patchwork on the same frame (Section 8).**

*Above:*
**Author's living room filled with traditional patchwork designs interpreted into two couches (actually four large self-boxing pillows) and a large self-boxing-edge pillow, plus assorted knife-edge throw pillows — all made from leather or suede (Sections 9, 10, and 11).**
*Left:*
**Many colors combine to make a multi-triangle knife-edge throw pillow (Section 9).**
*Below:*
**Close-up full view of a cabin steps suede self-boxing pillow (Section 10).**

*Left:*
**Brown suede poncho decorated with diagonal fringing shows the impact of natural leather (Section 12).**
*Below Left:*
**Beaded brown suede poncho shows how different decorations effect different looks (Sections 12 and 13).**
*Below Right:*
**White leather poncho used as a background for multicolored beadwork (Sections 12 and 13).**

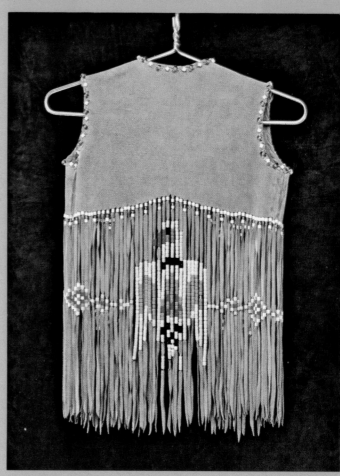

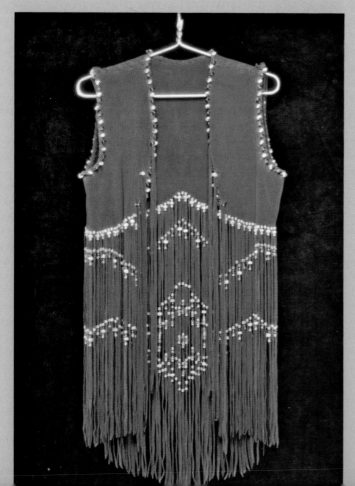

*Above Left:*
**Black suede neckpiece used as a piece of jewelry.**
*Above Right:*
**Tan suede vest decorated with squaw beads worked in a thunderbird motif (Section 14).**
*Left:*
**Purple vest decorated with beaded diamond motif (Section 14).**

Purple suede bead-woven jacket (Sections 15 and 16).

Leather and studs decorate an ordinary dungaree suit (Section 17).

Double-fringed and multicolored beaded jacket (Sections 15 and 16).

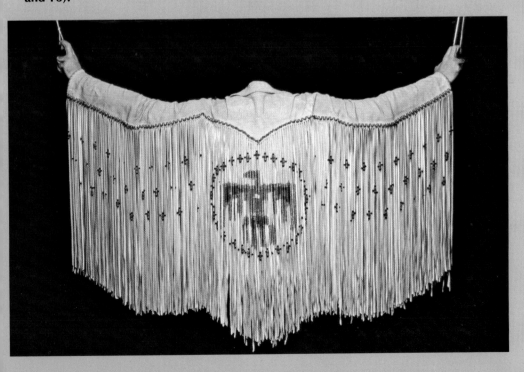

*Right, Above and Below:*
**Front and back views of leather-appliqued cartoon characters on a denim jacket.**
*Below:*
**Denim jacket decorated with a leather and suede seascape design (Section 18).**

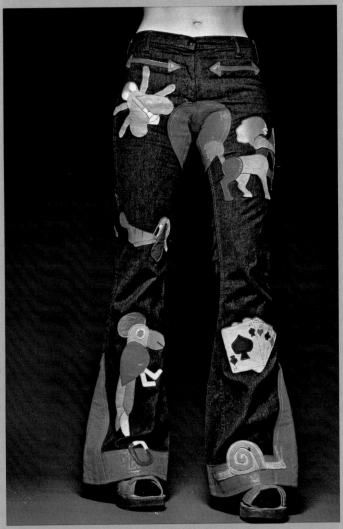

*Left:*
**Crab jacket — leather appliqued over denim (Section 18).**
*Below Left and Right:*
**Front and back views of plain dungarees brought to life by exciting leather appliques (Section 18).**

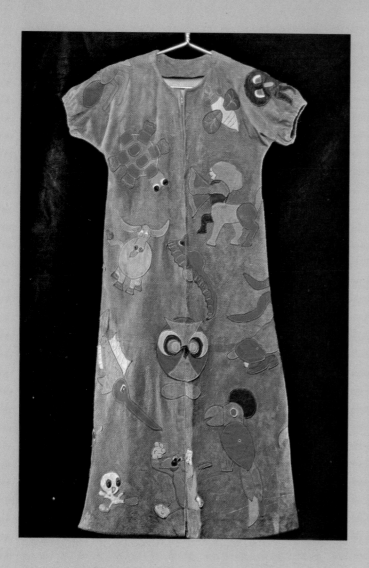

*Above Left and Right:*
**Suede dress or coat covered with many of my
leather appliqués — front and back views.**
*Right:*
**A vest and pants, cutouts and underlays of leather and
suede, make a fashionable outfit (Section 20).**

any holes. You may have to make allowances in order to get around a curve, perhaps by spacing the holes on one row wider apart than on the other row, or even by sewing into the same hole twice. So don't punch the holes too far ahead of your stitching; keep the marking, punching, and stitching at a pretty close pace. However, it is important that you punch and stitch only up to about ¼ inch from the four sides of the pillow top. Do no do any stitching too close to the edges, or around them — you will be edge-stitching there later to join the top and bottom together, and you don't want bulk.

Use a drive punch to make holes here. Mark where you are going to punch holes, and then place your leather — in this case right-side up — over a block of hardwood. Place the punch over the position marked for a hole, and hit it with a mallet just as if you were driving a nail. The punch will remove a small circle of leather. If you do make mistakes, don't panic — mistakes fall into the crazy-quilt design.

To sew the diagonal stitch, bring the lacing from the wrong side through the first hole — on the row with the single hole. Now insert the lacing diagonally into the first hole of the next row, bring it straight across on the wrong side to the adjacent hole, and bring it back up through the right side.

For the flat cross-stitch (spaced), start by bringing the lacing from the wrong side through the first hole. Then insert the lacing diagonally into the second hole of the other row. Then, on the wrong side, bring it across diagonally through to the right side through the third hole of the first row. In a sense, you are doing a diagonal stitch, only sewing into every other hole. When you reach the end, turn around and sew back, filling in the empty spaces.

The length of the lacing is basically up to you. I use rather long lacing (but not long enough for it to tangle) to avoid having to make too many joins in it. What joins I have to make I make as invisibly as possible, so the lacing looks like one long continuous strip. Never join lacings together with a knot unless absolutely necessary; then add a drop of glue and hammer the knot flat. The correct way to begin, end, and join flat seam lacings (see Figs. D-19 and D-20) varies according to the type of stitching being done, so follow the directions for each type care-fully. (For further information on hand sewing refer to Section 4.)

## STITCHING PILLOW TOP AND BOTTOM TOGETHER

When you have finished sewing all the patchwork pieces together, your top will be done. Now trim the edges to be sure they are even. You should have a patchwork leather square of the correct measurement to form the top of your cushion — 21 by 21 inches. But if it isn't quite exact, don't worry; you can adjust it slightly when stitching top and bottom together.

Remember that even if you hand-stitched the patches, you can still use a machine to stitch the top and bottom of the pillow together. Many people hand-stitch as a decorative form and make it part of the patchwork design, but use machine stitching for more functional chores like putting in zippers or stitching the tops and bottoms. Hand stitching is beautiful, but machine stitching can sometimes be more practical. So think about hand stitching just the crazy-quilt patchwork on the top, and use machine stitching where it is part of the "canvas".

To machine sew the cushion together, you will be using a traditional seam, with raw edges hidden on the inside. To make these seams, place the top and bottom pieces of the pillow together right side to right side so that the edges are even all around.

Baste the edges with masking tape (see Fig. C-4) or even paper clips. Just stitch right through the tape and remove it after you have finished sewing. The clips should be left on for as short a time as possible and removed as you come to them.

Use a glover's needle and a seam guide on the machine to gauge your seam allowance. Or take your dressmaker's ruler and mark the seam allowance on the wrong side of the leather — this way there can be no mistakes. To do this place the ½-inch ruler line on the raw edge of the leather and draw a line along the ruler edge.

If there is any fullness in the seams, ease it into the smaller piece of the two, or stretch the smaller seam a little by pulling on it lightly. To insure sharp corners, pivot the needle at the intersecting point of the seam lines.

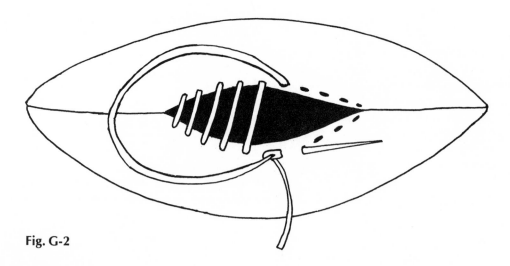

**Fig. G-2**

Sew a ½-inch seam around three sides and enough of the fourth side so that a 6 to 8-inch opening is left for loose stuffing. If you are using a prestuffed form, leave between two-thirds and three-quarters the length of the fourth side open. Always sew around both corners of this fourth side and in at least 2 to 4 inches on the seam edge. Remove the thread spool and bobbin from the machine and sew the rest of the edge seam as if you were stitching the pieces together. This makes holes in the leather so that later, when you have to blind stitch this opening closed, you can merely sew right into the holes already made (see Fig. G-2).

If you are hand sewing, you must sew around three sides and part of the fourth, just as you would with a machine. But in this case, place the top and bottom pieces of the pillow wrong side to wrong side. To join the two together, use an edge-stitch — that is a whipstitch (see Fig. D-11) or cross-edge stitch (see Fig. D-12). If you used a flat cross throughout the top, then use a cross-edge stitch on the outside raw edges. If you used a diagonal throughout the top, then use a whipstitch. (If you used both types, then take your choice here).

With wrong side to wrong side and edges lined up evenly, ease in any fullness. Evenly and lightly glue about six inches of edge together, using a ½-inch seam all around. Use a rubber or nonpermanent leather cement. Let the glue dry till it is not runny but still sticky. Now mark the placement of your holes and punch them. You can, of course, still opt for the drive punch, but this is an ideal place to use the rotary punch, since the holes are around the edges and the punch doesn't have to reach too far.

Be sure to put the right-size puncher in posi-

tion — the holes should correspond to the size of those you punched through the patchwork. Twist the wheel forward till the correct-sized punching barrel clicks into place. Then place it over the mark on the leather where you want the hole to be. Make sure the punching tube is on top and the anvil on the bottom.

Use the same width lacing as you did for the patches, and judge the spacing and size of your holes accordingly. Now punch your holes through the leather all around the pillow, and edge-stitch around the outside of three sides plus part of the fourth. Be sure to sew around both corners on your fourth side, and in at least 2 to 4 inches on the seams. Now gently pull apart the unstitched section and put in the stuffing. Lightly glue the fourth side back up, lining up the holes, and then sew up the rest of the edge.

For both the whip and the cross-edge stitches, you must punch a row of holes (approximately ¼ inch in from the raw edge and ¼ inch apart) around the entire perimeter of the leather square. For the whipstitch, simply insert the lacing into the first hole from inside the two layers of leather to emerge on the right side (see Fig. D-21) then whip the lace over the edge of the leather and insert the lacing into the next hole from the underside.

For the cross-edge stitch, start as you did with the whipstitch, only whip the stitch into every other hole. When you have finished sewing that way, turn and repeat in the opposite direction.

When edge-stitching you will usually, as here, be working with two pieces of leather which are lightly glued together (see Fig. D-21). To begin stitching, gently pull the two layers apart. Pass the lacing through the first hole from

**40**

between the two layers. Leave a 1 inch tail and glue it down immediately between the layers. Each time you run short of lacing, gently pull the two layers apart and pass the lacing through the next hole, but through only one thickness of the leather. After pulling the stitches taut, cut the lacing so as to leave a 1 inch tail which, again, should be glued between the two layers. Then, starting from between the two layers of leather, pull the new lacing through the hole opposite the one through which you ended the other lacing so there is again a 1 inch tail. Glue the two layers of leather together, making sure the tail is inside.

Another way to join the laces is to simply overlap them, glue thoroughly together, and continue to stitch — making sure that both parts of the lacing goes through the punched holes. Put a few drops of clear glue carefully on the inside of these stitches to help hold. Or you can sew the laces together by machine or hand. To finish off, simply stitch over three or so of the beginning stitches (like backstitching). Pull both lacing ends taut, and trim both ends.

## STUFFING, MAKING A FORM, AND FINISHING OFF

The amount of stuffing to be used is determined by how firm, full, soft, or flat you want the final pillow, so it is really a matter of taste. But for a 20 by 20 inch pillow you will usually need 1 or 1½ pounds of polyester Poly-fil.

Of course you can just use loose stuffing right in your leather cushion cover, as long as the particles are substantially larger than your largest lace hole. To do this, simply pack in the loose stuffing and, if machine sewing, blind slip stitch (see Fig. G-2), or if sewing by hand, simply continue edge-stitching the opening so that the top and bottom of the cushion are completely sewn together.

But if you are hand-stitching your cushion, it is really best to use a stuffed form so that loose stuffing won't slip out of the lacing holes. In addition, a form helps to maintain the shape of a pillow better than loose stuffing will.

It's advisable to learn to make your own forms for your pillows, since many times you won't find the size and shape you want among the narrow range of commercial prestuffed forms.

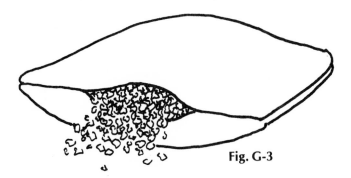

Fig. G-3

Making forms for knife-edge pillows, at least, is quite easy. Simply make a muslin cover the same shape and size as your pillow design (or maybe a little larger — ½ inch). Lay the brown paper pattern which you used for the pillow itself on the muslin (with the flap folded under), and trace around it with your felt-tipped pen.

Do this twice, or once on a double layer of material, so that you have two squares of muslin exactly the same size. Cut them out and sew them together using a ½ inch seam allowance and leaving an opening of 6 to 8 inches for the stuffing in the center of one edge (see Fig. G-3). If you like, you can turn the muslin inside out so that the seams are hidden, and then stuff it to the firmness you want.

Now, making sure the edges are inside, blindstitch the opening together by hand. You don't have to turn it if you don't want, since the raw edges won't show anyway from inside the outer cover. So you can just stuff and sew up the opening. But don't forget to backstitch at the edge of the opening for strengh.

If you don't have a sewing machine, and must make a form, cut out the top and bottom pieces as above. But hand-stitch them together using a fast backstitch. It doesn't have to be neat — no one is going to see it because it's on the inside — so do it quickly.

Now, if you are machine stitching the pillow cover, turn it right-side out and insert the stuffing or form. Then, making sure that the edges are turned to the inside, and using a glover's needle threaded with a double strand of thread, blind slipstitch into the already-made holes (see Fig. G-2). This will finish sewing the bottom and top of the cushion together. To finish off the thread, sew back a couple of stitches and tie a knot. If you hand-sewed the seams of the cushion, simply continue lacing as previously described, and your pillow is done.

41

## TOOLS NEEDED

GRAPH PAPER, BOTH THE SMALL AND
    THE 1-INCH SIZE
HEAVY BROWN PAPER
WATERPROOF FELT-TIPPED PEN
SHEARS AND SMALL SCISSORS
RUBBER OR LEATHER CEMENT AND
    BRUSHES
CLEAR DRESSMAKER'S RULER

### OPTIONAL

MASKING TAPE
RUFFER OR SANDPAPER

• FOR MACHINE SEWING

EVEN-FEED OR WALKING FOOT
    (OPTIONAL BUT HIGHLY
    RECOMMENDED)
GLOVER'S NEEDLES FOR BOTH MACHINE
    AND HAND SEWING
HEAVY MERCERIZED THREAD
AWL OR A VERY SMALL DRIVE PUNCH

### OPTIONAL

BUTTONHOLE TWIST THREAD
TISSUE PAPER

• FOR HAND SEWING

DRIVE PUNCH
LACING
HARDWOOD BOARD
MALLET

### OPTIONAL

LARGE-EYED EMBROIDERY NEEDLE
LACING PLIERS
AWL
ROTARY PUNCH

# 8

# LEATHER DIRECTOR'S CHAIRS

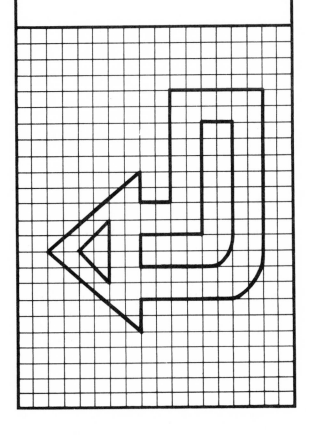

A director's chair is one of the most versatile and economical pieces of furniture you can buy. Director's chairs come in either of two sizes — table height or bar height. In light and dark wood or painted white in a high-gloss enamel, they can be used anywhere in the home and blend perfectly into any decor. But they are even more distinctive if you finish these chairs' canvas upholstery with patchwork, plain, or appliquéd leather — sewn by machine to create a high-fashion look, or hand-sewn with leather thongs or heavy thread for a craftsy appearance. The result is a piece of furniture that you couldn't buy anywhere, your unique creation. The leatherwork itself is really simple to make and great fun to do, and the type of seat and back you construct for them determines their final look.

First remove the canvas seat and back from the chair's wooden frame. Remove the wooden dowel sticks from the piping at both ends of the canvas seat and put them aside till later. If the canvas is old and sagging, wash and dry it. This should bring it back to its original shape; if not, you should replace it with new canvas, using the old material as your pattern.

Undo the row of stitching which forms the loops on the canvas chair back; do *not* remove the stitching which forms the piping on the seat, or the edge stitching on the seat or chair back (see Fig. H-1).

This canvas seat and back — whether new or old — will act as a backing for the leatherwork, so you can use soft, easily workable leathers that would otherwise sag or rip without support.

In addition to these two pieces of canvas, you must cut out a third piece of material (canvas or any other material that doesn't have much stretch) to act as a facing for the chair back. This piece of canvas should be the same width as the back but 6 or 7 inches shorter (see Fig. H-1).

To make a director's chair out of plain leather, simply replace the canvas with leather. Use the canvas as your pattern, and use a strong leather that has very little tendency to stretch. The first director's chairs I made were out of plain leather, but they didn't turn out too well, and in about two weeks they had sagged so much I was sliding onto the floor. Director's chairs get a tremendous amount of pressure and therefore need either a very strong leather or canvas backing. If you use plain leather, get a thick yet pliable kind. Before purchasing it, pull

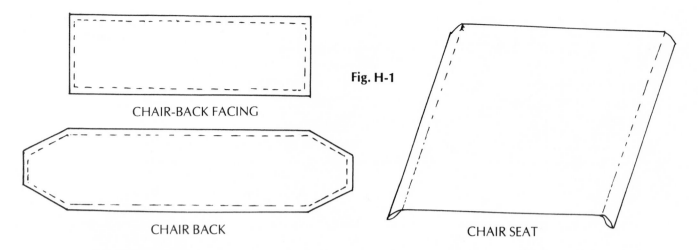

CHAIR-BACK FACING

**Fig. H-1**

CHAIR BACK

CHAIR SEAT

on it to make sure there isn't too much give. The leather should be dyed through completely so that you won't have to double the back, but rather will have leather on one side and suede on the other, but the same color on both.

The most important thing to remember, however, is to be sure to cut the leather so that you are following the grain of the hide. This grain, as I mentioned earlier, is right along the backbone from head to tail, straight down the back. Leather stretches *around* the animal rather than lengthwise — just as with humans. (When you eat a large meal you grow rounder, not taller!) So make sure never to use the belly for large areas which receive pressure, as it will sag. The seat from side to side, therefore, should always be cut lengthwise from the skin of the animal — preferably along the backbone. (In other words, head to tail equals side to side on the chair seat and back.) Withal, plain leather chairs are excellent for later painting, stenciling, and weaving.

For a director's chair with a definite patchwork design (such as those shown in the color section), first make a pattern for the design. The way I adapted patchwork for use on director's chairs shows how really versatile this design form is. You can also make a crazy-quilt design without having to use any pattern at all, and using only scraps. But in either case, the techniques are basically the same, and you should know the complete process first before trying any shortcuts.

To make a pattern, you should start out working on graph paper — an extremely useful accessory for constructing and enlarging patterns, and essential for creating designs in leather. Graph paper comes in various sizes and is used for drawing up original designs for clothing, ap-

pliqués, beading, studding, and many more things. From these original patterns which are done on small-sized graph paper you can enlarge the pattern to its full size on larger-sized graph paper — generally with 1 inch squares. (see Fig. R-1) You need two pattern pieces — one for the seat, and one for the back. (The pattern for the back will also act as the pattern for the back facing.)

The standard measurements for a director's chair are: seat — 20 by 15½ inches, which includes the extra inch which must be added to the length; back — 28 by 7 inches; back facing — 7 by 21 or 22 inches. (The two patterns in Figs. H-2 and H-3 are designed to have a seat width of 16 inches. It is easier to measure this way, and in these designs the edges can be cut off with little or no design loss. However, for designs to fit within the outlines of the seat, it must be an exact 15½ by 20 inches, which includes 1¼ inches at each end for dowels (see Figs. H-4, H-5, H-6, and H-7). But I advise you to stick to the open-edge type of designs until you become proficient enough to be really accurate. Be very precise with these later patterns, and add the seam allowances where you feel is correct.) However, it is a good idea to measure for yourself, to be doubly sure and get yourself into the habit of taking exact measurements. When you measure the seat, don't forget to add 1 inch onto the length.

Now draw a rectangle on the graph paper, making each square of the grid equal to 1 inch of the seat size. Within that area, draw the design you would like to see on the chair. Color it in *lightly* with your favorite colors — making sure that you can still see the lines of the grid underneath. Don't be afraid; if it doesn't turn out right, you can always make another graph.

**Fig. H-2**

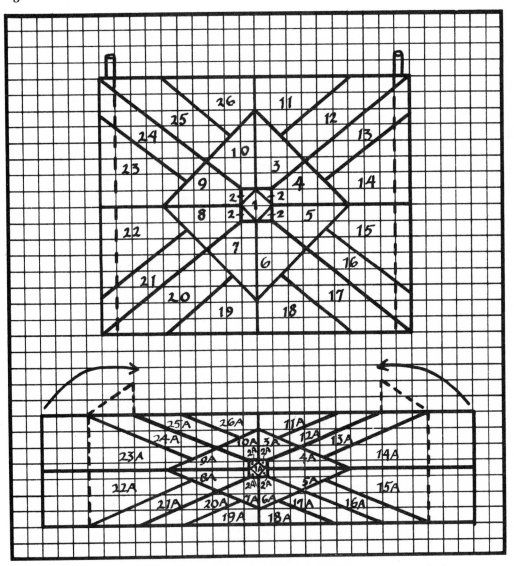

DIAMOND CHAIR PATTERN

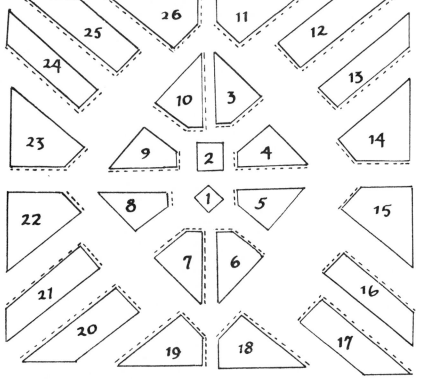

**Fig. H-2a**

**Fig. H-3**

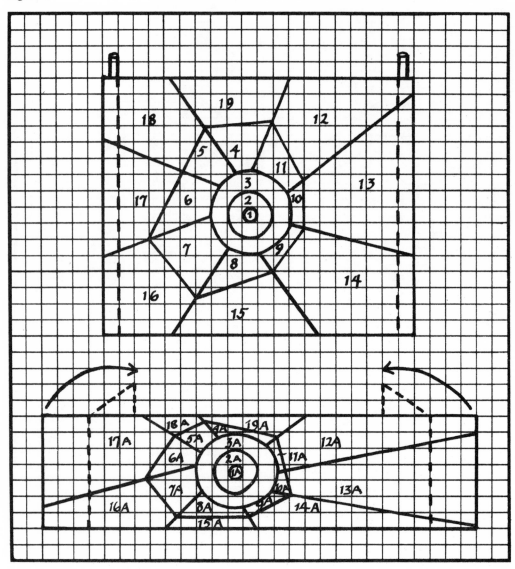

BULL'S-EYE CHAIR PATTERN

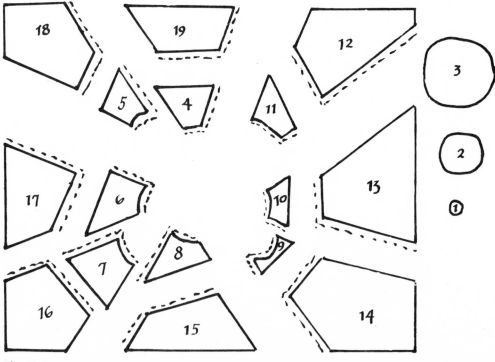

**Fig. H-3a**

**FIG. H-4**

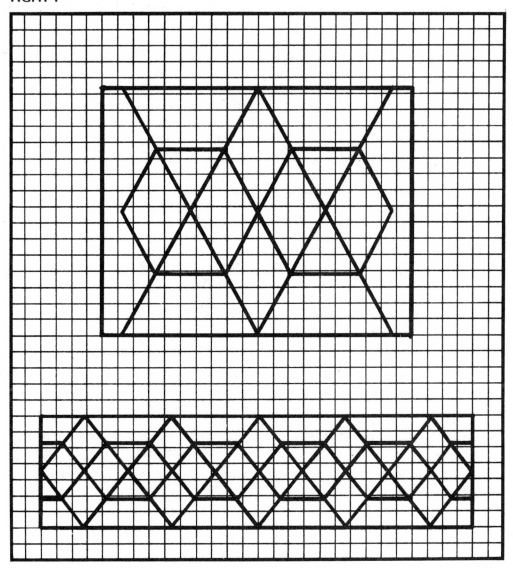

HEX CHAIR PATTERN

**Fig. H-5**

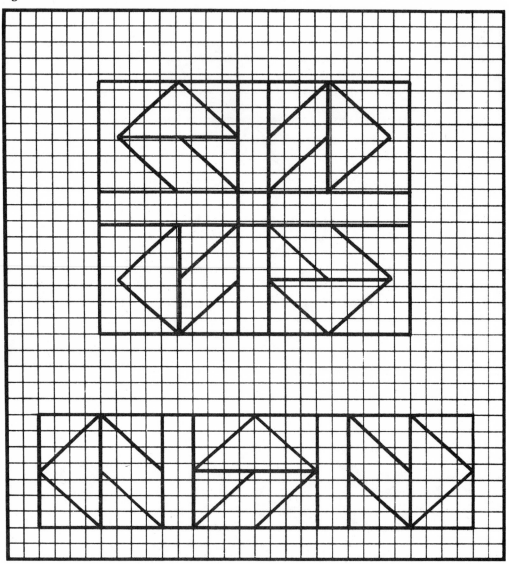

TWIST CHAIR PATTERN

**Fig. H-6**

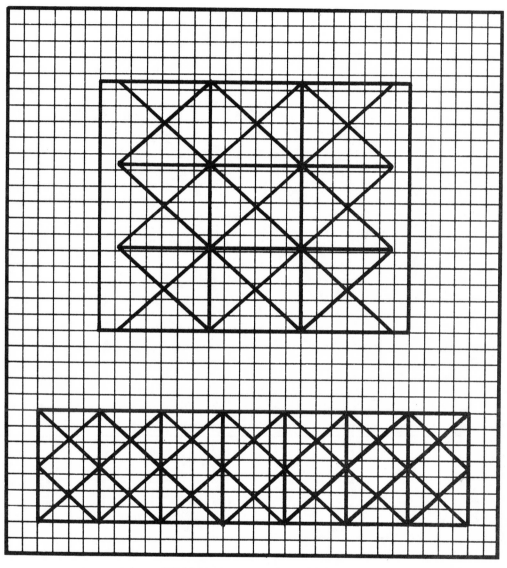

CRISSCROSS CHAIR PATTERN

**Fig. H-7**

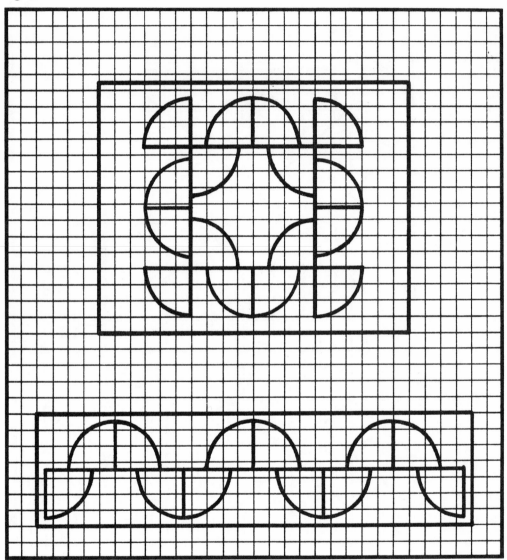

WAVE CHAIR PATTERN

After you have hit on a design you like, draw another rectangle on the graph paper corresponding to the measurements of the chair back. Adjust the seat design so that it complements or matches the elongated length and compressed width of the back. This should not be a duplicate, but rather a new arrangement of the basic concept of the design, adjusted to fit the different shape of the back. Of course, as in everything else, you must use your own judgment as just how to adjust the design, but it usually means making the individual pieces smaller, and not merely chopping pieces off the width or adding pieces onto the length. If you do simply chop and stick on, the final effect will look as if you did just that.

On the bull's-eye chair, I chose to keep the central circles large and to make the outside web smaller, since I felt it would be most effective this way (see Fig. H-3). On the diamond chair, however, everything is scaled down equally, since it is a strictly geometric design and should maintain a regulated quality in order to look right (see Fig. H-2).

After you have adjusted the design on the back, take a heavy pencil and draw a line across the width of the back 3½ squares in from either end. You now have a third rectangle containing the pattern for the facing of the chair back. The facing for the chair back should be a duplicate of the chair back itself, but 3½ inches shorter on both ends to allow for the loops. This new line marks the cutting line for the back facing pieces of the design.

After you have completed the designs on graph paper, you must enlarge the design to its actual size. The graph paper grid makes this job easier. Simply draw your own giant-size graph paper on brown butcher paper, with each square measuring 1 inch. Count the number of squares on each pattern and draw the same number of squares on the brown paper. Or if you already have the 1 inch graph paper, (which you can purchase from your local fabric store or from the address given in the mail-order listing) merely draw the correct size rectangles.

Next, number the graph squares on the outside of the large rectangle around your illustration as seen in Figs. H-2 and H-3, and do the same on the enlarged squares. Now duplicate the design you made on the small graph paper

by marking each square on the larger graph with exactly the same markings as on the small one, drawing the lines in one square at a time. In this way you will get an enlarged design with exactly the same proportions as your original. And don't forget to transfer the lines eliminating the 3½ inch excess on the back facing (the cutting lines for the back facing).

Keep your original graph paper sketch as your guide for assembling the final design. Number each separate pattern piece on the original, and then mark the corresponding enlarged pattern piece with the same number. To distinguish between patterns, use plain numbers for the seat pieces, and a number plus a letter for the back pieces (11 and 11B, for example) to eliminate any confusion.

Cut out each piece of the enlarged version of the design.

You must now make the *final* pattern. Place the numbered pieces on the material chosen for your final pattern — heavy paper, cardboard, or very fine sandpaper — and trace around each, leaving enough room around each piece to allow for a seam allowance of ⅜ to ½ inch. Again, number each piece to correspond with the original pattern, and transfer the lines marking the cutting line for the back facing. Take your clear dressmaker's ruler and add a ⅜ to ½-inch seam allowance on all edges that will be ultimately *underlapping* another piece (see Figs. H-2a and H-3a). To do this, place the ⅜ or ½-inch line in the ruler over the raw edge of the leather so that the ruler edge is on the inside, and draw a line along this edge to indicate the underlap.

If you want, you can eliminate the graph paper stage of this process and just draw your design to scale. Take brown paper and draw rectangles the exact size of the seat and back, then draw your design on this and simply cut it up as your pattern. You might think this way is easier, but it really isn't, as you won't have a sketch to refer to for final construction. In addition, you will have to remember to add seam allowances for underlap directly on the leather. You can get very confused and make many mistakes. I always plan the whole thing out on graph paper and work every step through to be absolutely sure of good results — especially for intricate designs.

In order to correctly add these underlap allowances, you must plan the order in which you are going to assemble the pieces in forming the final design, and know how each leather piece will fit in relation to the other pieces of the pattern. Be sure to add allowances to the underlapping pieces only. Otherwise the size of each piece will not correspond to the original, and you will ruin the final design. You must decide for yourself which will underlap, but in general, if the design has a definite central point, I make that piece the overlapping one and gradually tier down to the border like stepping stones.

After you have cut out your adjusted pattern pieces, you are ready to start cutting the final leather. Place each piece of the pattern with its numbered upper side facing *downward* on the *wrong* side of the leather. Trace around it with a felt-tipped pen. Either use your original drawing as your guide for a color scheme, or make one up as you go along, to make the best use of your scraps. Mark the wrong side of the leather with its corresponding number; and mark all underlap allowances as shown on the pattern pieces to facilitate construction later. (Be sure to put these

markings on the right edges — remember that the pattern is now reversed, so be careful). Mark the cutting line for the back facing, and don't forget — you will need two of each back piece. Now cut your leather — cutting only to the cutting line on the back facing.

After all the pieces are cut and marked, assemble the patchwork, underlapping pieces as planned, and glue them together with their underlaps. Build up the designs like a jigsaw until you duplicate your original graph paper sketch. If you have marked everything properly, you will merely have to match up the numbers to the original, and the assembled leather will correspond exactly. You should now have three solid sheets composed of many pieces of leather.

Now brush rubber or leather cement, evenly and carefully, all over the canvas seat. Be careful not to put glue beyond the row of stitching that forms the piping holding the dowel sticks (see Fig. H-8) — this is the trick to really doing the seat properly. Now press the patchwork leather seat down on the canvas. Trim away any excess leather along the long edges, but *not* on the

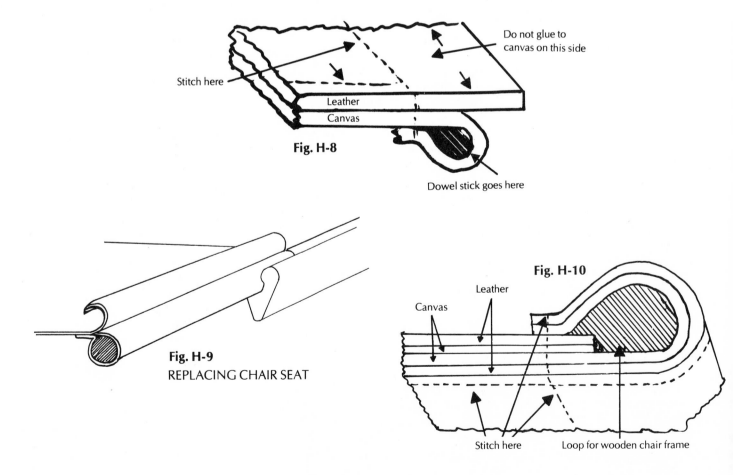

Fig. H-8

Do not glue to canvas on this side

Stitch here

Leather

Canvas

Dowel stick goes here

Fig. H-9
REPLACING CHAIR SEAT

Fig. H-10

Canvas

Leather

Stitch here    Loop for wooden chair frame

ends. There should now be two separate layers at either end of the seat — the original piping of the canvas, plus a ½ to 1 inch overlap of leather.

Glue the appropriate leather patchworks to the canvas chair back and to the chair-back facing. Now take the seat and sew the leather to the canvas along the stitching line which forms the piping. To do this, turn the seat over so that you can follow the stitching line easily. This stitching can be done either by hand or by machine, depending on how you plan to sew the rest of the chair. Make sure you do not make the piping any narrower, or the dowel sticks won't fit in. These sticks must fit into the grooves that hold the seat to the wooden chair frame.

Sew the leather patches onto the canvas seat, back, and back facing, making sure that each piece is sewn securely. If you are using a sewing machine, sew ⅛ inch in from all edges; if sewing by hand, punch holes and lace each patch down using a diagonal or flat cross-stitch. (See Section 4 on hand sewing for hole pattern and sewing techniques.)

Really heavy or intricate lacing doesn't work too well here, since it may be too bulky and uncomfortable for sitting on. Try to punch as little as possible, since too many holes can weaken the chair. Choose one of the simpler lacing stitches and carefully follow the instructions given in Section 4 on lacing. Punch right through both canvas and leather. For this project you should use a drive punch; the size depends on the type of lacing you plan to use. For really intricate designs, I recommend thin (yet strong) lacing, so you don't distract from the design. If you are using a simpler design, however, use heavier lacing and let it add to the overall effect.

Try to keep the lacing flat — a back, diagonal, or flat cross-stitch would be good for sewing the patches together. For the edges, use either a back or a simple edge stitch. For the piping seam, use a running stitch or backstitch, since you don't need any bulk there. For the loops on the back, use a flat cross-stitch or a backstitch. Again, for the crazy-quilt design, try sewing different patches down with different types of stitching; but, as I mentioned, stick to a simple stitch in the intricate geometrics so that the design of the leather can stand out.

Sew the edges of the leather and canvas seat together, either by machine or by hand using a simple edge stitch. Now replace the dowel sticks in the piping and slip the seat into the grooves already made for them on the chair sides (see Fig. H-9). The ½ to 1 inch of loose leather extending beyond the grooves will be concealed when you raise the armrests. This way you can easily slide the sticks in and out of the fabric and the grooves in the wood. If you had attempted to cover the piping for the dowel sticks with leather, they would no longer fit into the grooves of the chair. And if you snipped the leather off before the piping, you would see an unsightly raw edge. This way, the edge is neat and concealed.

After the patches are sewn down, glue the chair back to the back facing (see Fig. H-10). Make sure the facing is centered so there is 3 to 3½ inches of uncovered material on both ends. If you are sewing by machine, topstitch a row of stitching ⅛ to ¼ inch from the edge around all the outer edges of the chair back, being sure that both the back and its facing are sewn together at the same time. You may find your machine won't accept this thickness; if that is the case follow the directions given for sewing the loops back in place. Or, since it is usually the thread that is the problem because it tends to break easily, you can sew with your machine without thread, using a fairly long stitch. This will punch evenly spaced holes into which you can hand-sew with a buttonhole twist or a doubled heavy thread. However, if you sew at a slow, steady speed, using an even-feed or walking foot and a glover's needle, you should generally have no problems.

If you are sewing by hand, edgestitch or saddle stitch around the edges of the back, again making sure that the back and its facing are sewn together.

After this is done, sew the loops back in place (see Fig. H-10). Usually you will find that this thickness will not pass through your machine, and you must begin sewing by hand. If you've never done it before, it's a good place to start — this is in a sense a forced lesson in hand sewing for all of you who wouldn't try it otherwise. But it's easy — just use the right tools, and there's no problem (Of course, if you've been sewing the entire chair by hand, follow these directions also).

First fold the ends over 3 to 3½ inches so

they form loops at both ends — the back should now measure 21 to 22 inches. Glue the loops into place, being sure to glue only a narrow strip of about 1 inch at the very edge. Now take a drive punch, a rotary punch, or even an awl, and punch a series of holes for the lacing. The size of the hole should be determined by the type of lacing you plan to use.

The holes should be ¼ to ½ inch apart and about ⅜ to ½ inch in from the edge. If you have been sewing by machine, but your machine won't sew through this thickness, I recommend using the smallest punch on the rotary punch or an 00 drive punch, and sewing a line of back-stitching with a strong thread such as a doubled buttonhole twist and a heavy needle (embroidery or tapestry with a large eye).

If you have been sewing by hand, use the same lacing material and either a flat cross-stitch or a backstitch. Lace the loops in place, slip the back onto the chair, and it's done. If your leather is grain, not suede, prepare it by using a conditioner or saddle soap to retard soilage.

To make a director's chair without sewing, simply use any of the permanent glues such as Barge's All Purpose Cement or Weldwood to glue the pieces together and attach the leather to the canvas. This is the type of glue used by belt manufacturers, who just glue the lining to the top without stitching. There is no need to stitch the leather down, and you don't need any canvas facing for the back of the seat, since you can glue the leather right on the front and back of the original chair back. However, the glues you will be using are quite permanent and there is no room for mistakes. The only sewing necessary is to remake the loops on the back, which can be either machine- or hand-sewn.

## CRAZY QUILT AND APPLIQUÉ

To make a crazy quilt patterned chair using scraps and no pattern, simply arrange scraps in a design you like. Make sure all the scraps overlap each other, and cover an area at least equal to the size of the seat, back, and back facing. Trim down the patches so they overlap ⅜ to ½ inch. Glue the pieces together. Place the seat, back, and back facing on the wrong side of the glued-together scraps. Trace around the pieces with a felt-tipped pen, and cut out along the traced lines. Glue the canvas to the wrong side of the leather and sew as has been described above, either by machine or by hand. If you sew by hand, you can try using different stitches on different patches to add to the "crazy" quality of the pattern.

After all is sewn down, sew around the edges of the seat, sew the back and its facing together, and sew the loops back in place. You now will have a patchwork director's chair.

Making an appliqué director's chair is quite simple. If you just put the appliqué directly on the canvas, then all you need do is cut out the appliqué, assemble it, then glue and sew it onto the seat and back of the chair. If you sew it on with the same color thread as the canvas, you won't be able to notice the stitching. However, if you want to avoid seeing the stitches on the chair back facing, you can make a mirror image of the appliqué for the back facing. Simply cut out the same appliqué, only this time turn the pattern pieces over, trace around them, and cut. This way you will get a reverse image of the original. Place the appliqués back to back on either side of the chair back, and sew them in place. If they are placed exactly opposite each other, the sewing lines should be the same — or very close to the same — on either side.

If you are using permanent cement, merely glue down the appliqués. However, on surfaces that get as much wear as seats, I strongly recommend sewing appliqués for added strength. And if you are hand-sewing, use narrow lacing and either a zigzag or a diagonal stitch.

A soft-leather-plus-appliqué director's chair is equally easy to make. Use a soft leather such as you would if you were making a patchwork chair, and use the canvas as a backing. Using the canvas as your pattern, cut out three large pieces of leather (all the same colors or mixed as you please): one for the seat, with 1 inch added to the length; one for the back with the loops open; and one for the back facing without the loop allowance. Cut out and assemble your appliqués. Glue the seat leather to the canvas seat — only as far as the stitching lines for the piping — and sew the leather to the canvas, either by machine or by hand, along the stitching lines for the piping and around the edges of the long sides. (If you are hand-sewing, don't forget to use narrow lacing and a flat cross or diagonal stitch for sewing the appliqués.) Glue the assembled appliqué on the seat where you want it and sew it down. You must sew through both the canvas and the leather here, or else the leather may tend to pull away from the canvas. This is also true for the seat back, so glue the leather to the can-

vas chair back, glue the appliqué to the leather, and then sew it down.

The chair back facing gets very little wear, so simply glue the appliqué onto the leather and sew it down. Now glue the seat back and its leather facing together and sew completely around the entire outside edge, being sure that the back and its facing are sewn together. Now sew the loops back, and it's done.

55

## TOOLS NEEDED

GRAPH PAPER, BOTH THE SMALL AND
  THE 1-INCH SIZE
HEAVY BROWN PAPER
WATERPROOF FELT-TIPPED PEN
SHEARS AND SMALL SCISSORS
RUBBER OR LEATHER CEMENT AND
  BRUSHES
CLEAR DRESSMAKER'S RULER

### OPTIONAL

MASKING TAPE
RUFFER OR SANDPAPER

• FOR MACHINE SEWING

EVEN-FEED OR WALKING FOOT
  (OPTIONAL BUT HIGHLY
  RECOMMENDED)

GLOVER'S NEEDLES FOR BOTH MACHINE
  AND HAND SEWING
HEAVY MERCERIZED THREAD
AWL OR A VERY SMALL DRIVE PUNCH

### OPTIONAL

BUTTONHOLE TWIST THREAD
TISSUE PAPER

• FOR HAND SEWING

DRIVE PUNCH
LACING
HARDWOOD BOARD
MALLET

### OPTIONAL

LARGE-EYED EMBROIDERY NEEDLE
LACING PLIERS
AWL
ROTARY PUNCH

# MULTI-TRIANGLE PILLOW WITH CONCEALED SEAMS AND ZIPPER

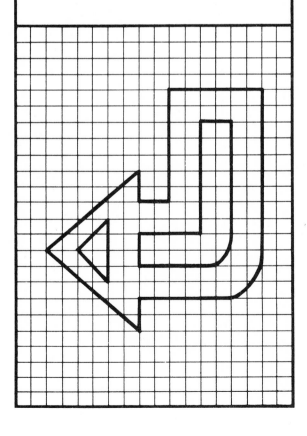

The small, multicolored, triangular patch pillow shown in the color photo is an example of patchwork with a nontraditional but definite pattern. Though this pillow is the same knife-edge type as the one described in Section 7, it has some refinements — including a definite patchwork design, concealed seams with machine stitching, and a zipper in either the side or the back.

The same principles given for making patterns in the last section on director's chairs apply here, but in this pattern you must add varying types of seam allowances, depending on whether you are using concealed or underlapped seams. Generally, hand-sewn seams are overlapped and machine-concealed, but not always. So this section covers the finer points in the construction of pillows.

Everything about these pillows must be planned in advance. Of course situations crop up that require spur-of-the-moment ingenuity, but why make work over some trivial mistake that could quite easily be avoided? Creativity comes after you are in complete control of your medium, otherwise it can be a waste of good ideas with no goal.

If you want to make your own design for this type of pillow, follow the directions given for making patterns in the director's chair project. But here, draw a square to correspond to the size of the pillow top desired. If you are machine stitching and want to use traditional concealed seams, be sure to compose your designs from basic straight-edged geometric shapes such as squares, rectangles, diamonds, or triangles. With concealed seams, curves can be tricky. And don't work with too many small pieces, as they can be time-consuming and frustratingly hard to put together. Add seam allowances to the pattern pieces in accordance with the type of seaming you are planning to use — traditional concealed or underlapping.

It is difficult to give hard and fast rules, but for this project look for leather that is strong, yet soft and flexible. Many leathers will fit this description, but I am rather partial to garment cowhides. They are leather on one side, suede on the other, and dyed all the way through — and are thus reversible, making them extremely versatile. You need not restrict yourself to these hides, as they only come in a limited number of colors, but I do think these skins are a pretty good guideline. Of course you won't find exact dupli-

**57**

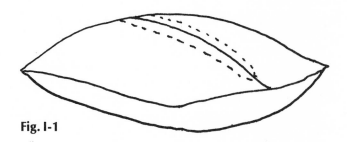

**Fig. I-1**

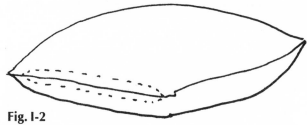

**Fig. I-2**

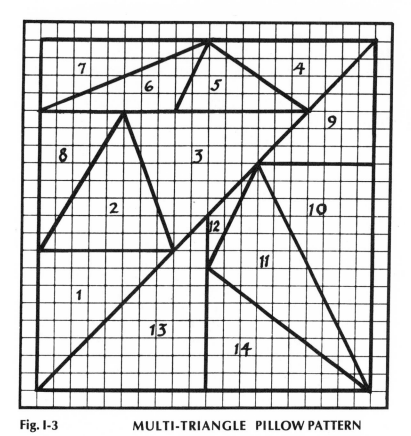

**Fig. I-3**     MULTI-TRIANGLE PILLOW PATTERN

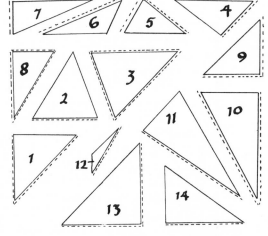

**Fig. I-4**

**Fig. I-5**

**Fig. I-6**

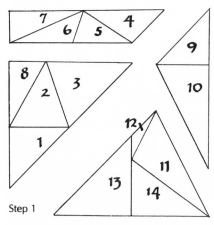

Step 1

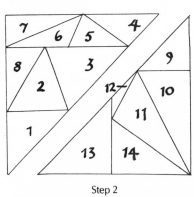

Step 2

cates, but look for leather with similar qualities and texture. I didn't use muslin to back this pillow, since the leather was all fairly strong. Of course, if your leather appears weak, back it. If you make your sampler (crazy-quilt) pillow as previously described, you should know something about leather by now. Having used various types of leather, you are in a far better position to judge your needs and what qualities you like in the leather you work with.

You will find that leather hides are sold in three different ways: whole skins, 25 square feet and over; half skins; and in some places, quarter skins (see Fig. A-2). You should buy two half skins — one in a fairly subdued neutral color for the back, and the other in one of your favorite colors. For the other patches, use scraps from your previous projects — which should by now be in your scrap bag — or get some new ones from leather suppliers.

To make the pillow pictured, use the same pattern you used for your sampler — 21 by 22 inches with 1 inch folded under on the 22 inch length to form a flap. This pillow too will measure 20 by 20 inches when completed. The top will be a patchwork construction, and the back a plain piece of leather. If you want, there will be a zipper either in the back or in the side seam, whichever you prefer.

In the illustrated pillow, fourteen pieces (in this case, triangles) form the top of the pillow cover. Each is a different color, but if you don't have that many colored scraps, you can use duplicates. However, as there is such a variety of triangular sizes, you can use even small scraps for some of them, thus stretching your scraps. The back is of olive green leather — the same color as one of the larger patches on top. You can use any color you want on the back as long as it is fairly neutral and doesn't draw attention from the patchwork design.

Use your brown paper pattern to cut out the back piece. Decide whether you want a zipper or not, and if so, where. If you want it in the back (see Fig. I-1), unfold the flap so the pattern measures 21 by 22 inches. If you want to put the zipper in the joining-edge seam (see Fig. I-2), fold the flap under so the pattern measures 21 by 21 inches.

Enlarge the graph paper pattern in Fig. I-3 using the procedure outlined in the chapter on

director's chairs. Each square on the graph paper here is equal to 2 inches on the finished pillow. When making up your pattern on brown paper, leave enough space between each pattern piece to allow for added seam allowances.

If you are planning on sewing by machine using traditional concealed seams, add ½ inch seam allowance around each edge of every piece of patchwork pattern (see Fig. I-4). If you are using overlapping seams — whether hand- or machine-sewn — add the ½ inch seam allowance to the underlapping seams only, as you did in the construction of the director's chairs (see Fig. I-5).

Where you underlap is basically up to you, but remember to add to underlaps only, and not to the overlaps. This way you will keep the exact proportions you planned on. Think carefully before deciding. For instance, in planning the underlaps for this pattern, I decided to construct it by sections to make it easier to work with (see Fig. I-6). First I built smaller sections, then I combined them to form larger sections until finally I had a square for the top. I try to make at least one or more underlapping seams on each patch, and let the other edges overlap, to add strength. I worked out the underlapping plan thinking of how each piece would fit in relation to the others.

Now cut out each piece of the pattern — remember to number each piece with the corresponding number from the original pattern.

To help save time and make things accurate, save the pieces cut out of the large graph paper. Then make up your pattern and cut it out. You will have two patterns for each piece of patchwork — one with seam or underlap allowances added, and a smaller one the exact size of what your finished piece should be.

Lay your larger pieces — the ones with seam allowances added — face down on the wrong side of the leather, being sure that patches are not cut on the diagonal of the stretch.

Use scraps for these pieces if possible, and try to make the best use of each scrap. Don't waste a large piece of leather by cutting a small patch out of it, only to find later that you haven't got a scrap large enough for one of the bigger triangles.

Trace around each pattern piece, remove it, and then work the leather with the corresponding number. Now, before cutting place the smaller graph paper pattern in the exact center of the patch — if you are using concealed seams — or lined up against an edge with no seam allowance for underlapped seams. Now trace around this piece too, and you will have both a cutting and a stitching line.

If you use this method, do it properly and accurately. I prefer to use the dressmaker's ruler method, as I find I have a lot of control. But always do mark the seam allowance on the wrong side of the leather patchwork so that you can be absolutely accurate when joining the patches. For concealed traditional seams, mark a seam allowance on each edge of the patch, using your dressmaker's ruler. If you are using overlapping seams — whether for hand or machine sewing — mark the seam allowance on the wrong side of the patch which will overlap the ½-inch underlap allowance. This way you will be able to underlap easily and accurately, lining up the raw edge of the underlap with the mark on the upper piece and gluing them together.

Next, before starting to join the pieces, you must figure out the best order in which to sew the patchwork design together. By sewing haphazardly, you can get into difficulties trying to get around awkward points and corners, so think before you sew. See how all the seams will join together and try to get an overall picture. Keeping your seam lines as straight as possible will make it

easier. Try to join pieces in sections that can be joined to other sections, thereby building up to the finished design in steps.

For example, with the irregular patchwork pattern shown in Fig. I-3, sew — or glue and sew for overlapped seams — in the following order: 1 to 2, 2 to 8, 2 to 3 — thus forming Section A. Put it aside and go on to the next one. Sew 5 to 6, 6 to 7, 5 to 4, giving you Section B. Now connect Sections A and B along the seam line formed by patches 6 and 5 on Section B and patches 8 and 3 on Section A. Once you have done this, you will have a larger section forming a triangle equal to half the pillow top — Triangle I. (see Fig. I-6).

Now join patch 9 to 10, forming Section C. Join patch 12 to 11, 11 to 14, 13 to 12 and 14, thus forming Section D. Now join Section C to Section D along the seam line of patches 10 and 11 to make a second triangle forming the other half of the pillow top — Triangle II (see Fig. I-6). Now join these two triangles along the longest side of each triangle, completing the pillow top.

To help prevent stretching and slippage, baste your seams together. With overlapping seams, basting is done by gluing (with a small brush to avoid a mess and for accuracy) the underlapping pieces under the overlaps. Line up the raw edge of the underlapping piece with the marked allowance on the wrong side of the piece overlapping it.

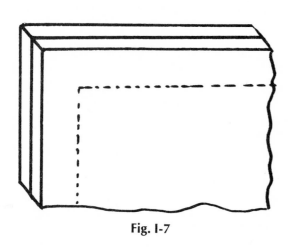

Fig. I-7

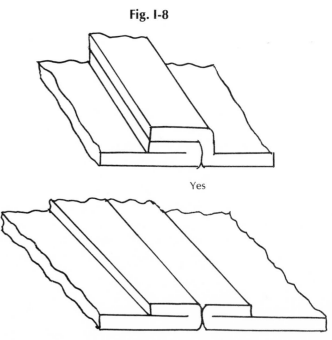

Fig. I-8

Yes

No

For traditional concealed seams, place the patches right side to right side and baste the seam together by taping over the raw edges with masking tape. Make sure that the seam allowances, and especially the points formed by the intersecting seam lines, are properly aligned. If you find the seams don't quite fit together, ease or stretch them together so that they are the correct length and fit together properly. If you find a great discrepancy in the seam lengths, check to be sure that you are basting the correct seams together.

If you are using a machine, check it over to make sure it is working properly. For concealed seams, simply sew a line of stitching along the seam line, sewing only as far as the point formed by the intersecting seam lines on either end of each side of the triangles (see Fig. I-7). Start sewing about ¾ inch from the end of the seam line and backstitch to the intersecting point of the seam lines. Then, sewing directly into the holes already formed by the backstitching, sew up the rest of the seam. Then backstitch directly into the holes already made on the seam line to join the beginning of the stitching, so that the seam is actually sewn with two strands of thread (double stitched) for strength, and so the ends are secured. Be very careful when backstitching, as too many holes in leather can cause it to weaken and rip.

After you sew each seam, glue it down to one side — in whatever direction you feel is best and which causes the least bulk. Never open patchwork seams flat while gluing — this will weaken the stitches by leaving them no backing. Gluing the seams to one side will strengthen them, since there can be no pull on the stitches — all the pressure will be exerted against the strip of leather underneath which is formed when you glue the seam allowances to one side. (see Fig. I-8).

If you are sewing by hand, assemble your pieces in the same order as above, sewing the pieces in each section together first, then joining the sections together. Use a spaced flat cross-stitch or diagonal stitch. Mark and punch two rows of holes, one on either side of the raw edge of the overlapped seams. Be sure to keep your stitches properly planned here. In the sampler pillow you didn't have to worry too much about neatness, but here you are dealing with very

straight lines. Try to keep a uniform look in your stitching — neat and disciplined. This doesn't mean absolute precision, but it does mean working with your dressmaker's ruler, measuring as accurately as possible. You should now be ready to control your placement of stitching to a degree, adjusting the distance between stitches so that holes do not cut through or too close to the edge of any patches. You must figure out how to sew around places like points, and try not to interfere with the stitching of other seams so that you don't have to overlap stitches and seams, causing bulk. Try to sew so that every part of the patch — even the point — is sewn securely and neatly.

Again, the type of lacing and the spacing of the stitches is up to you, but as a rule, try to follow the advice given in Section 8. Very precise geometric patterns should have narrower lacing so as not to distract from the design, but more organic designs can take thicker, more noticeable lacings.

Be careful to glue and sew patchwork pieces *exactly* along the stitching lines. If your seams and cutting are accurate, your pieces should fit together as neatly as a jigsaw puzzle. It is absolutely essential that you be accurate in sewing, because everything must fit together properly to obtain the perfect size in your finished piece. This will become really important in traditional geometric motifs such as Cabin Steps, Le Moyne Star, or other intricate designs; which is why I suggest starting your precise patterns with this irregular triangular one — the different size triangles will give you plenty of practice in construction, but because it is not an exactly precise pattern, you can afford to make a few mistakes. If a few points get knocked off the triangles, don't worry too much. Just learn by it, so you will have less trouble with the more intricate patterns where accuracy is a must.

## ZIPPERS

Whether you are sewing by machine or by hand, if you want a zipper in the back or side, you must put it in *before* sewing the top and bottom of the pillow together. Putting a zipper in is very simple, but remember that you really can't use a zipper with loose stuffing. I rarely use zippers

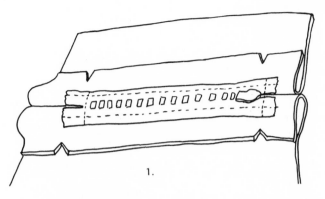

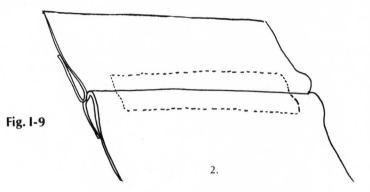

Fig. I-9

1.  2.

with small pillows and put them only in very soft suede or leather throw pillows that might need to be sent to the cleaner's. For more durable pillows I usually don't bother with zippers, since I can easily clean them without removing the stuffing, using either saddle soap for leather or a suede cleaner and brush for suede. (See specific details of leather care in Section 6). When the stuffing loses its fluffiness, I simply undo some stitching and replace it.

To insert a zipper, first decide what size zipper you want to use. The form will usually require a zipper at least two-thirds to three-quarters the length of the seam, or one that fits the entire length for large pillows. For a 20 by 20 inch pillow, you will need a 14 to 15-inch zipper. Use a dress zipper for this size pillow, as it is the best for small openings. For putting a zipper in the joining seam with a machine, place the zipper along the center of one edge of the cushion top — on the wrong side — to see how much room it will take up. Mark the ends of the teeth, plus ¼ to ½ inch on either end, by making a notch on the raw edges of the seam allowances. (Or you can simply measure the length of the teeth plus ¼ to ½ inch on either end with a ruler, and then mark the measurement on the leather — centering it, of course.)

Then, being sure to line up the ends of the seam, place the edges of the top and bottom together and sew both ends of the joining-edge seam just up to the notches for the zipper. Then finish off these little seams by tying the end of the thread, or backstitching into the holes already made. Now change the stitch on the machine to a long basting stitch and sew up the rest of the seam. (If the zipper fits the length of the seam exactly — as it should be for large pillows — baste the entire seam.) Glue and pound this seam out flat, but only within the marked

zipper area plus about ½ inch on either end.

Take your zipper and place it face down on the wrong side of the leather — within the markings made for it—so that the center of the teeth is placed exactly over the seam (stitches). Glue the zipper tape down on the leather. Be sure to glue it carefully, so that glue does not get on the zipper teeth. Wait for the glue to dry, then — using a normal-sized stitch — stitch down one side, across the end at the notch, down the other side, and across at the other notch to meet the stitching where you began. Blend the stitching together by sewing into the same holes made by your first few stitches. Now remove the basting stitches along the zipper line, but don't undo the regular stitching at the ends of the edge seam (see Fig. I-9).

Open the zipper and leave it open so that you can turn the cover to the right side when completed. You are ready to stitch up the other sides of the cover.

If you prefer to put the zipper in the back of the cushion — a better place for larger pillows — you should have already planned and allowed for it when cutting the back piece, and have added an extra inch to the length. If you have done this, you must now cut the cover in half across the width. (For extra long rectangular pillows, you have to add to the width and cut across the length. If you added to the length and cut across the width, you wouldn't be able to put in a zipper long enough for the form to be inserted.) Now insert the zipper in this new seam by cutting the back apart and proceeding the same way you would in a joining seam: Line up the raw edges after marking the length of the zipper teeth plus ¼ to ½ inch at both ends by notching the edges. Sew, with regular stitching, up the seam to these notches. (If the zipper is the exact width of the seam, simply baste the entire seam together.) Glue and pound seam open,

62

place the zipper face down on the seam, glue it in place, and sew it down.

Sew up the remainder of the seam with machine basting. Hammer open and glue the seam along the place reserved for the zipper. Place the zipper on the wrong side of the leather so that the center teeth are on the seam line; glue the zipper tape down. Sew the zipper down one side, across the end, up the other side, and across the other end to meet the original stitching (see Fig. I-9). This will join the two back pieces together again.

This is the easiest way to put in a zipper. However, there is another method many people consider neater and one which you use for zipper joins that are readily visible (see Step 4 of Fig. I-10). Prepare for zipper insertion in the joining-edge seam, but do *not* glue the seams open and down. Place the zipper face down on the seam allowance for the back of the pillow with the teeth on the seam line. Glue the zipper tape down, and sew through the tape and seam allowance only (*not* through to the right side of the leather) (see Step 1 of Fig. I-10). Now turn the zipper face up, thus making a narrow fold in the back seam allowance (the one you just sewed the zipper to). Stitch very close to the edge so that you sew through both the seam allowance and the zipper tape. You will thus be sewing through a double layer of leather on the back seam allowance and also sewing through the zipper tape (see Step 2 of Fig. I-10).

Now spread the back and the top of the cushion out flat. Turn the zipper face down flat, thus forming a small pleat in the back seam allowance at both ends. Glue the zipper tape down, then stitch the zipper to the pillow across the bottom of the zipper, along the front of the pillow side, and across the end of the zipper through the tape (see Step 3 of Fig. I-10).

You can use this same method to install the zipper in the back surface of a pillow; but for your first zipper, use the simpler technique.

Zippers and hand lacing may seem like a strange mixture, but a zipper is a very convenient closure; and you will most probably use both at some time. Actually ,it is very easy not to bother to put a zipper in hand-sewn leather pillows, as you can unlace a portion of your lacing and remove the form, clean the leather, replace the forms and relace through the ready-made

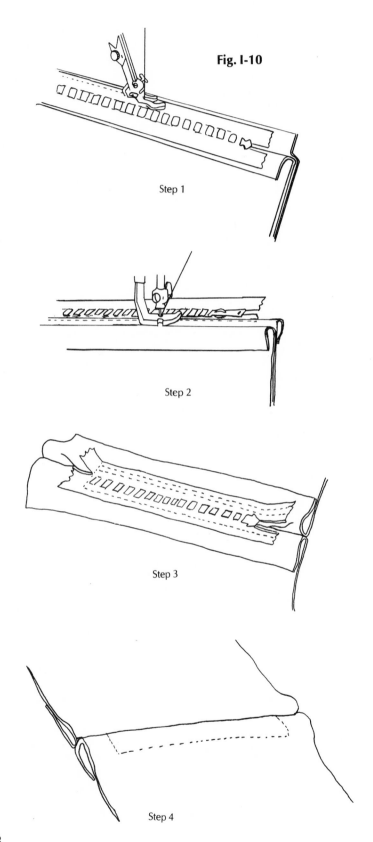

Fig. I-10

Step 1

Step 2

Step 3

Step 4

holes. If you do use a zipper, the best way — if you don't mind combining machine stitching with hand stitching — is to put it in the back surface of the pillow as just described, using your machine to sew it. Or you can put it in the joining-edge seam with a combination of hand and machine stitching.

To do this, turn under the ½ inch seam allowance of one edge of both the top and bottom pieces, glue them down, and hammer them flat. Then edge-stitch (with either a whip or a cross-edge stitch — whichever you are planning to use to sew the top and back together) the entire top edge, being sure to edge-stitch very close to the edge.

Now glue a 1 inch wide strip of leather — the same color as the pillow back — face up to each end of the zipper, about ¼ to ½ inch past the teeth, overlapping the tape at either end of the zipper so that you extend the length of the zipper tape to fit the entire length of the seam (see Step 1 of Fig. I-11). (Of course, this is unnecessary if your zipper fits the entire length of the seam to begin with.) Abut the edges of the turned-under seams or very slightly overlap the top — with its edge stitching — over the bottom, so they are lying down flat. Lightly tape them together with masking tape. Center the zipper face down with its extended ends so that the center of the teeth are exactly over the center of the abutted seam (see Step 2 of Fig. I-11). Glue the zip-

per tape and leather strips at either end of the zipper down so that the wrong side of the leather cover is against the right side of the zipper (see Step 3 of Fig. I-11).

The top and bottom pieces of the cushion should now be connected. Machine stitch the zipper in place, and then continue your stitching across the entire width of the seam so that you sew the leather strip down also. Open the zipper and remove the masking tape as best you can.

If you don't have a sewing machine, or want to use a zipper in the back with hand stitching, you should have added the extra inch to the bottom piece. Now put the zipper in the same way as you did for the side-joining seam, only do not bother to edge-stitch. Instead of machine stitching, punch holes through the leather, zipper tape, and leather stripping. Do the running stitch (see Fig. D-14) or backstitch (see Fig. D-15) across the entire width of the back, thereby inserting the zipper and joining the two sides of the back together (see Fig. I-12). .

To punch holes for the running stitch or backstitch, punch a single row of holes in a straight line. To sew the running stitch, start stitching from the wrong side and pull the lacing through the first hole to the right side, leaving a 1 inch tail on the inside. Now simply weave in and out of each consecutive hole. (Make the holes fairly close, so that you get good tight stitching.)

**Fig. I-11**

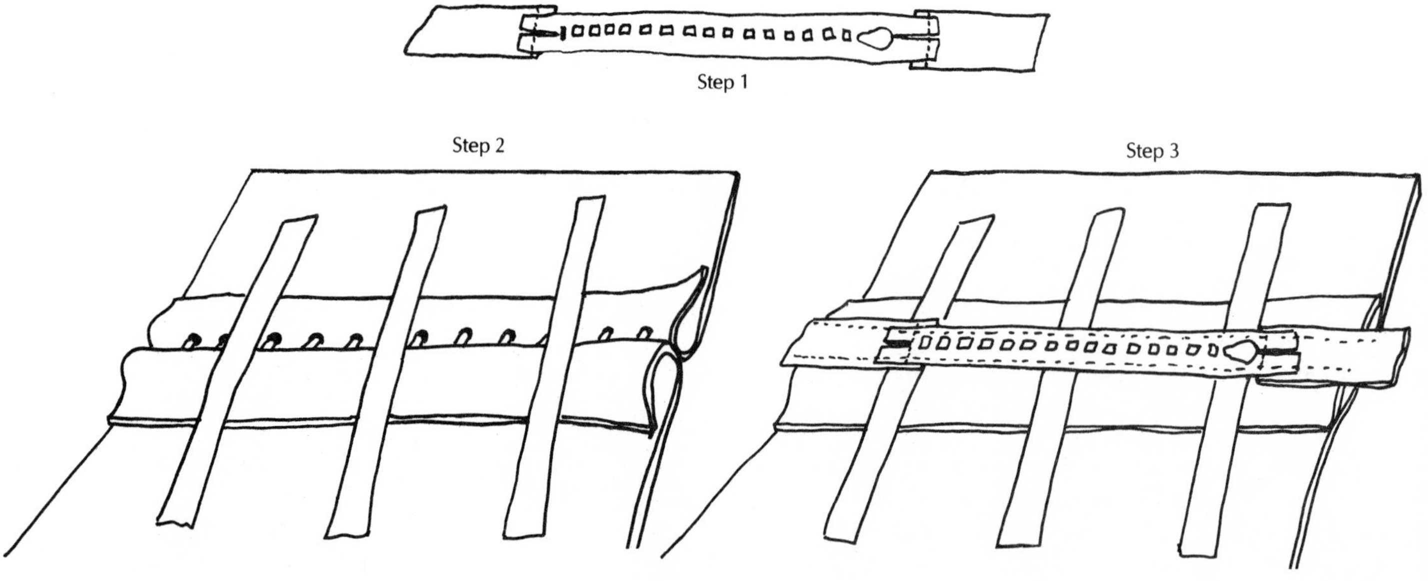

Step 1

Step 2

Step 3

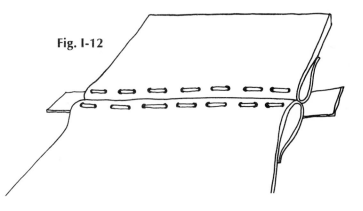

**Fig. I-12**

If you feel this may not be strong enough, do the backstitch. Punch holes the same as for the running stitch. Start by bringing the lacing up through the second hole on the seam, then lace back into the first hole, then pull it through the third hole from the wrong to the right side. In other words, stitch the lacing back into its starting point and pull it through the next empty hole. Attach the ends of the leather securely to the wrong side.

The method of abutting the seams over the zipper and strips of leather on either end of the zipper to extend its length is also useful when you want to insert zippers without using any seam allowance. This way you would simply abut the raw edges of the leather. This is especially useful for heavy leather and also for the times when you forget to leave any extra leather for seam allowances — which often happens.

After you have constructed the top and put the zipper in either the side or back, the bottom and top must be sewn together to form the cover for the pillow.

If you are machine stitching and have inserted a zipper in the joining-edge seam, then simply open up the zipper and turn the cover so that the right side of the front faces the right side of the back. Join the three remaining sides together with masking tape, making sure they are even, and sew them together using a ½ inch seam allowance. Then turn the pillow right-side out, and put in the form.

If the zipper was inserted in the back, and you are machine sewing the top and bottom together, open up the zipper and place the front and back pieces face to face. Then baste the edges together and sew around the entire perimeter of the pillow cover, using a ½ inch seam allowance. Then turn the pillow through its own zipper opening so that the right side is out.

If you are sewing by hand and have inserted a zipper in the joining seam, then glue the other three sides together with a ½ inch seam, making sure they are facing wrong side to wrong side. Then mark and punch holes around the three sides. Using the edge-stitch of your choice, sew top and bottom together around these three sides, starting and joining the lacing as described in Section 4.

If you inserted the zipper in the back with hand stitching (or even machine stitching), glue a ½ inch seam around the edges of the entire cushion. Make sure the wrong sides are together. Mark and punch holes, and sew the pillow together around all four sides.

## TOOLS NEEDED

GRAPH PAPER, BOTH SMALL AND THE
    1-INCH SIZE
HEAVY BROWN PAPER
WATERPROOF FELT-TIPPED PEN
SHEARS AND SMALL SCISSORS
RUBBER OR LEATHER CEMENT AND
    BRUSHES
CLEAR DRESSMAKER'S RULER

### OPTIONAL

MASKING TAPE
RUFFER OR SANDPAPER

### • FOR MACHINE SEWING

EVEN-FEED OR WALKING FOOT
    (OPTIONAL BUT HIGHLY
    RECOMMENDED)
GLOVER'S NEEDLES FOR BOTH MACHINE
    AND HAND SEWING
HEAVY MERCERIZED THREAD
TISSUE PAPER (OPTIONAL)

### • FOR HAND SEWING

DRIVE PUNCH
LACING
LARGE-EYED EMBROIDERY NEEDLE
HARDWOOD BOARD
MALLET

### OPTIONAL

LACING PLIERS
AWL
ROTARY PUNCH

# 10

## BOX-EDGE PILLOW/CUSHION WITH CABIN STEPS DESIGN

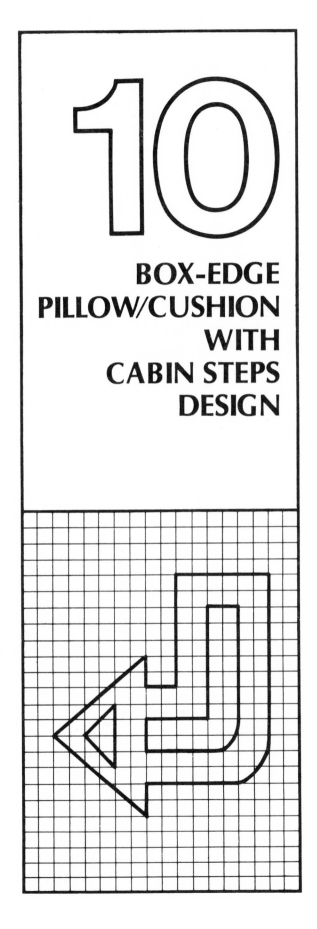

Box-edge cushions have a more tailored appearance. They can be made to fit special areas perfectly, so that they look like they really belong there.

Larger pillows that are to act as floor sofas or be put on platforms are best if they are versions of the box-edge. I use self-boxing (see Fig. J-1) for patchwork because I feel it shows off the design best. However, the pillow may require a true box-edge inner form in order for it to keep its shape perfectly — unless you use a stuffing made from foam rubber wrapped with polyester batting, or a comparable type of stuffing.

A self-boxing-edge pillow is constructed from two pieces of leather sewn together. The top piece, or lid, measures the exact size of the top of the completed pillow, plus the measurement of the height added to all four sides, plus a ½ inch seam allowance around all the edges. A square with sides equal to the pillow's height is cut out of each of the four corners of the top piece, and the edges of this square are joined together to form the vertical sides. This entire top piece, of course, is formed from pieced patchwork. The bottom piece of the pillow measures the exact size of the finished pillow, plus ½ inch seam allowance all around (see Fig. J-2).

By now you can make your own patterns, using the techniques already discussed in previous sections. But for these self-boxing-edge pillows, you will have to make certain adjustments to compensate for the different shape.

To make a design for this type of pillow, draw a rectangle on graph paper, scaling the size so that each square of the graph paper is equal to 1 or 2 inches of the finished pillow. Leave the corners intact for now, but remember that they

**Fig. J-1**

Inside

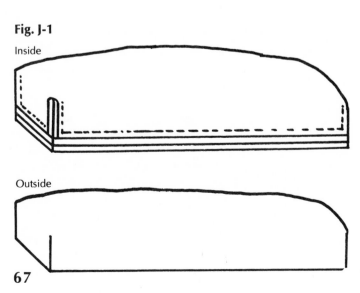

Outside

67

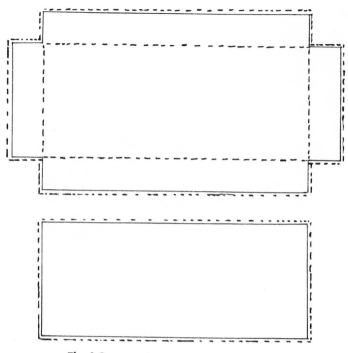

**Fig. J-2**

will later be eliminated. *Do not add seam allowances yet.*

Once your design is worked out, erase the area on the corners which should be eliminated to form the height of the pillow. (You will usually find that you have to adjust the height of the pillow by ½ inch in either direction to make it fit in with the pattern.) Then enlarge the design — with the corners eliminated — on 1 inch graph paper. Now make up your brown paper pattern, remembering to number the pieces and to add a ½ inch seam allowance around each piece for concealed seams and ½ inch underlaps in the appropriate places for overlapping seams.

The self-boxing-edge pillow I am describing is the Cabin Steps pattern shown in the color section. For this pattern you will be working with straight pieces, which are fairly easy to deal with. (Incidentally, this design would make a fabulous leather-topped quilt — just adjust the size and sew fabric to the back.) This particular pillow measures 32 inches wide, 44 inches long, and 4 inches high so that when the 4 inch height is added all around, the pattern area measures 40 by 52 inches). The top piece, when completed, will therefore measure 41 by 53 inches: the finished size of the pillow plus the height, plus ½ inch seam allowance all around — with a 4 inch square eliminated from each corner. The bottom measures 33 by 45 inches — the

exact size of the top minus its sides, plus ½ inch all around.

The Cabin Steps design for this size pillow is illustrated to scale in Fig. J-3.

It just so happens that this layout, when enlarged, is the exact size I wanted to fit a particular area in my home. Of course, if your room requires a different size pillow, then adjust accordingly. Measure the area into which your cushion will be placed. This measurement will be the exact size of the pillow — and hence, of its bottom piece. Now add the height to get the measurement for the lid. Add the seam allowances later.

To adjust the Cabin Steps pattern to fit your pillows, draw on graph paper the size rectangle you need, using a scale of one square on the graph paper to either 1 or 2 inches. Now within this area draw a design that looks like mine, but with the widths and lengths of the pieces adjusted to fit your different size. (An easy way to do this is to divide the rectangle into quarters, draw the central band in first, and then draw the four corner rectangles.) This particular pattern is easily adjusted to make a pillow 28 by 40 inches, simply by eliminating the central band of the pillow and joining the four rectangles together. Now make up your pattern and add your seam allowances around every edge of each patch as shown in Figs. J-4, J-4a, and J-4b for making concealed seams, or as shown in Figs. J-5, J-5a, and J-5b for overlapping seams.

As this particular pattern forming the lid of the cushion is actually four rectangles joined together by a band circling the width and length of the pillow, there are duplicate pieces, and you will need to make only one pattern piece for each duplicated piece. The pieces numbered in Fig. J-3 are the only ones for which you need to make patterns. If you are sewing by machine, add the required ½ inch seam allowance around each edge for concealed traditional seams; if you are hand-stitching with overlapped seams, follow the underlap allowances as shown. You will notice that the underlaps tier down like steps to the outside, as I recommended in the section on director's chairs for designs with a definite center. (Of course, on a design of your own, add allowances where you feel underlapping is appropriate.)

To obtain the patches required to construct

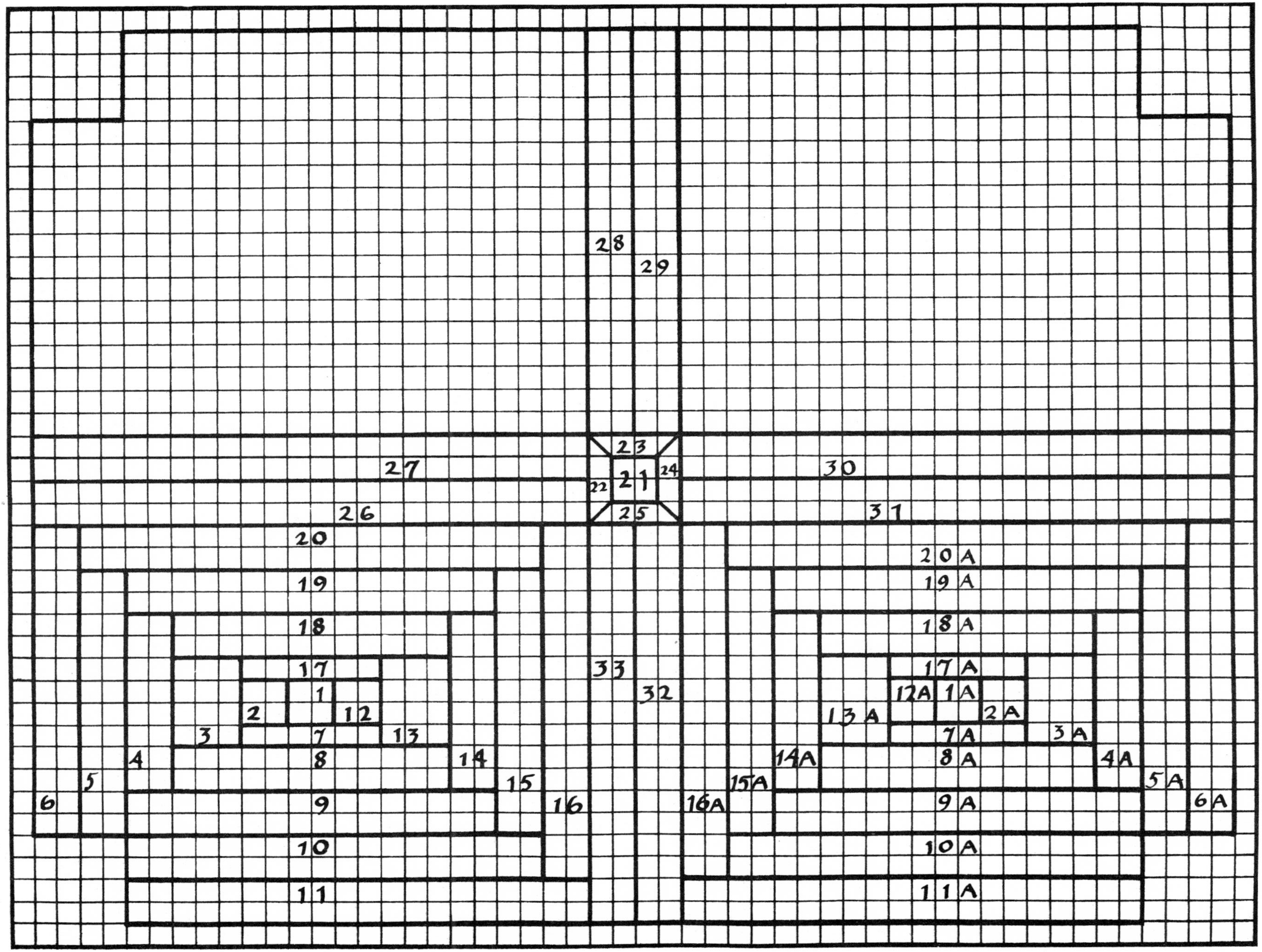

CABIN STEPS PATTERN FOR BOX-EDGE PILLOW

Fig. J-3

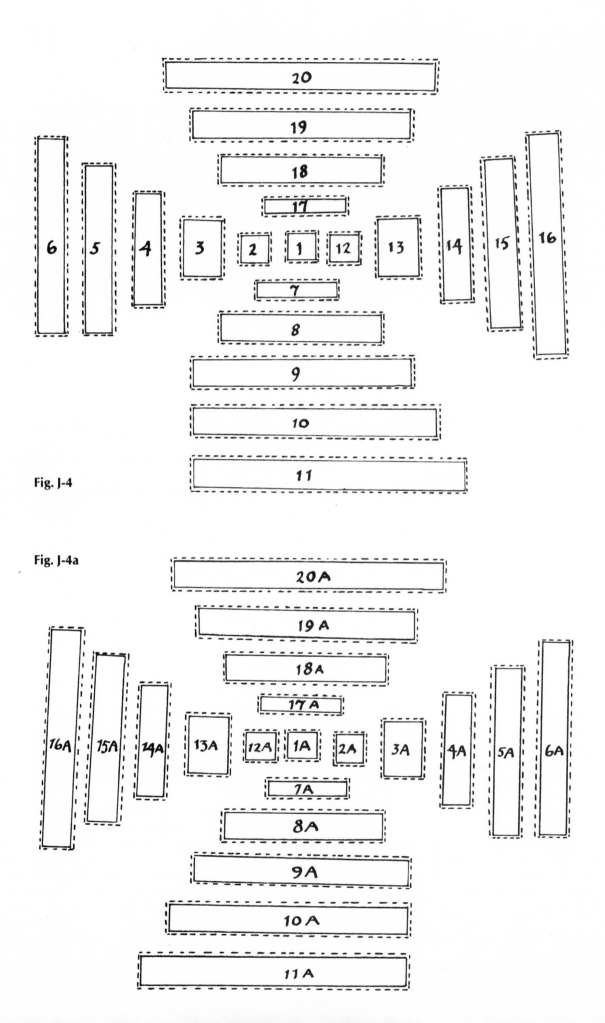

Fig. J-4

Fig. J-4a

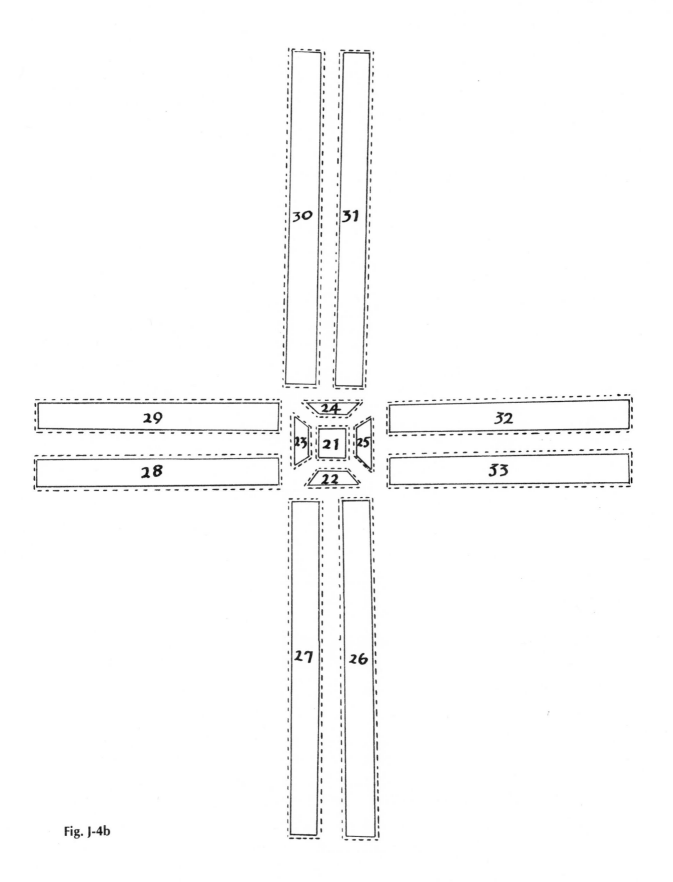

Fig. J-4b

71

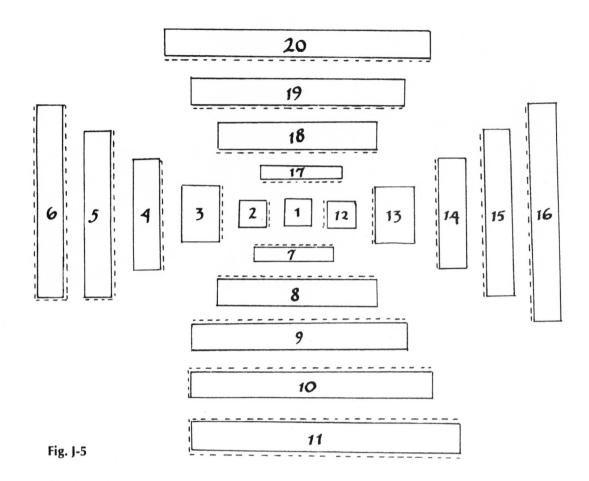

**Fig. J-5**

**Fig. J-5a**

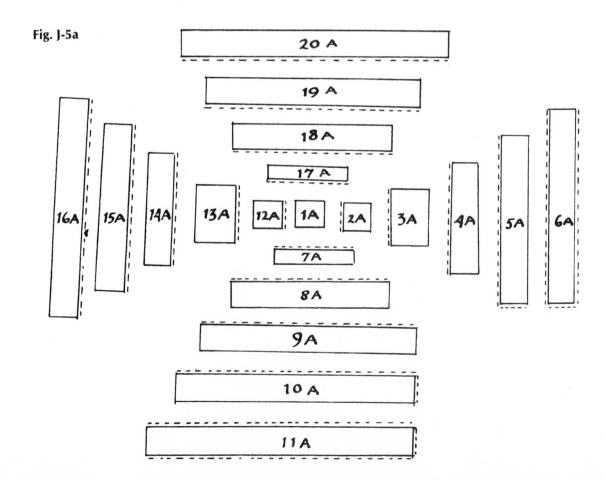

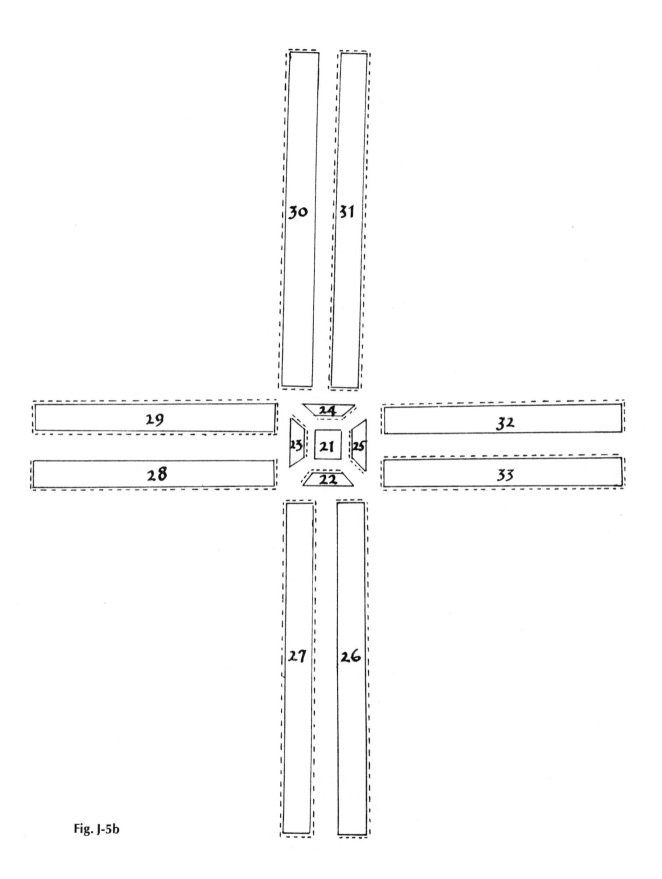

**Fig. J-5b**

73

the top of this cushion, cut: (2 pieces each of numbers 1-20 and 1a-20a; 1 piece for numbers 21-33)

| | | | |
|---|---|---|---|
| 1 and 1a — 2 pieces each | | 21 — 1 piece |
| 2 and 2a — 2 pieces each | | 22 — 1 piece |
| 3 and 3a — 2 pieces each | | 23 — 1 piece |
| 4 and 4a — 2 pieces each | | 24 — 1 piece |
| 5 and 5a — 2 pieces each | | 25 — 1 piece |
| 6 and 6a — 2 pieces each | | 26 — 1 piece |
| 7 and 7a — 2 pieces each | | 27 — 1 piece |
| 8 and 8a — 2 pieces each | | 28 — 1 piece |
| 9 and 9a — 2 pieces each | | 29 — 1 piece |
| 10 and 10a — 2 pieces each | | 30 — 1 piece |
| 11 and 11a — 2 pieces each | | 31 — 1 piece |
| 12 and 12a — 2 pieces each | | 32 — 1 piece |
| 13 and 13a — 2 pieces each | | 33 — 1 piece |
| 14 and 14a — 2 pieces each | | |
| 15 and 15a — 2 pieces each | | |
| 16 and 16a — 2 pieces each | | |
| 17 and 17a — 2 pieces each | | |
| 18 and 18a — 2 pieces each | | |
| 19 and 19a — 2 pieces each | | |
| 20 and 20a — 2 pieces each | | |

With this particular pattern, you will have to cut different pieces of leather using the same pattern pieces. So even though the colors used here are arbitrary, try not to duplicate colors on any of the same-numbered patterned pieces. Think about what color will be going next to what. It is a good idea to lightly color your original graph paper pattern so you will have some idea of what it will look like.

In my pattern I made each rectangle identical in proportion, but changed the placement of the colors within the design. I found that I really didn't need that many colors, since careful planning and placement can give the effect of a wide spectrum. In the color photograph, you will see that each color is repeated at least two and even three times within each rectangle. However, the colors are placed differently in each one and are used to make different-sized patches in each, so that you really don't notice that there aren't that many colors.

If I found I didn't have enough leather to make the longer strips, I would cut two smaller lengths of the same color — adding ½-inch seam allowances on the joining ends — and then join the two together. This technique is not really noticeable, but try to make as few joins as possible because they will become obvious if there are a great number.

I backed some of the weaker strips with muslin by taking the corresponding pattern piece and cutting out a piece of muslin the same size. I then spread glue evenly with a brush on the wrong side of the leather and glued the muslin to it, using the edge of my ruler to smooth it down. This way I am able to use scraps that I would normally not be able to use.

The height of this type of cushion is up to you. It is the stuffing that will give your cushion its final shape, so depending on the design, you can vary the height about ½ inch without any difficulty, since you can compensate for it with your inner form. In addition, a slight difference in height is really unnoticeable unless pillows are placed right beside each other. I adjust the height of the pillows to best fit the corners of my design.

In my Cabin Steps pattern, it just so happened that a perfect corner could be formed most easily with a 4-inch height. This is because each strip of the outside part of the design was 2 inches wide. So I simply cut a square equal to the size of two strips. If the strips had measured 1½ inches, I would have made a 3-inch square, and thus had a 3-inch height. But never make your height less than 2½ inches, as it would be too narrow.

After cutting out the leather, always mark seam allowances, whether for concealed or overlapped seams, on the wrong side. In addition, always number your pieces to correspond to your original graph pattern so that you can keep track of what you are doing.

With this cushion — as with all others, whether sewing by hand or machine — it is best to construct in sections and then piece these sections together to form the whole. For this design, I recommend constructing the four outer rectangles and the central band separately, and then joining the rectangles to the band one by one. Therefore, the order of construction should be: (see Fig. J-3 for numbers of the pieces) 1 to 2, 1 to 12; 2, 1, 12 to 7; 2, 1, 12 to 17; 17, 2, 7 to 3; 17, 12, 7 to 13; 3, 7, 13 to 8; 3, 17, 13 to 18; 18, 3, 8 to 4; 18, 13, 8 to 14; 4, 8, 14 to 9; 4, 18, 14 to 19; 19, 4, 9 to 5; 19, 14, 9 to 15; 5, 19, 15 to 20; 5, 9, 15 to 10; 20, 5 to 6; 20, 15, 10 to 16; 10, 16 to 11.

Repeat this two times to form the two diagonal corner rectangles. Then join 1a to 2a; 1a to 12a; 2a, 1a, 12a to 7a; 2a, 1a, 12a to 17a; 17a, 2a, 7a to 3a; 17a, 12a, 7a to 13a; 3a, 7a, 13a to 8a; 3a, 17a, 13a to 18a; 18a, 3a, 8a to 4a; 18a, 13a, 8a to 14a; 4a, 8a, 14a to 9a; 4a, 18a, 14a to 19a; 19a, 4a, 9a to 5a; 19a, 14a, 9a to 15a; 5a, 19a, 15a to 20a; 5a, 9a, 15a to 10a; 20a, 5a to 6a; 20a, 15a, 10a to 16a; 10a, 16a, to 11a.

Repeat this twice until you have the other two diagonal corner rectangles. Then join 21 to 22, 23, 24, 25; 25 to 22 and 24; 23 to 22 and 24; 26 to 27; 28 to 29; 30 to 31; 32 to 33; 22 to 26,27; 23 to 28,29; 24 to 30,31; 25 to 32,33; to form the central band. Then join each of the rectangles to the central bands, (20 to 26 and 16 to 33; 20 to 30 and 16 to 29; 20a to 31 and 16a to 32; 20a to 27 and 16a to 28), and your top pattern will be completed.

This order is basically the same for overlapped seams. Glue the four rectangular sections together and then sew the strips together, working from the center out. Then glue and sew the central band together, also working from the center out. Finally, glue and sew each rectangle into its appropriate corner.

For hand sewing, use the stitch of your choice to sew the pieces together, but glue, punch, and sew in the order outlined above. If you are machine sewing and making traditional concealed seams, don't forget to sew only to the point made by the intersecting seam lines (see Fig. 1-7). Then glue the seam allowances to one side for strength.

Once the patchwork design is constructed, you must sew a seam at the edges formed by the removed square at each corner. Be sure to sew only to the intersection points of the seam lines; otherwise you will have a problem when it comes time to join top and bottom sections of the cushion.

When these corner seams are sewn, you will have a lid-shaped top which must now be joined to the bottom.

To cut out the bottom of this pillow, make a brown paper pattern to be sure you are cutting accurately. It is very awkward to fit perfect right-angle corners and straight lines in the space of an irregular leather hide, and much easier to get perfect corners and straight lines on paper

that comes in a regular shape. Even so, irregular hides have few starting points from which to get your bearings, and making a pattern here can be a little awkward because of the size involved. Therefore, make a pattern the width of the pillow plus 1-inch seam allowance, and about 12 inches long — or even one-half or one-third the length of the back. Using this as your pattern, cut out strips which you will later join together to form the pillow bottom.

Since this bottom is going to be flat against the floor or platform and will not be seen, you don't want to waste really good skins, so piecing with less high-quality skins here is a good idea; you can even use different colors. I used suede splits — which I dislike if visible — backed with muslin for strength. I found this to be one place where suede splits (especially the large sueded cow splits) can be used, since no one will actually be sitting on them, and there is little wear.

If you are putting a zipper in the back, you will be able to insert it in one of the seams joining the leather strips of the back together. Make this zipper the entire width of the cushion so that inserting the form will be easy.

If the pillow is exceptionally long, then you will have to put a zipper in the entire length rather than the width of the pillow. To do this, you must add an extra inch to the width rather than the length, as you did with the smaller pillows. In this case, therefore, make the pattern 1 inch wider, and maintain the same-length pattern. Sew all the strips together, forming the correct length for the back. Cut the piece in half completely across the length; then go back and finish off the seams which you cut through so that the stitching won't come apart. Glue the seam allowances. Whether by hand or machine, insert the zipper using the method described in Section 9.

If you forget to add the extra 1 inch or you feel that the leather is too heavy to have seam allowances, abut the raw edge of the seam, using masking tape to join them together so they remain flat. Place the zipper so that it is centered and the zipper teeth are exactly over the abutted seam. Glue down the zipper tape thereby joining the two sides of the back together. Sew in the zipper either by topstitching on the machine, or by hand, using a running or backstitch as you did with the box-edge triangle pillow. If you are

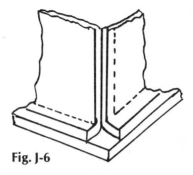

**Fig. J-6**

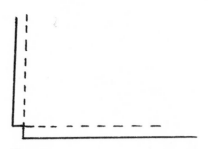

**Fig. J-7**

making a small box-edge pillow and using a zipper shorter than the width or length of the pillow, then glue a 1 or 1½-inch wide strip of leather to either end of the zipper tape to extend it to the length of the seam (see Step 1 of Fig. I-11).

Now — if you are machine sewing — place the top and bottom pieces together right side to right side, and baste the seams. If you followed the instructions and sewed only to the intersecting points of the seam lines, the top pieces should have corners already "snipped" to the seam line (see Fig. J-6), which will facilitate getting around corners. If you didn't do this, you can still snip into the seam line at the corners of the bottom piece (see Fig. J-7).

Now sew the two pieces together. If you put in a zipper, then sew completely around all four sides. If you did not put in a zipper, sew around three sides and in about 2 to 4 inches on either end of the fourth side. Then remove the thread from your machine and sew the rest of the fourth side, making holes through which you can stitch later. Turn the pillow right-side out, put in your form, and either close up the zipper or blind-stitch into the holes previously made.

Because of the many seams involved in making patchwork, there is bound to be a slight discrepancy between the size you planned and the actual finished product. But try to keep this discrepancy to a minimum. If you are very careful and follow the instructions given for planning, marking and sewing, you shouldn't have any problems. If you do find you have a discrepancy, then ease the seams joining the top and bottom pieces together so they fit.

If you are stitching by hand and you put in a zipper, then place the top and bottom wrong side to wrong side and glue them together, making a ½-inch seam around all four sides. Then mark and punch the holes and sew the pieces together with the edge-stitch of your choice. If

you did not put in a zipper, then glue the pieces together, mark and punch holes, sew around three sides and 2 to 4 inches on either end of the fourth side. Then gently pull the rest of the fourth side apart. Insert the form, and glue the fourth side again. Line up the holes and finish sewing the pieces together.

## BOX-EDGE FORM

For a self-boxing edge pillow to hold its shape perfectly, it may need a true box-edge inner form made of muslin. A true box-edge consists of top and bottom sections of equal size joined together by a length of fabric called a boxing strip (see Fig. J-8). The size of the top and bottom pieces is equal to the area to be covered plus ½ inch all around for seam allowances. (In other words, the top and bottom pieces of the inner form are equal to the bottom piece of the outer cover).

The length of the boxing strip is determined by the measurement of the perimeter (all four sides added together - width plus length plus width plus length) of the shape, plus 1 inch to allow for seam allowances. The width of this strip depends on the thickness of the cushion plus 1 inch seam allowances. This will insure that the pillow will hold the same thickness throughout.

If you want to be sure that your finished form fits snugly into the outer cover for a tailored look, then make the form a little larger than the outer cover. This means adding ½ inch to the length and width of the top and bottom pieces, ½ inch to the width of the boxing strip, and 2 inches to its length. This will give you a really snug form for your cover. If it's a very large pillow, you should add 1 inch to the width and length, ½ inch to the height, and 4 inches to the length of the boxing strip.

For the pillow described here, which measures 36 by 44 by 4 inches, you will need a top and

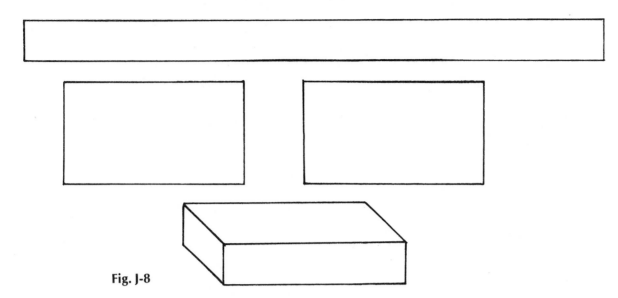

**Fig. J-8**

bottom inner-form section each measuring 37 by 45 inches and a boxing strip measuring 161 by 5 inches. If you want a really snug-fitting form, then make it 37½ by 45½ inches for the top and bottom, and 5½ by 163 inches for the boxing strip.

You will probably find that you have to cut the muslin in sections — especially the boxing strip — and piece them together. You can draw the pattern right on the muslin, since it will not be seen and has definite straight edges from which to work. Mark all seam allowances and other directions right on the fabric so that construction will be easy.

To join the pieces of a straight-sided pillow like this, pin the boxing strip to the top section so that the beginning of the boxing strip is aligned with a corner of the top. Starting at that corner, sew one edge first, starting in ½ inch from the corner. (Remember to backstitch the beginning of seam for strength.) Stitch till you are ½ inch away from the next corner. Leave the needle in the fabric, raise the pressure foot, snip off corner of fabric, pivot the needle, and turn and start down next side, pivoting and clipping as you reach each corner. Stop stitching ½ inch from the last corner and backstitch to finish the seam. Take the fabric from the machine and fit the two ends of the boxing strip together at that corner and stitch. Sew the bottom section to the strip in the same manner, but leave an opening on one side for insertion of the stuffing.

If all this sounds too complicated, you could

also make a muslin inner form in a self-boxing shape. Construct as for. the patchwork cover but do not insert a zipper; when joining top and bottom pieces, leave an opening on one side for stuffing.

The amount of stuffing used is, as previously explained, up to your personal taste. A rough approximation, however, is: 14 to 15 pounds of chopped foam; 12 to 13 pounds of a kapok and foam mixture; or 7 to 8 pounds of polyester Poly-fil.

There is another type of stuffing you can use for your pillow — foam rubber wrapped with polyester batting. (You can use a form or not as you wish, but I prefer to use one.) You will need a piece of foam rubber the same length as the pillow, but about 1 or 2 inches narrower than the width and ½ to 1 inch narrower than the height. Then wrap this foam rubber with polyester batting as many times as necessary until you achieve the exact size of your desired pillow (preferably even a little larger). Since this batting comes in 16 inch widths, you will have to wrap the foam in sections and cut the batting to fit if necessary. After use the bottom will flatten. If, however, you want to be sure of a very flat bottom buy a piece of foam the exact size of the cushion. Then simply lay batting on the top and allow it to overlap the sides. This is an excellent stuffing for larger pillows, as it combines firmness with softness and durability. As a matter of fact, I feel it is best for large pillows.

77

## TOOLS NEEDED

GRAPH PAPER, BOTH SMALL AND THE
   1-INCH SIZE
HEAVY BROWN PAPER
WATERPROOF FELT-TIPPED PEN
SHEARS AND SMALL SCISSORS
RUBBER OR LEATHER CEMENT AND
   BRUSHES
CLEAR DRESSMAKER'S RULER

   OPTIONAL

MASKING TAPE
RUFFER OR SANDPAPER

• FOR MACHINE SEWING

EVEN-FEED OR WALKING FOOT
   (OPTIONAL BUT HIGHLY
   RECOMMENDED)

GLOVER'S NEEDLES FOR BOTH MACHINE
   AND HAND SEWING
HEAVY MERCERIZED THREAD
TISSUE PAPER (OPTIONAL)

• FOR HAND SEWING

DRIVE PUNCH
LACING
LARGE-EYED EMBROIDERY NEEDLE
HARDWOOD BOARD
MALLET

   OPTIONAL

LACING PLIERS
AWL
ROTARY PUNCH

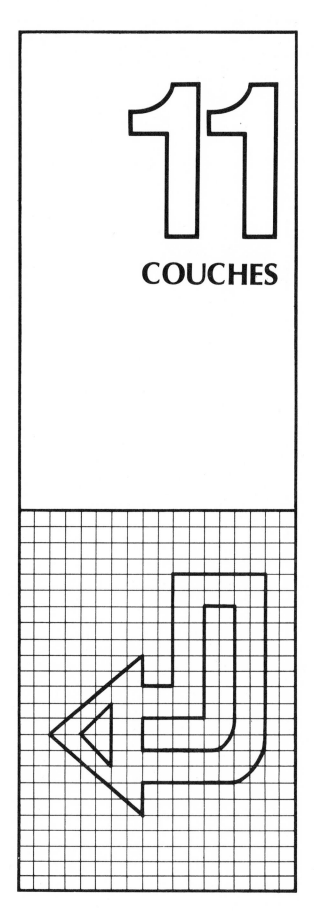

# 11

# COUCHES

Each of the two couches shown in the photo of my living room consists of two large overstuffed pillows of the self-boxing type.

They can be made either with patterns derived from traditional patchwork quilting, from patterns of your own design, or from scraps fitted together in their original shapes to create a crazy-quilt design. You can use traditional concealed seams, overlapped seams, or abutted and overlayed seams, either machine- or hand-stitched. Beautiful and effective, these pillows are of basically simple construction and are without a doubt far more effective and practical than anything you can buy.

To make this kind of couch, first measure the size you want. The width can be anywhere from 30 to 36 inches (any narrower than that will not give a comfortable seating area); there's no limit on the length. I am rather partial to the larger sizes because I feel they are unusual and really show off the design. However, you should know by now that large cushions such as those pictured are more difficult to work with, so it is often advisable to break the length of the seating area into two or three smaller cushions — simply because they are easier to handle and stuff. In addition, it is easier to fluff up smaller cushions, as larger ones can be quite heavy. But the choice is yours.

Though each of my two couches gives an entirely different feeling, both are made from a series of squares joined together to form the tops for the pillows. These patterns can easily be adjusted to any length and width — within the limitations of the measurement of the square: 12 inches in the case of the Le Moyne Star pattern, and 4 inches in the multiple-square pattern — by eliminating the appropriate number of squares that form the pattern.

## MULTICOLORED-SQUARE COUCH

The multicolored-square couch has only one pattern piece — a 4 inch square for hand sewing and a 5 inch square for machine sewing (see Fig. K-1) — joined together to form the desired size. The size square used in this pattern is, I feel, best: any larger and you wouldn't get the feeling of an intricate pattern; any smaller would be

79

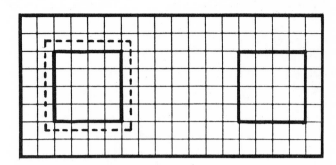

**Fig. K-1**
MULTICOLORED-SQUARE
COUCH PATTERN

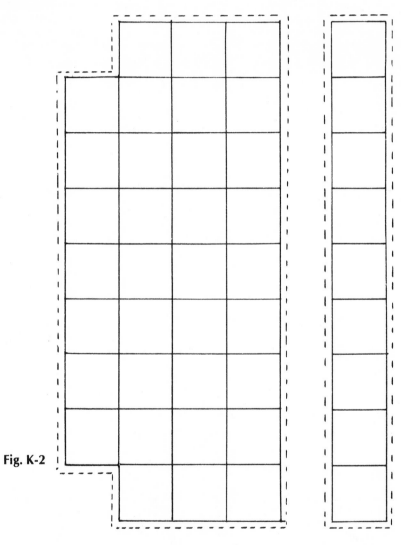

**Fig. K-2**

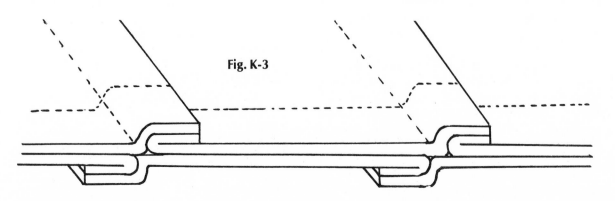

**Fig. K-3**

awkward to sew. The size of the seat of my couch is 2 feet 8 inches by 6 feet by 4 inches; and 1 foot 4 inches by 6 feet 4 inches for the back — but you can easily adjust these dimensions by adding or eliminating squares.

In pure pattern terms, my couch is a rectangle formed by ten squares by twenty squares on the seat and six squares by twenty squares on the back, less eight squares eliminated to form the corners of the boxing — a total of 312 in all.

The number of squares you require will depend on the size of your couch. When making up your pattern piece, make several duplicates, simply because the edges of a single piece will wear out by being traced around so many times, and eventually you will not be getting perfect squares. It is essential to be very careful in making up the pattern pieces and marking seam allowances and underlaps, since everything must be constructed to scale in order to fit properly.

Cut out the appropriate number of squares for the entire project; or, if you wish, cut out the squares gradually as you acquire scraps. If any of the leather on any of the squares appears weak, trace around the pattern square on muslin, cut it out, and glue it evenly with a flexible drying glue to the wrong side of that particular leather square.

If you are sewing by machine and using traditional concealed seams to construct the top sections of the seat and back pillows, sew the squares together to form strips the width of the couch. Sew very accurately so that each square measures 4 inches in the final pattern. Then join these strips together to build up the length (see Fig. K-2). As you are sewing the strips of the squares together, be sure to keep the squares lined up correctly so that the cross seams meet. And be sure that the seam allowances are folded and glued to one side on one strip and to the other side on the next strip so they don't cause bulk (see Fig. K-3). Leave a square off from either end of the first and last row of squares to form the corner seams which will give the pillow its box-edge shape.

For hand sewing, you can use either overlapped or abutted seams (see Fig. O-2), but for joining squares, abutted seams (see C, Fig. O-2) are best and easiest. To make an abutted seam, you must eliminate all seam allowances completely from both seams to be joined. Cut a strip of leather 1 inch wide. Then glue each square

halfway over the strip so that they meet at the center. The leather strips used to back the seam are invisible, and so can be short lengths which you can glue or sew together to form the required length.

For hand sewing with abutted seams, therefore, your pattern piece for this multicolored-square patchwork couch is a simple 4-inch square. Before you can start to construct the tops for the pillows, you must accumulate enough squares to form four or five strips of squares the width of the top. Then, using your dressmaker's ruler, mark ½ inch in on every edge of the squares, as if you were marking seam allowances. Now place them face down — with the colors arranged to your liking — and abut all the edges tightly together. Now take your 1-inch-wide strips of leather and, keeping the strips within the seam allowances marked on the squares — ½ inch on either side of the abutted edges — glue the rows of squares together, first in one direction and then in the other (see Fig. K-4).

**Fig. K-4**

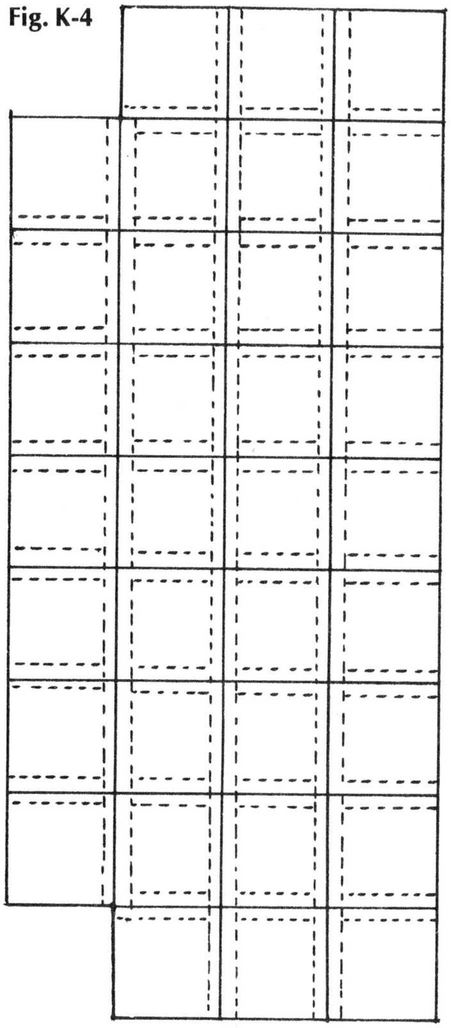

Decide which stitch and lacing you want to use, then mark and punch a row of holes on either side of the abutted edges, being sure to punch through both the square and its backing strip. Now stitch them together, first across the rows (running in a width-wise direction) and then lengthwise. After you complete construction of two or three sections of rows, join the sections together: Abut the edges, gluing a 1-inch strip to the back along the abutted edges to hold the sections together, mark and punch holes, and sew.

To join the corner seams, take a small strip of leather 1 inch wide. Abut the corner edges and glue the stripping to the inside so that the abutted seam meets exactly in the center, and so that it reaches slightly above the top of the corner. Ease in any fullness. Then, using your rotary punch, punch holes for your stitching on either side of the abutted edges of the corner seam. (Do not punch holes any closer than ½ inch to the outside edge of the pillow tops.) This will facilitate the joining of the top and bottom.

To construct the bottoms for these pillows, you will have to join strips of varying widths together — as you did with the Cabin Steps pillow — because short of elephant hide, you won't find a skin large enough for one huge piece. But, in addition, pieced leather distributes the stretch evenly and doesn't allow all the pressure to build up on a weak spot.

The size of the back depends of course, on the size of your pillow. If you want a zipper, then put it in either the width or the length, depending on the size required, and follow the directions given in the Cabin Steps pattern. If you are sewing by machine using traditional concealed seams, add ½-inch seam allowance all around; but if you are hand-stitching, leave no seam allowances around the outside.

To join the top and bottom together using traditional concealed seams, place the pieces right side to right side. Baste the seams together and sew around all four edges if you put in a zipper, and around three sides and part of the fourth if you did not, as already described.

To join the top and bottom together using hand stitching and no seam allowance, place the pieces wrong side to wrong side, and join them together as if there were a seam allowance added. Glue a ½-inch seam around the four sides, and punch and stitch together with the

edge stitch of your choice. The amount taken in is minimal and will not really be noticeable. If you do not sew any closer than ½ inch to the outside edge, you should have no problem joining around the corners of the top when sewing them together. If you find there is any problem, clip in ½ inch at the corners of the bottom piece so that they can be eased around. If you are not using a zipper, then sew around three sides and part of the fourth; if you put in a zipper, sew around all four.

## LE MOYNE STAR

For designs such as Le Moyne Star, each pattern fits into a square. This square can be any size you want, but 12 inches is the size I chose because it gave me the width, height, and length I wanted. For a wider pillow, use four 10=inch squares across the width; or three 12-inch squares for average-width pillows.

If you are machine sewing using traditional concealed seams, you will need three pattern pieces: a triangle, a square, and a diamond. Enlarge the pattern pieces shown in Fig. K-5, using a scale of 1 inch per square on the graph paper pattern. Add seam allowances on each edge of the three required pattern pieces (see Fig. K-6).

The squares and triangles forming the background for the star will all be the same color, and the eight diamonds which comprise the star will each be cut out of a different shade. For my couch, I used a total of nine colors in all. I alternated the background colors on each square, so that the colors within the star would all take turns being the background color. And I made duplicates and triplicates of each of the squares so that every color background is repeated a few times. Squares with the same background colors are, however, separated from each other in the final construction.

You can either cut out and sew the entire couch at one time, or cut out patches as you get scraps and do it bit by bit, square by square. But if you are waiting to accumulate scraps, don't forget to always keep the background a single color within each square. If you make it many different colors, you will not be able to distinguish the star pattern. So I would advise you to buy several different-colored skins and supple-

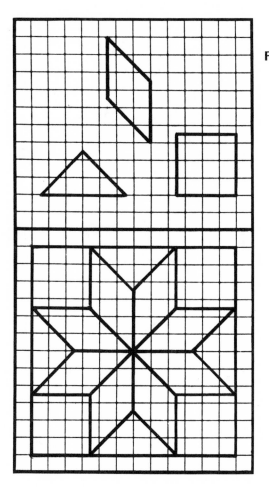

**Fig. K-5**

**Fig. K-6**

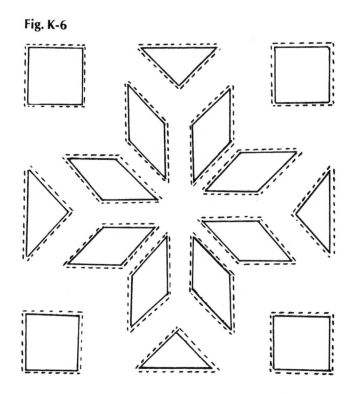

ment them with scraps, as I did. This way you can keep the ground of each square a single color; but on the other hand, you don't have to make all the background squares the same color, as that would become monotonous.

When cutting, don't forget to check for weak pieces and glue muslin to the wrong side if you find any. Mark seam allowances on each edge, as precision is important here.

For traditional concealed seams, start by sewing together the central point of the star. Start stitching from the outer edge, and sew toward the point, sewing only to the intersecting points of the line. Sew four pieces of the star together and put aside. (After you have finished the seam, don't forget to backstitch into the already-made holes so that you have two rows of stitching right on top of one another.) Then join the other four pieces of the star together. If you find that you

don't quite manage to sew all the way to the intersecting seam lines at the point of the star, sew as far as you can, then do your backstitching. Later you can go back and sew it with a glover's needle and a double thread — this is easy to do and gives the piece a finished look instead of just leaving it, as many people do when they are quilting with fabric.

Now you must join the two halves of the star together. Without any thread in the machine, sew along the seam line of each piece to be joined so that you will make perfect holes in the leather. Now sew the two halves of the star together as far as you can by machine. Hand-sew the rest of the seam simply by sewing through the holes already made by machine — a trick you can use for any other places where you might have difficulty sewing by machine. This is the secret to making this pattern — whether

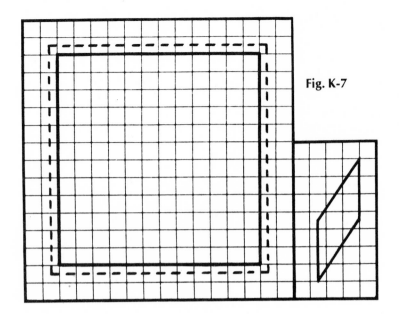

Fig. K-7

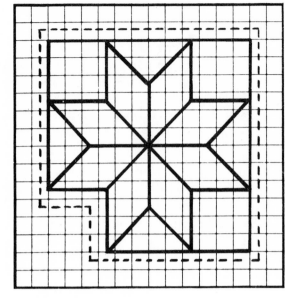

Fig. K-8

made into a fabric quilt or a leather patchwork piece — and it is fast and simple.

Once you have sewn the star point together, sew the squares and triangles forming the background. To do this, join each seam with masking tape and sew only to the intersecting points of the seam lines — not completely to the end of the seam. If you do this consistently, you will have no problem sewing around corners or points. Simply sew each seam line individually and backstitch carefully so that it is double-stitched.

It really is important to sew each seam individually. It may seem picky but it makes sewing so much easier, especially in the more intricate designs.

Some people find that using concealed seams can be rather awkward on this particular pattern, and prefer to use topstitching — this is really attractive here, especially with contrasting thread. But it should be used only to construct the individual squares; the squares should then be joined using the traditional concealed seams.

For topstitching by machine you can use either overlapping seams or abutted seams with the star appliquéd on a solid leather square. The second method uses more leather, but is really quite convenient and useful. To do this you will need a square pattern measuring 13 inches — 12 inches plus seam allowances — and a pattern for the diamond shape with *no* seam allowances (see Fig. K-7). Cut out your leather using these patterns. Mark the center of the square and 4 inches in from every corner. Now lay out your star, being very accurate in your placement — the points of the outside of the star must be ex-

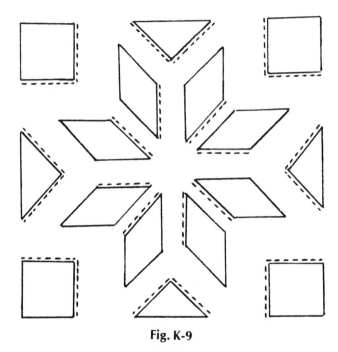

Fig. K-9

actly 4 inches from each corner and ½ inch in from the edge. The center points must meet exactly at the center of the square.

Be sure the pieces are abutted correctly and tightly, then glue them down. Topstitch in ⅛ inch from the edge of each diamond, thus sewing it to the background square. Now sew the squares together using traditional concealed seams.

On the corner squares, cut out a 3½-inch square so that you can form the self-boxing edge by sewing right to the outside points of the two diamonds (see Fig. K-8).

84

For overlapping seams, use the underlapping allowances in the places indicated in Fig. K-9. After you have cut out the leather, don't forget to mark the underlaps (or rather, overlaps) on the wrong side of the overlapping piece. Overlap the star in a circular order first, making sure the center point fits properly; then glue. Overlap and glue the triangles and squares in place to complete the pattern. Now topstitch ⅛ inch in from the edge around each diamond, which will sew the patchwork pieces of the square together. Then cut a 3½-inch square from the corner patches of the corner squares (see Fig. K-8), leaving in place ½ inch of the square that you topstitched to be part of the background for the star pattern. This ½ inch will allow you to sew a concealed seam to form the boxing lid of the pillow.

Now join the squares together with traditional concealed seams, the same way you did with the multicolored square pattern — rows of squares to fit the width which are then joined together to fit the length.

For hand-stitching this pattern, you can use either abutted or overlapped seams for the actual construction of each patterned square, but you must use abutted seams for joining the squares together.

If you want to use overlapping seams to construct the pattern, use the underlapping sequence show in Fig. K-9. Cut out your leather following the advice given regarding color. Mark the overlaps as previously explained. Construct the star first, then glue the triangles and squares in place to complete the pattern. Do not add one of the small square pattern pieces to the four patterned squares that will act as corners on the final cushion (see Fig. K-10). Mark and punch a row of holes on either side of the raw edges, and sew each piece down. I recommend that you use finer lacing and smaller holes to fit with the pattern.

To get a really neat center you can, if you wish, do a daisy stitch right in the middle of the star (see Fig. K-11). When punching the holes for this stitch, make the hole in the exact center of the star a little larger than the other holes. To sew it, have the lacing emerge from the center and stitch into every hole in rotation — always ending with the needle back in the center hole except on the final stitch. Then glue a piece of leather or muslin to the wrong side of the leather, right under the center of the star.

To abut the seams within the patterned square, cut out a 12-inch pattern rather than the 13-inch square you used for machine stitching. And to form the star, cut out eight diamonds using no seam allowances (see Fig. K-12). Mark

**Fig. K-10**

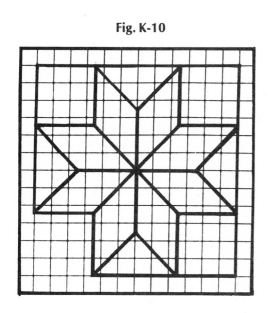

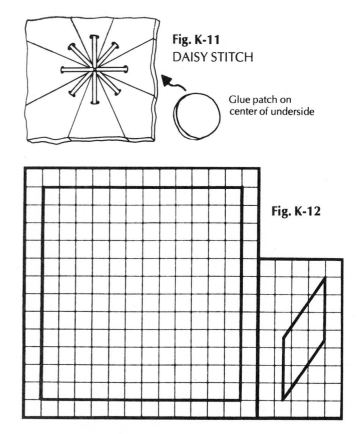

**Fig. K-11**
**DAISY STITCH**

Glue patch on center of underside

**Fig. K-12**

the center of the square, and mark in 3½ inches from the corners on each edge. Carefully glue the star so that its outside points are exactly 3½ inches from each corner and the center points meet exactly at the center of the square. Tightly abut the edges. Mark and punch your holes, and sew the patches together using a fine lacing and the stitch of your choice. For the center you can use a daisy stitch as you would for overlapped seams, gluing muslin under the point for strength.

On the squares that are going to act as corner pieces, cut a 3½-inch square of the background color from the appropriate corner, and do not stitch the edges of the star to its backing here. This will allow you to make the box shape of the pillow.

To join the patterned squares together, use the **slot-seam** method described for the multicolored-square patchwork couch: Mark ½ inch seam allowances around each edge of the squares. Place them face down, arranged to your liking, with the edges abutted. Glue the 1-inch stripping to the back of the seams, mark and punch holes, and sew squares together with the stitch of your choice.

Cut and construct the back as already described in the previous project (multiple-square couch). Join the top and bottom together, either by hand or machine, in the manner already indicated.

To make inner forms, follow the instructions in Section 10 on making self-boxing pillows. If you are making very long cushions, sew a row of machine stitching across the top and bottom sections of the muslin, two feet apart before joining them to the boxing strip. This little trick will help the cushion retain its shape, since the stitches prevent the muslin from stretching at these points, helping to keep an equal height throughout.

The amount of stuffing depends on the type you are using, the size of your pillow, and your individual taste. However, if you have made a few pillows, you should have some idea by now. If not, look at the general amounts suggested for other pillows in this book. Of course, if you want you can use foam rubber wrapped with polyester batting with or without a form — an excellent type of stuffing for very large cushions like this, and the type I use.

## WOODEN PLATFORMS

Once you have made up the cushions, you can place them directly on the floor, or you can buy or build a wooden base for them. Decide on the width, height, and length — preferably *after* making up the pillows: Leave plenty of room for the cushions; don't try to crowd and squeeze them into too small an area. It is best to give yourself some extra room to be able to pull cushions out farther if you wish.

The platform for your couches isn't just a flat four-sided box, but a contoured frame (see Fig. K-13). It should slant down from the desired height in the front (say 10 inches) toward the back of the box, which should be 1½ inches lower (8½ inches) than the front. If the pillow were placed on a flat surface (as it must be for couches with no back pillows) it would tend to slide forward, which is very uncomfortable for anyone sitting on it. Ideally there should always be a 1½-inch pitch from the front to the back, but it can be as great as 2½ inches if your taste calls for it or if it is an extra-wide couch. The front of couch seats — including the correct height of the cushion — usually measures 16 to 18 inches. But you must decide what height is the most comfortable, so go to a store and try various couches, and measure the front-seat height of the one you prefer.

For a 10-inch fronted platform, buy a board 10 inches high and sawed to the desired length. For the side pieces, get two 10-inch high boards of the desired width of the couch. These two boards must be cut at an angle to gradually reach 8½ inches in the back.

Nail or screw these four pieces together to form a rectangular frame. Then take three or four more pieces of heavier board — 10 inches in the front slanting to 8½ inches in the back — and attach them inside the box for added support. Now all you have to do is place a top on these supports — a sheet of plywood or several planks of wood totalling the exact width and length of the platform — and secure it to the wooden frame.

To make a back for your platforms as illustrated, follow the same directions, but make the box a true triangular shape with the flat piece lying against the wall, the narrower part on top, and angled out toward the base. The angle

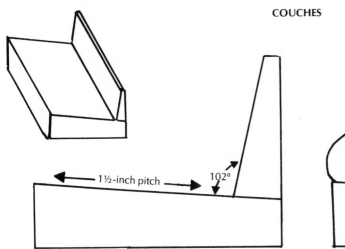

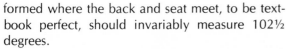

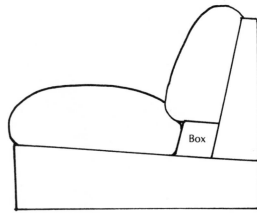

**Fig. K-13**

**Fig. K-14**

formed where the back and seat meet, to be text-book perfect, should invariably measure 102½ degrees.

If you want to make the seat of your couch even wider for more comfort, add a small box shape at the point where the seat meets the back (see Fig. K-14). This is what I did and it really makes for a super-comfortable couch. But be sure that this box is narrower than the depth of

your back cushions or the box edge will hurt your back.

However, if you are using a wall as the back for your couch, you will have to make do with a flat platform base. To make a flat platform simply follow the same basic instructions given for a contoured base, but do not slant it toward the back. When finished place the side of the platform against the wall and set your pillows on it.

PART **III** LEATHER GARMENTS

## TOOLS NEEDED

DRIVE PUNCH
GRAPH PAPER — SMALL
DRESSMAKER'S RULER
WATERPROOF FELT-TIPPED PEN
MALLET
SHEARS
SMALL SCISSORS
RUBBER OR LEATHER CEMENT AND
    BRUSHES
HARDWOOD BOARD
LACING
HEAVY BROWN PAPER

OPTIONAL

PLIERS
LARGE-EYED EMBROIDERY NEEDLE
AWL
MASKING TAPE
DRESSMAKER'S WHEEL AND PAPER

• FOR MACHINE SEWING ONLY

GLOVER'S NEEDLE FOR BOTH MACHINE
    AND HAND SEWING
EVEN-FEED OR WALKING FOOT
    (OPTIONAL BUT HIGHLY
    RECOMMENDED)
HEAVY MERCERIZED THREAD
TISSUE PAPER (OPTIONAL)

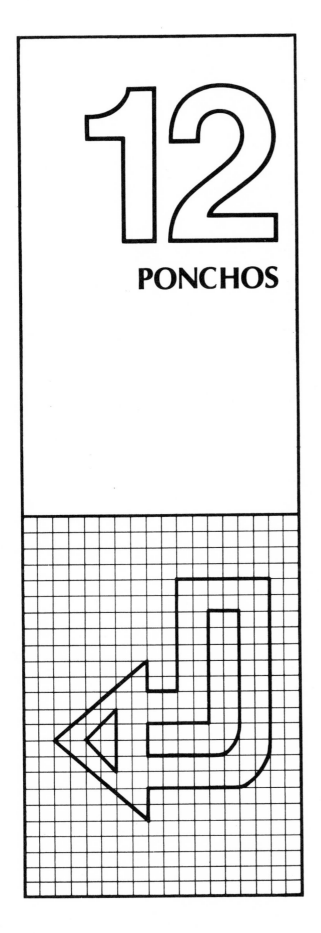

# 12
# PONCHOS

Ponchos are very good leather garments to begin with. They are practical to wear and easy to make, while still teaching you the basics involved in making leather clothing. Ponchos can also involve weaving and bead weaving, and the basics of fringing and knotted fringing.

This section and the next cover instructions for making three different ponchos. Two — an adult's and a child's — are beaded, and the third is plain, with diagonal fringing down one side of both back and front. These three can be sewn with a machine using concealed seaming and then later hand-sewn for decoration; or they can be hand-sewn only, using abutted seams. Use whichever method is more convenient for you. I used both machine and hand sewing, since I feel the combination is neater, easier, and stronger.

For an adult's poncho, you can either make patterns or not. (I like to make up patterns for the same reason I use them for cutting out large pieces for the back of cushions.) To make a pattern for this poncho, for the main sections you will need three brown paper pattern pieces, from each of which you will cut out two pieces of leather. If you are planning to sew by machine, make up three rectangles (see Fig. L-1) measuring

(A)  22½ by 40 inches, (B)  11½ by 40 inches, and (C)  11½ by 32½ inches.

**Fig. L-1**

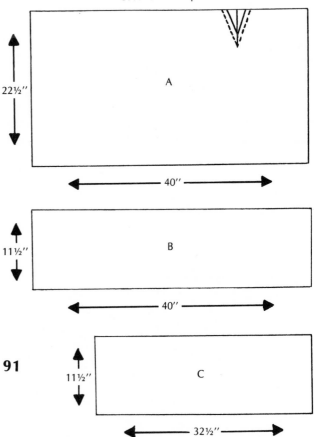

**Fig. L-2**    Cut two of each piece

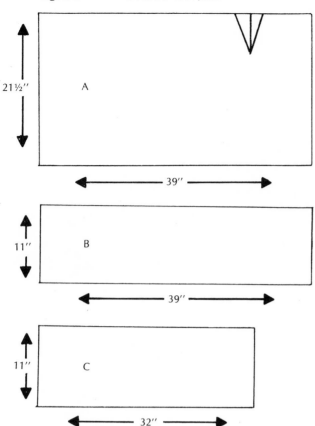

21½″    A

39″

B    11″

39″

C    11″

32″

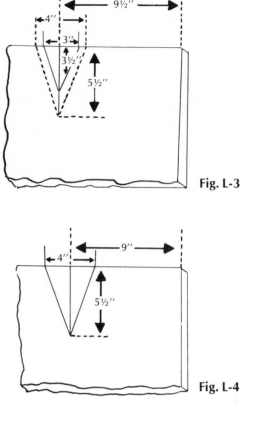

9½″

4″

3″

3½″

5½″

**Fig. L-3**

9″

4″

5½″

**Fig. L-4**

If you are planning to sew only by hand with abutted seams, make up three rectangles (see Fig. L-2) measuring

(A) 21½ by 39 inches, (B) 11 by 39 inches, and (C) 11 by 32 inches.

On the long side of rectangle A you must make the placement of the darts which will form the shaping for the shoulders. To do this, cut out a triangle starting at 8 inches from the end of the pattern for concealed seams, and 7 inches from the end of the pattern for abutted seams. When constructed, this dart is actually 4 inches wide at the top and runs to 5½ inches at the tip. But for machine sewing only, cut to 3½ inches deep and 3 inches wide at the top. The ½ inch seam allowance will bring it to its final size (see Fig. L-3). If you are making abutted seams, cut out the triangle 5½ inches deep at the point and 4 inches wide at the top (see Fig. L-4).

To make the darts, measure in 9½ inches from the corner for concealed seams and 9 inches for abutted seams. Draw a 5½ to 6 inch line at right angles to the edge at this mark. Now draw in the dart using this line as the center (see Figs. L-3 and L-4). Make the darts correspond to

the needed measurements for each type of seaming. Try to draw the sides of the dart to form a convex curve which, when sewn, will give a nice rounded shape to the shoulders.

When purchasing the leather for this poncho, get whatever you feel would best suit your purpose. But for the diagonal-fringed poncho, use leather finished on both sides and dyed all the way through. The texture and weight of the leather is basically up to you, but it should be soft enough to fall in easy folds. I used cowhide on the fringed poncho, white cabretta on the child's, and sueded splits on the beaded poncho. If you are going to use the poncho for heavy wear, choose a rough leather. If you want an elegant design, then use a softer leather or suede.

One factor to keep in mind when buying skins is that if you are making something from a fine suede, you will have to match up the nap the same way you would on velvet. Suedes will change color slightly, just as fabrics such as velvet or corduroy do, when you brush them with your hand. In making clothing, you should try to keep the nap going in the same direction on all the various parts. Therefore, you must purchase a bit extra to maintain a color throughout. Nap is not so noticeable on rough suedes, but always

92

check to make sure there isn't too much crocking—the tiny fibers that rub off and take the dye with them. Run your hand over the skin. If a lot comes off onto your hand, don't buy it. There should only be a small amount, which will wear off within a few days.

The diagonal-fringed poncho has a rougher look, whereas the beaded one is dressier. Whichever you choose, however, the skins have to be large enough to have areas free from scars large enough for the pattern pieces to fit. This means at least 6 square feet of scar-free area for the larger pattern pieces.

Don't forget that if you want a rough look, you can use irregularities such as the jagged edges, holes, and scars as part of the overall design. These flaws could be interesting around a ragged hem, for instance. But again, try to select skins with all the irregularities on the outside edges, because you don't want a hole in the middle of the back of a jacket.

In addition to these natural flaws found in leather, you must also remember to check the dye lots. Different dye lots equal different colors. It is sometimes hard to match even different skins of the same lot, especially in offbeat colors, since each hide absorbs differently. So be sure the skins are from the same dye lot and of equal color. This makes it important to know how much leather you need if you are making anything that must be matched perfectly.

The amount of leather you will need to buy is another consideration here. You must find out the square footage required to cut out the pattern pieces. Change the inch measurements of the pieces to footage measurements; multiply the length by the width of each piece; and then add the results together. In addition, you must work out the approximate amount of footage needed for the fringing. For the first poncho I describe you will need about 24 square feet for the large pattern pieces, and about 10 square feet for the fringing — a total of 28 square feet. This is not the exact amount, since you must also take into consideration the amount of waste you may have and allow a little extra for mistakes. Adding about 15 percent to get the needed total, you will need about 32½ square feet of leather.

If you can, get leather large enough to enable you to cut two very large rectangles the size of the large (A) and two smaller (B and C) rectangles combined — 33 by 50½ inches or 32½

by 50 inches. Usually, however, you will find that it is better to join the pieces, as it is expensive and difficult to find such large hides — let alone pieces with no flaws in them. In addition, the join line in this particular pattern indicates the correct placement of the top row of the fringing.

Besides making these calculations, always lay your pattern on the skins when buying. If you are sending away for the leather, send a copy of your pattern so they do the same. This will also allow you to be sure that the skins are large enough to accommodate the size pattern pieces being used.

You are now ready to cut out two identical leather pieces for each pattern piece. The smaller rectangles, B and C, will be added to the ends of the other two large rectangles, A, to make the poncho large enough for a nice full look.

While the pattern pieces are still laid out, transfer all necessary instructions (such as darts) to the wrong side of the leather. To do this, use a dressmaker's tracing wheel and run it over the markings on the pattern; this will transfer little indentations into the leather which you will be able to see quite readily. If the wrong side of the leather is sueded or if it is the wrong side of the cabretta, you will need to use dressmaker's tracing paper along with the wheel; otherwise the nap or roughness will cover up the perforations. In this case, place the tracing paper, color side facing the leather, between the pattern and the leather and run the tracing wheel over the markings. Put ½ inch seam allowances on both types of seaming to help you later, even though there are really no seam allowances on the abutted-seam pattern.

Don't forget all the tips I expounded on earlier: Don't ever cut on the diagonal of the stretch (or grain); mark your entire pattern before cutting so you can be sure you are taking full advantage of your leather; check the leather for scars or flaws in important places; and cut with smooth, even strokes of the scissors. This last is very important because if you are using abutted seams, the raw edges will be seen, and you get jagged-looking edges when you jerk on the scissors.

If you don't want to make up a pattern, you will need to measure and draw up pieces directly on the leather. Cut out two rectangular pieces measuring 22½ by 40 inches for concealed seams, and 21½ by 39 inches for abutted seams. Then on the wrong side of the long side of these rectangles, at opposite ends, mark the appropriate dart markings.

Now cut out four narrow rectangles: two measuring 11½ by 32½ inches and two measuring 11½ by 40 inches for concealed seams, or two 11 by 32 inches and two measuring 11 by 39 inches for abutted seams. (Of course you can cut one rectangle 33 by 50½ inches if your leather is large enough.) Be very careful to measure accurately — as is explained in previous chapters, it's difficult to make accurate right-angle corners and straight lines, especially on softer, more pliable leather.

Whether you use the pattern or no-pattern method, you will need additional pieces from which to make the fringing. If your leather is dyed throughout, you must cut approximately 228 strips of leather 20 inches long and ¼ inch wide. That should be enough to make the complete top row of fringing all around the edges of the adult's poncho. For leather finished on one side only, you will need to make self-fringing. To make this type of fringing just cut out pieces of leather 11 inches wide and of whatever length your leather scraps will allow. When combined, these pieces must be of the 11-inch width and total 114 to 120 inches in length. From these you will cut ¼-inch self-fringing to go around the entire upper fringe line of the poncho. In addition, you will also need strips of ¼-inch-wide leather lacing for sewing and weaving, and, if you are making a diagonal-fringed poncho, an additional 78 strips ¼ inch wide and 36 to 37 inches long.

When constructing the poncho, it is best to get the real basics down first. This means making the darts, attaching the small rectangles to the larger ones, and then attaching the resulting two large ones together.

First construct the dart. The finished dart is 5½ inches deep and 4 inches wide at the top; it should curve to follow the shoulder line and come to an easy point. Either glue or sew the darts, depending on whether you are sewing by machine or hand. For machine stitching, simply follow the lines of the ½-inch seam allowances and sew to the point. For abutted seams, abut the raw edges of the cut-out triangle and glue a strip 1 inch wide beneath, making sure that the center of the strip is directly under the abutted raw edges of the dart.

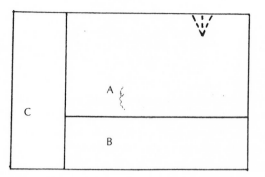

**Fig. L-5**

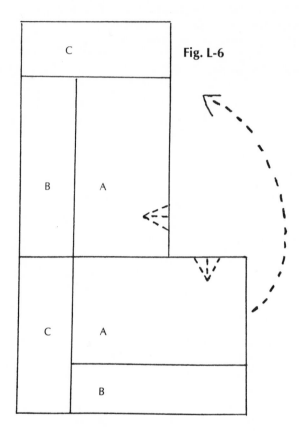

**Fig. L-6**

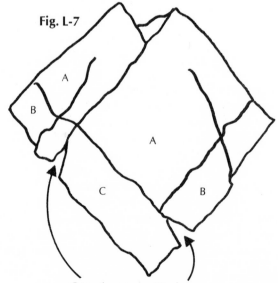

**Fig. L-7**

Open these seams 5 inches

Whether hand or machine sewing, the pieces of the adult's poncho should be assembled in the following order: (When I say assembled I mean either machine-sewn with concealed seams, or with abutted seams centered and glued to the 1-inch understrips, ready to sew.) Join rectangle B to rectangle A along the long dartless edge. Then sew rectangle C to the short edge of the rectangle formed by A and B, at the end farthest away from the dart (see Fig. L-5).

While sewing, keep the machine going at a slow, steady speed to maintain even stitches. On long seams, sew from top to bottom (neck to hem on garments), or at least keep them all sewn in the same direction so they will fall the same way. If you have excess leather, it will all be on one end and therefore easy to adjust. Tie the ends of seams or — if you are very careful, since improper backstitching can rip the leather — backstitch directly into the holes left in the leather by the forward stitching. To prevent puckering and catching, and to get a nice even stitch, hold the leather taut in back and in front of the needle as you stitch.

You should now have two large rectangles made by combining A to B, and C to AB. Now sew or glue the poncho sections together by joining the long side with the dart on it (AC) to the short side of the other rectangle (AB) closest to the darts (see Fig. L-6). Be sure not to join the area around the darts. Now join the long side of the second rectangle to the short side of the first, so that the B corner of the first rectangle and the C corner of the second rectangle match up, and your poncho is done.

After sewing these joining seams, go back and undo 5 inches of each seam that extends to the outer edges of the poncho. Then refinish off the ends of these seams to prevent the seam from unraveling (see Fig. L-7).

If you are machine stitching, you should join the pieces with traditional concealed seams. Use ½-inch seam allowances and join the pieces in the sequence listed above. With machine stitching you must glue the seam allowances open, then hammer them flat with a mallet. This means the long, concealed joining seams, the ½-inch seam allowances around the neck (easy because they are simply extensions of the joining seams), and in addition, the seams of the darts. If you are using very delicate leather, you can glue a strip to the wrong side of the leather along all seams to be used for punching and lacing as you would with abutted seams.

If you are hand-sewing you will be using abutted seams — a good idea here, as they are so simple to do with long flat seams. Abut all seam edges and glue a 1-inch wide strip of leather underneath, being sure that it fits within the ½-inch seam allowances marked around the seams of the pattern on the wrong side. On the neckline, glue a 1-inch stripping along the raw edges to form a facing. Be sure the dart is properly glued with a strip under the abutted edges of the triangle, and curved slightly to fit the curve of the shoulder. Work the strip around the curve, keeping it centered under abutted edges. Be sure everything is glued accurately and neatly so that all edges abut correctly.

To sew with leather lacing, whether you are using machine-sewn or abutted seams, you must mark and punch holes. All holes should be punched before you start stitching. The width of the lacing to be used here is ¼ inch. Be sure to use your dressmaker's ruler, marking accurately and clearly. (Measuring and marking is really easy with your dressmaker's ruler so don't even attempt to measure for fringing and beading without this tool.) Adjust spacing if necessary to make everything fit nicely within the allotted area.

For abutted seams, mark the center of the 1-inch strips so that you can easily measure the placement of the holes. Be absolutely accurate, however; otherwise the holes will not come out right and may fall on the raw edges of the abutted seam.

For traditional seams, use your stitched seam line as your guide. Then on the back of the garment mark two rows of holes, one on either side of the seams. Do this around every seam. All the rows should be ⅜ inch apart from center hole to center hole. For the upper fringing line the rows should be ⅜ inch apart and the holes within each row should be ½ inch apart for *loose fringing* strips (see Fig. L-13). For *self-fringing* in the top row, the holes should be ½ inch apart, and the holes in the lower row through which you will pull lacings should be ¼ inch apart (see Fig. L-14). For the diagonal seams across the front and back of the poncho, formed by joining the two rectangles ABC and ABC, the rows should be ⅜ inch apart and the holes within the rows ½ to ⅝ inch apart.

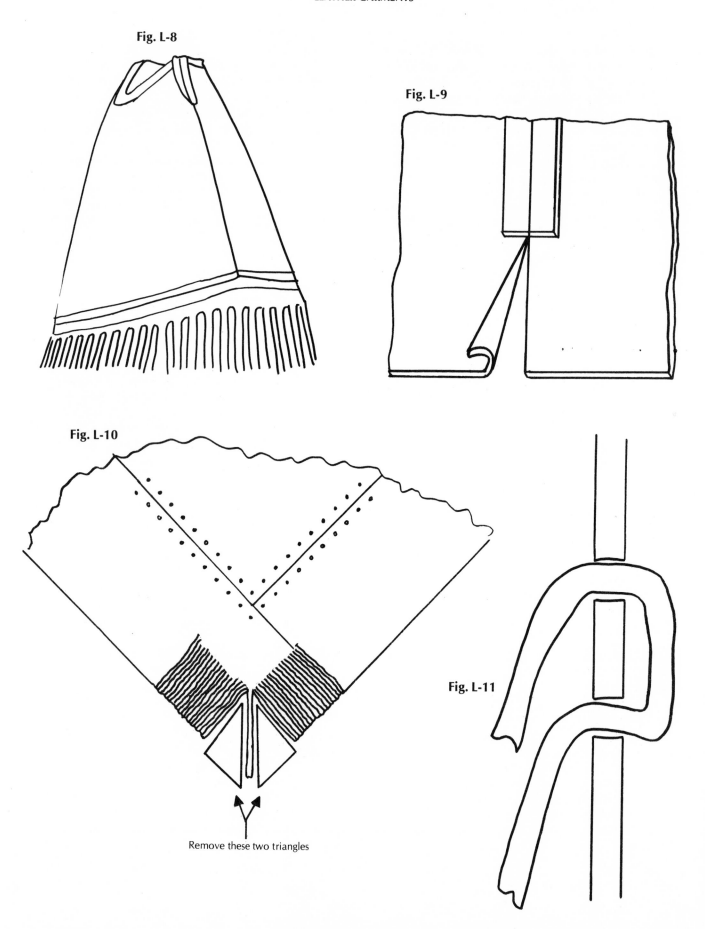

**Fig. L-8**

**Fig. L-9**

**Fig. L-10**

**Fig. L-11**

Remove these two triangles

Now draw a line on the wrong side of the poncho from the point of the dart straight down to meet at right angles the top row-of-fringing line (see Fig. L-8). Do the same with the other dart. Punch a row of holes on either side of this line so that the rows are ⅜ inch apart and the holes within each row are ½ to ⅝ inch apart. A row of diagonal stitching here will give the effect of a seam, but will in fact be purely decorative, separating the front from the back to give the poncho a finished look. At the same time measure, mark, and punch the holes for the edge-stitching to be used around the neckline. They should be ¼ inch from the edge and ½ inch apart from each other. Use a drive punch to make the holes, being sure to place a hardwood board beneath the leather. Hit the punch sharply with a mallet to get a good clean hole, removing a small circle of leather.

## FRINGING

Now measure 5 inches up around the entire lower edge of the poncho and draw a line around the inside, using a colored or lead pencil of a similar color to the leather. Before making your bottom row of fringing, however, check to make sure that none of the diagonal joining seams extend more than 5 inches from the outside edge, as previously pointed out. If they do, open them up to 5 inches now, and refinish off the ends of the seams by backstitching or tying the end thread (see Fig. L-7). On concealed seams, trim the ½ inch seam allowance on the excess 5 inches (see Fig. L-9). Now take your dressmaker's ruler and measure off ¼ inch strips from the 5 inch mark to the lower edge. Mark off about ten to fifteen strips, then take sharp scissors and cut along the lines to form the fringes. Cut with smooth continuous strokes, never quite closing the blades and never jerking, until there is a 5 inch fringe around the entire outer edge of the poncho.

When doing this, there is a trick to make sure that the fringes fall properly at the point in both the back and front of the poncho. First of all, at the both center points cut a single ¼ inch wide and 4 to 4½ inch long strip of fringing. Then, starting at shoulder seam lines and working toward the points, mark and cut your ¼ by 5 inch fringing as accurately as possible. Cut

straight fringes until you reach the open diagonal seam and 11 inches from the point on the other side. Then start cutting the fringes so that the bottom of the fringe is ⅜ inch wide and the top is ¼ inch. (Be very careful as you approach the point; cut carefully, being sure not to make the top part of the fringe so narrow that it can easily break.)

When you have used up all the material along the top line of the fringing, you will find that there is an excess of leather on either side of the central point fringe, forming triangles with their base on the outer edge and point on the inside. Eliminate these triangles of excess leather from around the center (see Fig. L-10). The size of these triangles depends on how you cut the strips up to that point. So work down from the side (shoulder) seams toward the points in front and back, being sure to always cut your point fringes first.

If you do forget to make this fringe, and find you inadvertently cut off the central fringe, punch a hole near the top of the point and pull a strip of loose lacing through. Tie a knot at the end of the lacing on the wrong side, and pull it tight against the leather so that the knot won't allow the lacing to fall out. Trim the lacing to the correct length (5 inches in this case).

You must now finish the top fringe of the lower decoration. If you are using leather dyed all the way through, you should have cut about 228 (or the number of punched holes) 20 by ¼ inch fringes. Trim both ends to a point and pull both ends through both holes adjacent to each other on the double row of holes (see Fig. L-11). Pull taut so both ends are even. Do this through all the holes around the entire edge of the poncho.

If you are using a leather finished on one side only, such as cabretta, then you must cut your strips of fringing differently. You should already have cut the 114 to 120 inches of 11 inch wide pieces of leather ready to be fringed. Now mark a line 1 inch in from one edge and mark ¼ inch strips ten to fifteen at a time (see Fig. L-12) as you did around with outside fringing until you have 114 to 120 inches of 10 by ¼ inch fringing (456 to 480 fringes). Trim the ends to a point. With the right side of fringed strips to the wrong side of the poncho, pull each fringe through the bottom row of already punched holes to the right

**Fig. L-12**

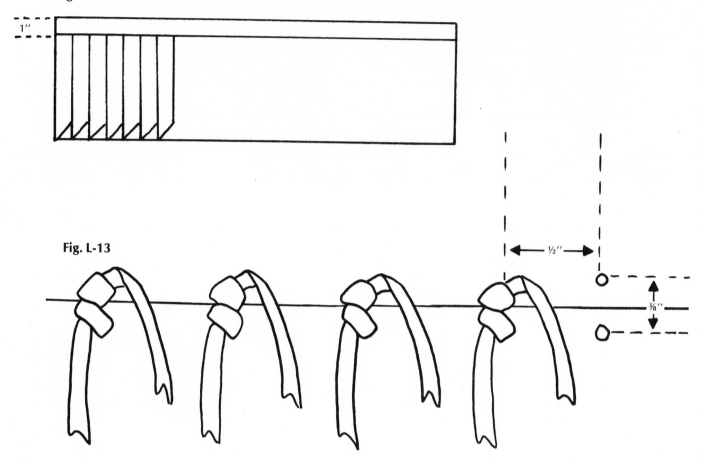

**Fig. L-13**

**Fig. L-14**

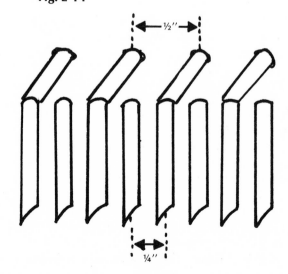

side — the holes on the bottom row of the double row should have been spaced only ¼ inch apart. This will leave the top row open, ready to sew or bead. (The spacing of the holes in the top row is ½ inch.)

Now stitch a row of diagonal stitching along the darts and down the shoulder seam line which you created. Starting from either the top or bottom — through one of the fringe holes or neck-edge stitching holes — sew a diagonal stitched line through the hole already punched. Then edge-stitch around the neck with the stitch of your choice.

You must now decide if you want a beaded poncho or one with diagonal fringing along the join of back and front.

For the fringed one, remember you can use only leather dyed on both sides. Go back and tie the two pieces of each fringe around the second row so that a knot is formed on the right side of the leather. This way, the fringe can't pull out and acts as a stitch joining the two sides of the seams together (see Fig. L-13). Now cut out the fringing for the diagonal strips. Using scraps if possible, you will need about 78 fringes 36 to 37 inches long and ¼ inch wide. The holes within the rows should be ½ inch apart here and the double row ⅜ inch apart. Now take these lacing

fringes and, from the wrong side, bring the lacing through all adjacent holes of the double row and knot, thus tying the seam together (see Fig. L-13). This forms side fringing and also "sews" the seams together.

Do this on the front and back. If you used self-fringed strips of leather for your top row of fringing, then you must stitch diagonally around the top fringe row. Stitch into every hole in the top row (½ inch apart) and into every other hole in the bottom row (¼ inch apart) to finish off the poncho (see Fig. L-14).

## TOOLS NEEDED

LARGE-HOLED BEADS
DRIVE PUNCH
WOODEN MALLET
HARDWOOD BOARD
FELT-TIPPED PEN
CLEAR DRESSMAKER'S RULER
GRAPH PAPER
HEAVY BROWN PAPER
RUBBER OR LEATHER CEMENT AND
    BRUSHES
SHEARS
SMALL SCISSORS
MASKING TAPE (OPTIONAL)

• HAND SEWING

MALLET
HARDWOOD BOARD
DRIVE PUNCH
LACING

### OPTIONAL

PLIERS
LARGE-EYED EMBROIDERY NEEDLE
AWL
ROTARY PUNCH

• MACHINE SEWING

EVEN-FEED OR WALKING FOOT
    (OPTIONAL BUT HIGHLY
    RECOMMENDED)
HEAVY MERCERIZED THREAD
GLOVER'S NEEDLES FOR BOTH MACHINE
    AND HAND SEWING
TISSUE PAPER (OPTIONAL)

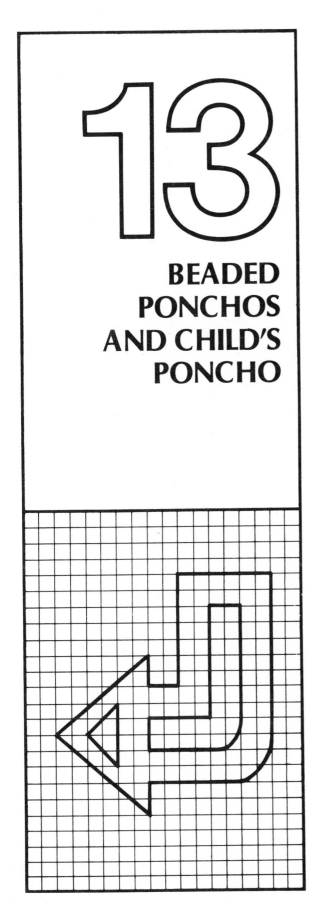

# 13

# BEADED PONCHOS AND CHILD'S PONCHO

For beading the adult's poncho, you will need 428 to 430 beads for ☒, 198 to 200 beads for ⊡, 84 to 86 beads for ▲, and 304 to 306 beads for ◪. The ☒ beads should be squaw tubular beads; ⊡, ▲, and ◪ beads should be the large glass or the plastic imitation-glass Indian beads. (My color scheme for the rust poncho is: ☒ — purple opaque; ⊡ — yellow opaque; ▲ — green transparent; ◪ — orange transparent. For the white poncho my color scheme is: ☒ — black; ⊡ — light green; ▲ — light blue; ◪ — orange.)

Squaw beads could easily be substituted for glass beads with little design loss. In fact, if you want you can use only squaw beads for all of your designs, as they are inexpensive and light-weight. In addition, if you feel that glass beads would be too heavy, there are plastic beads which simulate the look of glass rather well. However, I used glass and tubular beads as I wanted to get as authentic a quality as possible in my work, basing my beadwork on the motifs used by the American Indians. The Indians made their own beads from shell, turquoise, bone, and traded coral, but traded for glass beads with the settlers because they loved the way glass beads sparkle and catch the light. The glass beads are heavy, however, and as you can see from the color photos, the right combination of tubular squaw beads is equally effective. (You can order these from Plume Trading Co., but Tandycraft and many hobby stores also carry them. See the addresses under the mail-order supplies in the back of this book.) Taking up where we left off in chapter 12, for beading you must make another double row of punched holes to form the fourth side of the outer framing diamond of the design (see Fig. M-1). To do this, turn the poncho inside

**Fig. M-1**

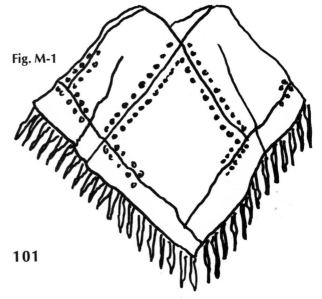

101

**Fig. M-2**
DIAMOND BEADING PATTERN

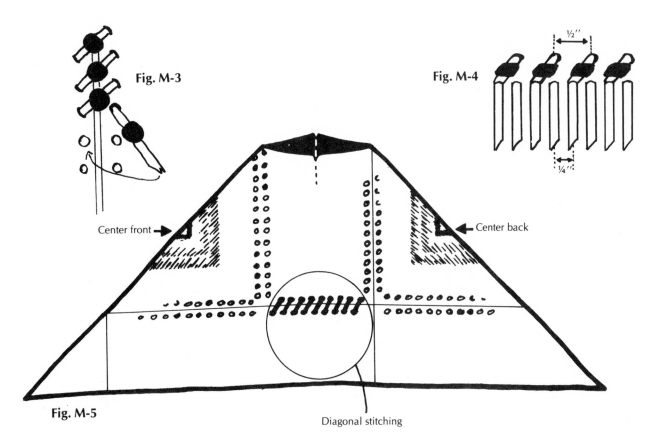

Fig. M-3

Fig. M-4

Center front →

← Center back

Fig. M-5

Diagonal stitching

out and measure from the point of upper row of fringing to the diagonal seam line joining the back and front rectangles together — 20½ inches (adult size). Then, starting from the top fringing point, measure the same distance — 20½ inches — on the other side and mark on both front and back.

Now draw a line from the center point of the neckline to the marked point on the top row of fringing line on both back and front. Mark and punch holes along this line to match the other diagonal line — a double row ⅜ inch apart and the holes ½ inch apart within each row, measured from center hole to center hole. This will give you your outer framing diamond.

Now choose two or three colored beads which will be in the design (see Fig. M-2 for the color arrangement of the diamond). These are to be alternated here. Using a diagonal stitch and starting from the top fringing line, work up toward the neck and down the other side of the diagonal seams, forming the upper half of the diamond. You must alternate the two colored beads around the entire diamond. Use a diagonal bead stitch (see Fig. M-3) to achieve this effect. Bring the lacing through the hole from the wrong to the right side, then thread the lacing through a large-holed bead.

Pull the bead on the lacing till it is right up against the leather of the poncho, then sew your leather lacing into the next hole through to the wrong side of the leather, and pull the lacing fairly taut. This will give you your beading along the seam lines. Start all over again and repeat the process. It is just like doing a diagonal stitch, except here you add a bead. When it comes to joining these lacings, sew them together. This is good for joining in the middle of seams, as the joins can be hidden in the center of the beads. If you prefer, however, you can use the method you would normally use to join if you were just using lacing.

If you used self-fringing strips for the top row of fringing around the poncho, do a diagonal bead stitch around the entire outer framing of the diamond, as you did with plain lacing for the diagonal fringed poncho. Stitch into every hole in the top row (½ inch apart), and into every other hole in the bottom row (¼ inch apart) — see Fig. M-4. Then do a row of plain diagonal stitching with just lacing in the remaining holes running along the top fringing row on either side between the beaded front and back diamonds (see Fig. M-5).

If you used separate strips for your lacing, then you need do only the diagonal bead stitch

103

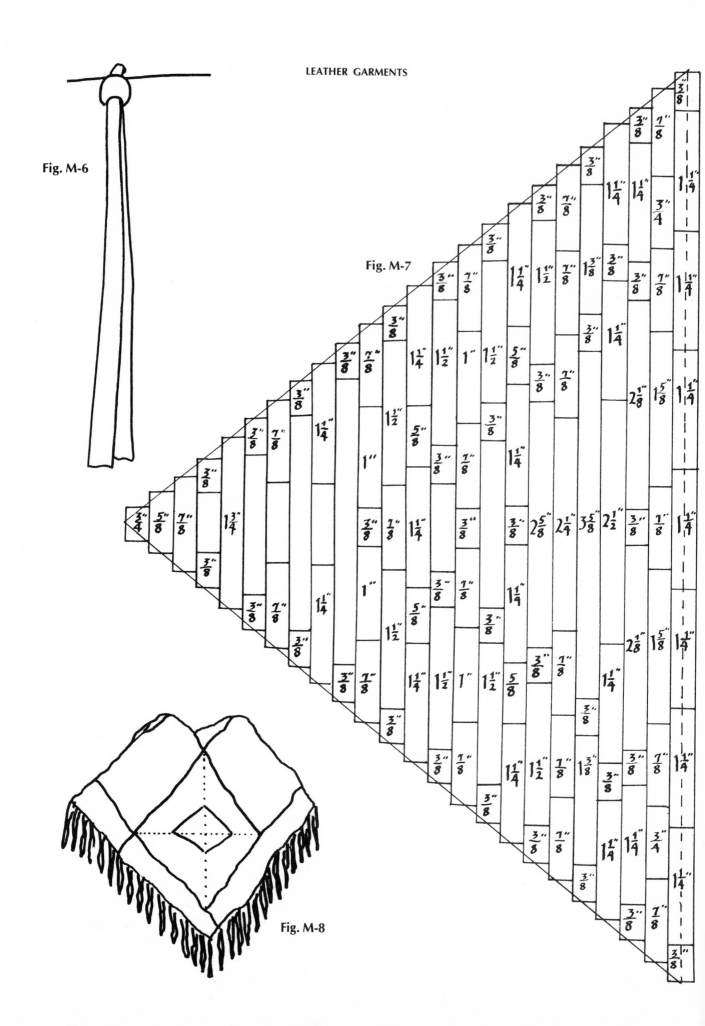

Fig. M-6

Fig. M-7

Fig. M-8

on the top two seams of the triangle. Now on the bottom fringing, thread both ends of each fringe through the hole of the bead. Push the beads on tight so that they are snug against the leather and replace the knot as you sew (see Fig. M-6). Use alternating colors on the beads as you did with diagonal bead stitching. The remaining fringes of the top fringing row running on either side between the two beaded front and back diamonds (see Fig. M-6) should be knotted to sew the two seams together (see Fig. L-13). Once this is done, all stitching should be finished so that no remaining punched holes are left.

Now, for the center diamond of the beaded design, the treatment of the beading is determined by the size of the beads. For other projects the size of the beading can be whatever you choose, from seed beads on up to the glass ones used here. Seed beads call for a fine beading needle and thread. Take a stitch and slip five or six of the beads onto a needle. Then take a small stitch and thread another few beads, until your design is complete. However, for large beads such as those used in this poncho, you must draw out the entire design on the back of the leather first and plan the exact placement of each bead. To do this properly, you will also have to plan the placement of each hole to be punched so that you can bring the lacing through where needed.

First draw your pattern on the back of the leather. It is usually best to work out patterns for beading on graph paper first. The size graph paper to be used depends on the size of your beads. (Each square should be equal to one bead.) For this poncho, use 3/16 to ¼ inch squaw beads, glass Indian beads, or any of the larger-holed beads.

The plan in Fig. M-7 shows the correct way to punch the holes for the diamond pattern shown on the beaded ponchos in this book. The lines indicating where the holes are to be punched mark the exact center of the round hole to be punched out. Always make an accurate pattern and duplicate it on the wrong side of the leather exactly as in the original.

For the diamond pattern used on the ponchos in this book, lay your poncho out flat, wrong side out. Then draw two dotted lines dividing the diamond into quarters (see Fig. M-8). These lines run across the width and height of

the diamond from point to point, and where they intersect is the exact center of your pattern. Now from the center of the diamond mark out 4¾ inches on either side of the height line and 5⅞ inches on the width line. Join these marks to form a diamond measuring 9½ inches high by 11½ to 12 inches wide, with each side of the perimeter measuring 7¾ inches (see Fig. M-9). The outside line of the smaller diamond will be the exact center of all the outside holes, but no hole is to be punched on either outer side points of this diamond.

Now divide this smaller diamond into ¼" strips as you would when marking for your fringing. Start measuring from the broken line marking the center height of the diamond. First measure ⅛ inch on both sides of this line, drawing in parallel lines to create your center ¼-inch fringe. Now on either side of this central fringe, use your dressmaker's ruler to draw lines marking ¼-inch strips — making a total of forty-seven over the entire length of the diamond, twenty-three on either side of the central fringe (see Fig. M-7). Holes should always be punched directly centered between the ¼-inch stripping lines which indicate the placement of each row of beading in the pattern. When copying, first draw the diamond with its ¼-inch separations. Then draw in the marks indicating the placement of the holes in the center row and then work out toward the sides. (These measurements are from center hole to center hole.)

To figure out the amount of spacing, lacing, and hole sizes for different-sized beads, measure a bead's width and length. The spacing of the holes should be a little larger than the size of the beads to be used. Measure one bead and add enough to it so that it is not squeezed. Don't forget to leave space for the hole to be punched

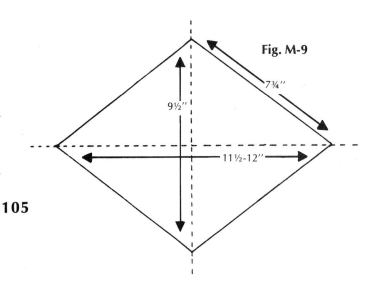

Fig. M-9

9½"

7¾"

11½-12"

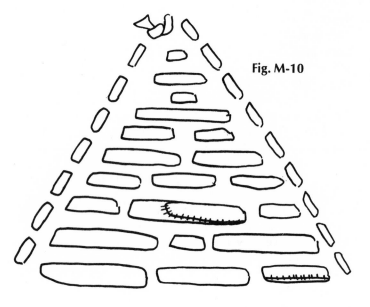

Fig. M-10

When everything is marked, check to be sure it is right. Mark all directing lines; double-check to be sure you are right before punching; and start punching at the center row and work out to the sides.

Always be sure you are punching through only one layer of leather. To do this, put your wooden board between the two layers. If you are going to have beading on both the back and front of an article — such as this poncho — you must mark and punch *both* sides before beading. If you don't, you will destroy the finished bead-work on one side by hitting on top of it with a wooden board and mallet while working on the other side.

When actually weaving, do one row at a time. Start from the center line and first work one side of the diamond design and then the other. Follow the beading diagram given in Fig. M-2. The color of the beads you use is up to you, but you will note that there is a total of four different colors.

Pull the lacing from wrong side to right side, starting at the top of the diamond. Leave a 1-inch tab of leather lacing on the wrong side when starting; glue it down tight, being sure not to cover any holes. Thread the appropriate number of beads onto the lacing, with colors and order corresponding to the given beading pattern, and push them to the end of the lacing right up against the leather. Now insert the lacing into the next hole in that row and pull it fairly taut. Then bring it through to the right side through the next hole. Thread the appropriate number and color combination of beads and continue as above until the end of the row.

The lacing at the end of the row should be on the wrong side. Take this, bring it through the first hole of the next row, and bead-weave that row to correspond to your beading pattern. When you finish off the first side of the diamond, do the other, working in the opposite direction; but be sure always to work from the center strip of the design out to the edges. You can use paper to cover each row as you finish it to make sure you don't get confused, but I really don't see how you can make a mistake — the punched holes will indicate the number of beads needed to fill the space between center hole and center hole.

— again, measurements are based on the distance from center hole to center hole. The size of the hole in the bead determines the size lacing to be used. The size of the holes in the leather in turn depends on the size of the lacing, and should be a little smaller than the lacing so that it fits snugly. The distance between rows of beads corresponds to the width of the lacing being used. Cover each line of beading with a piece of paper when you finish copying, just as you would with very fine print when reading, to help avoid confusion.

Or you can trace the design from this book, fold it in half along the center dotted line, trace the other side, then open it up to full pattern. Now tape this over the wrong side of the leather on the poncho back and front, matching center points and center lines. Take your dressmaker's tracing wheel and run it over all the lines on the pattern. This will leave indentations in the leather which you can mark over with a felt-tipped pen. If the wrong side of the leather is sueded or roughly textured, you may have to place dressmaker's tracing paper face down under the pattern before using your tracing wheel, so it will leave colored marks on the leather indicating the pattern lines. You can also number each line on the outside of the diamond on both the pattern and leather to help you work more easily.

I like to sew my lacing together when I run out. However, you can glue the ends down and glue a tab over them. To finish off at the side points of the diamond, tuck the end into the previous stitch — which is fairly snug — and glue it down (see Fig. M-10). When you finish the front and back bead-weaving of the diamonds, your poncho is finished.

## WEAVING WITH LEATHER ONLY

If you would rather use contrasting leather or leathers instead of beading, simply sew through the holes of the design with lacing only. You can use just one color or several, conforming to the basic color scheme. Make designs by simply drawing on graph paper. Draw in the basic design and color where you feel you would like to see different colors. But make sure you leave spaces between the colors to allow you to bring leather lacing to the wrong side to secure it.

Now enlarge to the size you want and trace or copy it on the back of the leather. The holes to be punched should be placed within the strips allotted for the rows of lacing, which you should draw over the entire pattern. The width of these strips depends on the size lacing you use. Very fine strips and lacing give beautiful intricate designs; larger ones are bold and effective, especially for larger, more casual areas. (This is also true for bead weaving.)

## CHILD'S PONCHO

This poncho requires about 16½ square feet of leather. Make up one pattern piece only — a rectangle measuring 22 by 36½ inches for machine-stitched traditional concealed seams (see Fig. M-11), and 21½ by 35½ inches for hand stitching with abutted seams (see Fig. M-11a). Be sure to mark the placement of the dart. On the child's poncho the finished dart measures 3 inches at the base and 3½ inches to the point. For traditional concealed seams, cut out a triangle 2 inches wide at the base and 3 inches to the point, with the beginning of the

dart at 7 inches and its center at 8 inches from the short edge (see Fig. M-12). Mark in your seam allowances around the triangle. For abutted seams, cut out a triangle 3 inches wide at the base and 3½ inches to the point, with the beginning of the dart at 6 inches and its center at 7½ inches from the short edge (see Fig. M-13).

Sew or glue up the darts as you would for the adult's poncho and join the two large rectangles together by first joining the long dart side of one rectangle to the short side closest to the dart of the other rectangle; and then repeat, only reversing. Start sewing the seams from the neckline edge (dart edge) and sew just to 3¼ inches from the bottom edge of the poncho to allow for the bottom row of fringing. Now mark a line 6½ inches from the edge all around the bottom for the placement of your upper row of fringing. Mark and punch holes along this line as you would for upper fringe of the adult's poncho — using ½-inch placement on both rows for separate fringing, and ¼ inch on bottom row and ½ inch on the top row for self-fringing. Then mark up 3¼ inches from edge around entire outside, and mark and fringe as for adult's.

Continue working the poncho as you would if it were an adult's. Draw a line from the point of the dart straight down to meet the top fringing lines at right angles; mark and punch a row of holes on either side of this line ⅜ inch apart and ½ inch apart within the rows. Stitch with a diagonal stitch. Mark and punch holes down the diagonal joining seam across back and front of poncho, using the same measurements.

If you are using leather that is finished on both sides for the upper row of fringing, cut 174 strips 9 to 10 inches long and ¼ inch wide. If your leather is finished on one side only, cut self-fringing strips 6 inches wide and 87 to 90 inches long — a total of about 248 fringes cut. Mark and cut the fringes by marking in 1 inch on the 6-inch width (see Fig. L-12), and mark and cut approximately 248 fringes measuring ¼ by 5 inches. Pull these fringes through as you would if it were an adult's poncho.

If you are making a diagonal-fringed poncho, cut strips ¼ inch by 18 to 20 inches to be laced through the diagonal seam holes. If you are making a beaded poncho, measure up 15 inches on the side of the points opposite the side

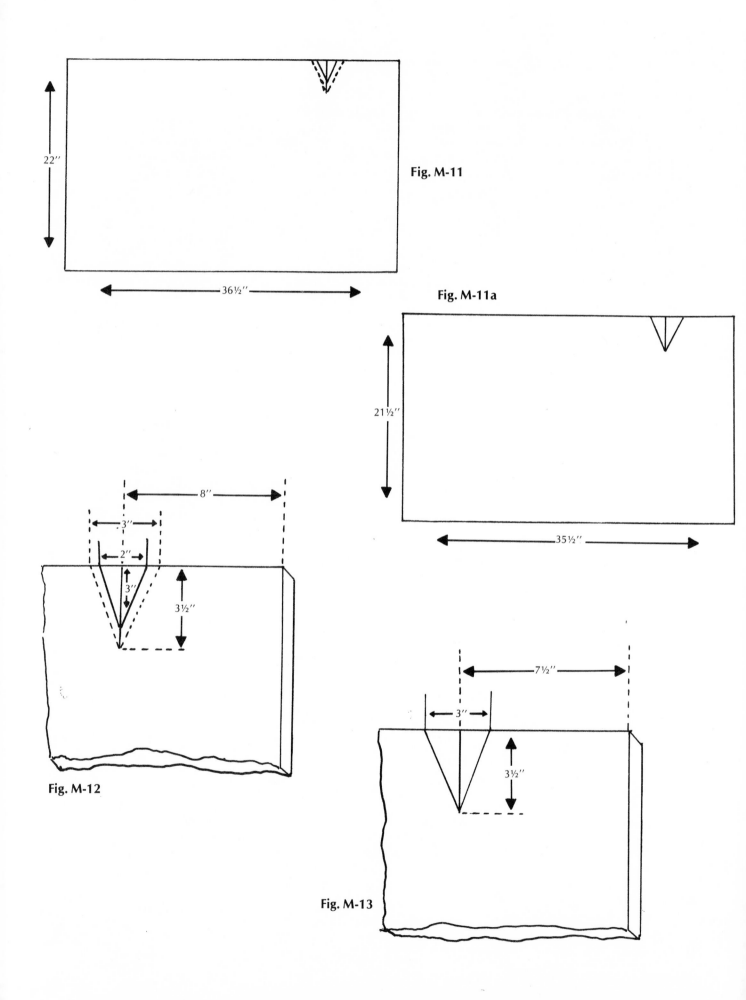

22″

36½″

**Fig. M-11**

**Fig. M-11a**

21½″

35½″

8″

3″

2″

3″

3½″

**Fig. M-12**

7½″

3″

3½″

**Fig. M-13**

with the diagonal joining seam and draw a line from this point to the center of the neckline (see Fig. L-12). Now mark and punch holes to correspond to the other diagonal seams. Proceed as you would for an adult's poncho. The central diamond design is the same size as the adult's and should be marked and beaded in the same way. Mark the top and bottom of the different colored areas to correspond to your original design. Now punch holes using marks as the centers, and weave the lacing in and out of the punched holes.

## OTHER IDEAS FOR PONCHO DECORATION

All edge and top stitching can be beaded, or you might replace the beads with studs or rhinestone studs (see Section 17 for details on studding). You could punch or cut out a diamond or whatever pattern you want from the top layer of leather, underlay it with one or two different types and colors of leather, and sew around the edges as I will explain later. Once the basic structure is down, it is all up to you.

## TOOLS NEEDED

GRAPH PAPER, BOTH THE SMALL AND
    THE 1-INCH SIZE
HEAVY BROWN PAPER
RUBBER OR LEATHER CEMENT AND
    BRUSHES

CLEAR DRESSMAKER'S RULER
FELT-TIPPED PEN
MASKING TAPE (OPTIONAL)
SHEARS AND SMALL SCISSORS
DRIVE PUNCH
HARDWOOD BOARD
MALLET
LACING
LARGE-HOLED GLASS AND/OR SQUAW
    BEADS (OPTIONAL)

OPTIONAL
_____

LARGE-EYED EMBROIDERY NEEDLE
DRESSMAKER'S WHEEL AND TRACING
    PAPER
PLIERS
AWL

• MACHINE SEWING ONLY

EVEN-FEED OR WALKING FOOT
    (OPTIONAL BUT HIGHLY
    RECOMMENDED)
GLOVER'S NEEDLES
HEAVY MERCERIZED THREAD

OPTIONAL
_____

TISSUE PAPER

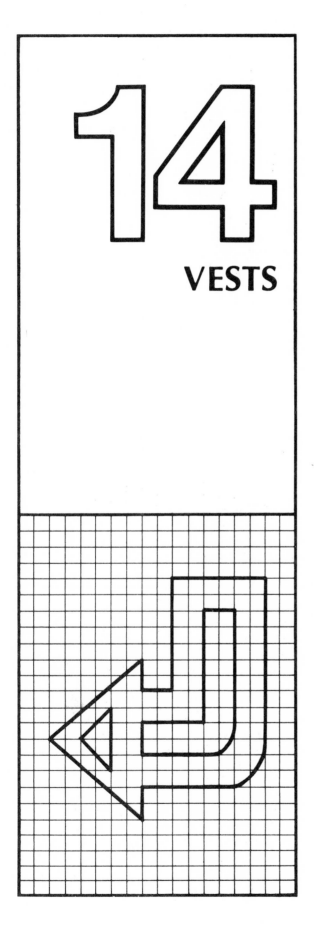

# 14

# VESTS

Making vests is the first step toward making more structured and fitted pieces of clothing. Always remember that you must make the basic garment before adding any decoration such as fringing; therefore, the shape and fit of the garment must be accurate. A vest must fit nicely across the shoulders and back and around the armholes. However, fit elsewhere can be a bit loose; therefore vests provide a good start in learning how garments must be constructed in order to fit the body properly.

You can either make up a pattern yourself or buy one. I have made up two graph patterns — one for an average adult's vest (see Fig. N-1 and N-1a) and one for a child aged 7 to 10 (see Fig. N-2 and N-2a). Simply enlarge these patterns onto 1-inch graph paper as you would any other design and number the squares. Draw a box equivalent to the one around the pattern in the illustration onto your graph, using the equivalent number of squares. Now duplicate the pattern in the illustration by marking each square with exactly the same lines as in the small design, drawing them in one square at a time. In this way you will get an enlarged design exactly the same as the original. Don't forget to number the horizontal and vertical row of squares, and follow from that just as you would when reading a map.

If you want your pattern to be your own exact size, go to a store and buy a vest pattern with a V-shaped neckline like the one in my pattern. You must now adjust your commercial pattern for use as the pattern for this particular vest. First remove (cut off) all seam allowances around the neckline, front seams, and armholes. Then if you want to sew by hand only, using abutted seams, eliminate the seam allowances from the side and shoulder seams. Adjustments to commercial patterns must always be made before cutting out the leather so that markings can be transferred accurately to the wrong side of the leather for ease in construction. This means you must plan everything in advance, so think about what you want before starting any work.

Take a piece of heavy brown paper and tape your back pattern to it. Now trace around the neck, shoulders, armholes, and down the side seams until you reach the line indicating the waistline placement. If there is a fold line on the pattern, then first trace around one side of the pattern (including the fold line). Then remove the pattern, flip it over, line it up with the fold line, tape it down, and trace around the other side.

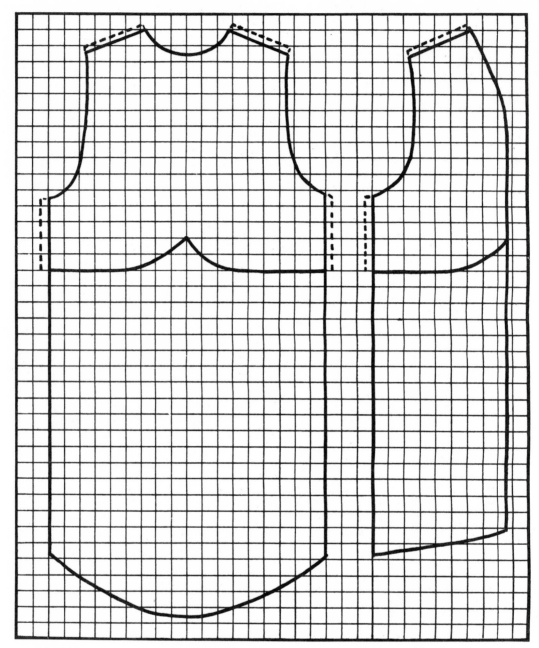

Fig. N-1

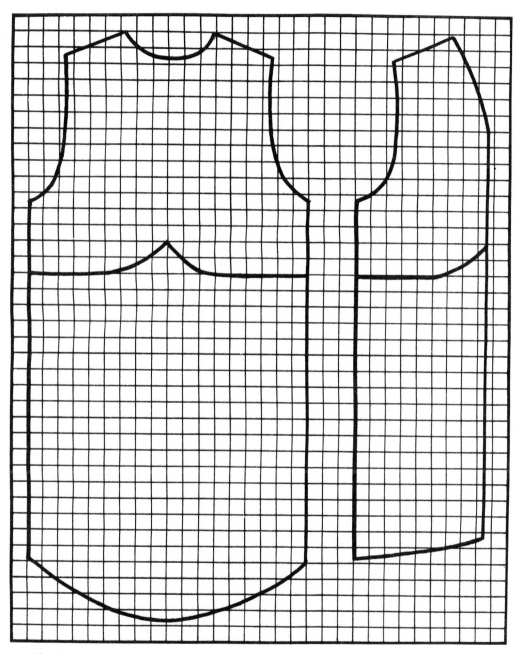

**Fig. N-1a**

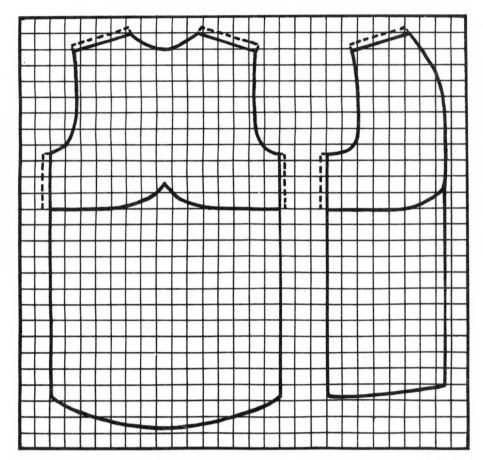

**Fig. N-2**

**Fig. N-2a**

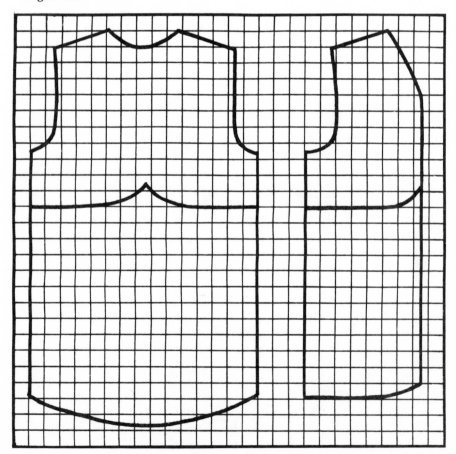

Remove the pattern. Measure and mark on the side seams 4¼ inches for the adult's vest (see Fig. N-3) and 3¼ inches for the child's (See Fig. N-4), and draw a line straight across the back connecting the two side seams at these points.

Now mark up 2 inches for the adult's vest and 1½ inches for the child's in the center of this line. Draw two curving lines from the sides up to meet it and form a scalloped shape such as shown in my pattern. This line will be the point to which you will cut your fringes.

You must now lengthen your back side seams to the desired length. I recommend about 14 inches below the waist for adults (see Fig. N-5) and 4 to 6 inches below the waistline for children (see Fig. N-6), as they are more active, and you don't want too-long fringes. (You can, of course, use this same principle for an adult's vest and make it shorter also. A shorter vest for a more-active person should fall about on the waist. I must say, however, I rather like fringes long, though solid vests look great when they are shorter.)

Once you lengthen the side seams, draw a line straight across connecting the ends. Then mark down 4 inches for the adult's vest and 1¾ inches for the child's from the center of the line and draw a new bottom line for the vest by connecting the side ends to the mark just made in the center with a curved line. This way a new hemline will be curved down toward the center.

For the front of the vest, tape your pattern down to the brown paper as you did with the back and trace as with the back just to the waistline. Now remove the pattern and extend the side seam to 14 inches below the waistline for adults (see Fig. N-5a) and 4 to 6 inches for children (see Fig. N-6a). On the front extend it to 12¾ inches below the waist for adults and 1½ inches for children, then connect the front and side seam lines with a curved line. Now take your dressmaker's ruler and draw a line across the front vest section at 4¼ inches below the armhole for adults (see Fig. N-3a) and 3¼ inches for children (see Fig. N-4a) at right angles to the side seams. On the center front seam line mark up 2 inches for adults and 1½ inches for children and then gently curve the line to meet at this point.

Don't be afraid to make adjustments on commercial patterns. Just think of what you want to do first. To adjust patterns properly, you must

make up some rough sketches of the pattern and mark in your change lines on these miniatures first. When you feel your adjustments are correct, then transfer the lines to the larger pattern pieces. Make sure that all the lines indicating the top of the fringing are correctly indicated on the pattern so they can easily be transferred to the wrong side of the leather.

To make the adult-sized vest you will need skins with at least 3 feet by 20 inches of good flawless leather for the back and at least two

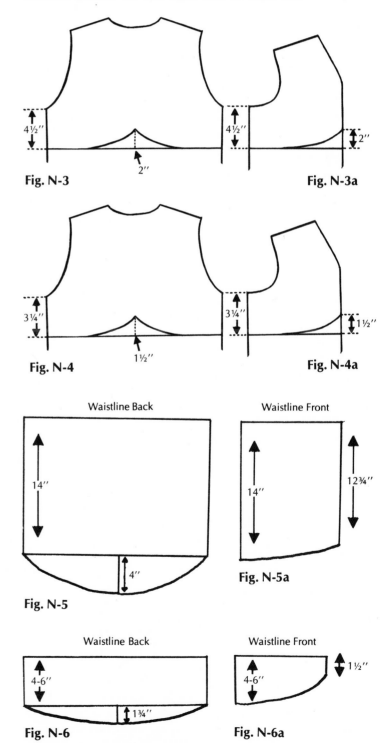

Fig. N-3  Fig. N-3a
Fig. N-4  Fig. N-4a
Waistline Back  Waistline Front
Fig. N-5  Fig. N-5a
Waistline Back  Waistline Front
Fig. N-6  Fig. N-6a

areas of 3 feet by 10 inches for the front. For the child's vest you will need an area 2 feet by 17 inches for the back and two areas 2 feet by 9 inches for the front. It is difficult to give exact square footage, however, as the skins must be long enough to fit the entire length of the vest. This is not a garment that can be pieced together with added seams to accommodate the skin sizes. Therefore, be sure to take your pattern pieces — or at least a tape measure and the correct measurements — with you when buying the leather. If you send away for leather, send a copy of the pattern to be sure. The leather for this vest must be dyed all the way through, since the fringes are really long and you will definitely be able to see both sides. On the beaded poncho you could use leather finished on one side only, since the fringes were not too long, but on the diagonal-fringed poncho you can see the unfinished side. As a rule, you can use leather finished on one side only, if you are lining the garment; but if you are not, it is a good idea to use leather finished on both sides. And since you are beading the leather fringes on this vest, the leather must hold the beads snugly. I therefore recommend using not too soft a leather — a heavier cowhide, heavy enough to hold the beads, should do the job.

Lay the pattern pieces out on the wrong side of the leather and trace around them, making

sure that the two front pieces are reversed (see Fig. N-7). Transfer all markings to the back of these leathers using a pencil, a tracing wheel, or a color very similar to that of the leather itself. Now cut out the long strips of leather lacing to make the ties in the front of the vest. For the adult's vest you will need six strips ¼ inch by 42 inches; for the child's, four strips ¼ inch by 34 inches. If you find you can't get strips this long, then cut them half the desired length and join pairs of them together. (The join will be hidden on the wrong side.) If you are planning to sew by hand, you will also need lacing for sewing the seams together and small strips for backing the abutted seams. So cut out four more strips either 42 or 34 inches long.

Once everything is cut out, sew up the shoulder seams first. Use machine-sewn traditional concealed seams plus a spaced cross-stitch, or abutted seams (see C, Fig. O-2) with a spaced cross-stitch.

Adjust the stitch sizes and spacing so that the seam length is all sewn tightly. A way to do this easily is to cut out four extra strips of leather 42 or 34 inches long, and use one for each of the seams. First punch a hole on either side of the seam line and ⅓ to ½ inch from either end of the seam, then make four sets of holes adjacent to each other on either side of the seam, spaced evenly to fit between the end holes. Now

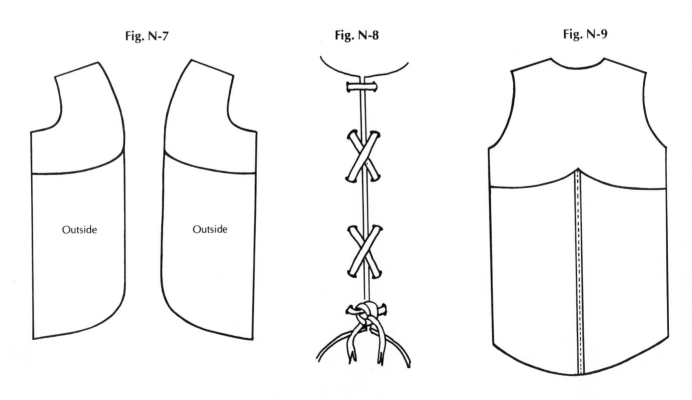

**Fig. N-7**  **Fig. N-8**  **Fig. N-9**

Outside  Outside

sew by lacing both ends through the holes closest to the neck edges, starting on the right side. Cross the laces over each other in the back and bring them through the next holes to the right side. Now repeat as if you were lacing shoes until both ends come through the last pair of holes on the right side at the armhole edge. Tie a knot and let the excess lacing simply hang as decoration (see Fig. N-8).

If you want to sew traditional seams, then start, join, and finish in the usual manner for straight flat seams. Then sew or glue the side seams down 4¼ inches for the adult's vest and 3¼ inches for the child's. Do not punch and lace the side seams now; wait until you finish the fringing.

Starting at the center back row, cut out the fringing (see Fig. N-9). The exact center of the back is the point at which the sides curve upward to meet, forming the scalloped shape of the top fringing — 8¾ inches for the adult's vest and 7½ inches for the child's, or just measure with your ruler and mark the center. Go over the line, marking the scalloped shaping to be sure it is easily readable. Your first fringe will run ⅛ inch on either side of the center mark. Mark and cut out this center fringe first, then mark ¼ inch strips across the back. Mark and cut only two or three fringes at a time here. Be as accurate as possible and mark and cut carefully, since the fringes here are really rather long. You shouldn't have much problem if you used the heavier, stiffer leather I recommended; and if you've already made a poncho, you should have had plenty of practice.

For the front fringing, start at the center front and work to the sides. If you are using concealed seams, eliminate the seam allowances once you finish fringing. Leaving these seam allowances until the end gives you a little extra room to work and you can cover up any little mistakes by trimming the fringe. When you have finished the fringing, if you find that you have not calculated correctly and you have too much on the top, then take in the side seam allowances so they fit correctly. If you find too much on the bottom, then simply cut your final fringe — make sure it fits in the top and eliminate the excess from the bottom. From my pattern you will cut sixty-seven separate fringes on the back of the adult's vest and thirty-four on either side of the front; for the

child's, fifty-nine on the back and thirty-one on either side of the front.

Now — after any needed adjustments — sew the side seams together using the same method used for the shoulder seams. If you want to continue the shoe-lacing technique you used for the shoulders, then start from just under the arm and work down. (Garment seams should always be worked from the neck to the hemline.)

Now mark and punch the holes around the armholes and neckline in preparation for the bead-edge stitching. The spacing is the same here no matter which type of stitch you decide to do. Make sure you space the holes evenly: ½ to ⅝ inch between each hole and ¼ inch from the edge. (Measurements are center hole to center hole and center hole to raw edge.) You will be beading completely around the armhole, but around the neckline you will bead only to about ½ to ¾ inch above the beginning of the fringing. Adjust the distances between the holes so that they are evenly spaced to fit the area to be laced. You will be using two alternating colors of beads, so punch an even number of holes and the beading will work out evenly.

Your basic construction and preparation is now complete and you are ready to put in your decoration — in this case, beading. Make up any design you want, using the methods outlined in Section 13. I have made up two different designs for you to follow for this vest, a diamond (as on the poncho) and a thunderbird. Both designs are further enhanced by extra borders, bands of beading motifs going around the entire vest, and by edge-bead stitching around the raw-edge facings. The diamond is made from a mixture of tubular squaw beads and glass Indian beads; the thunderbird mostly from tubular squaw beads with a few glass ones on the top border and around the neck and armholes.

The diagrams, photos, and patterns given for these vests should make the going pretty easy. Just be sure to follow them carefully. And if you make up your own design, plan it completely so that there is no problem when you are beading. The beads used here are found in hobby and bead stores; if you can't find them there, send away for them from the places listed in the mail-order list in the back of this book. For the purple adult's diamond-design vest you will need the following beads:

| Number and use | | My color choice | Type |
|---|---|---|---|
| ☒ — 203 | top border | Pink | Tubular squaw |
| 341 | third border and diamond | | |
| ‾544 | | | |
| ⊡ — 68 | top border | Smoky opaque (pearlized) | Glass Indian |
| 62 | around the neck and arms | | |
| 31 | second border | | |
| 40 | third row and diamond | | |
| 4 | for ties | | |
| ‾205 | | | |
| ⊡(o) — 203 | second row | Pearlized orange | Tubular squaw |
| ◩ — 102 | second row | Clear green | Glass Indian |
| 146 | third row and diamond | | |
| 62 | around the neck and arm | | |
| 2 | ties | | |
| ‾312 | | | |
| ◢ — 40 | center diamond | Smoky opaque yellow | Glass Indian |

(For a beige vest make ☒ — yellow, ⊡ — amber, ◢ — purple, ◩ — green, ⊡(o) — smoky opaque white)

For the child's thunderbird design you will need:

| Number and use | | My color choice | Type |
|---|---|---|---|
| ☒ — 164 | top border | Yellow | Tubular squaw |
| 49 | around the neck and arms | | |
| 8 | second row running from thunderbird motif | | |
| ‾221 | | | |
| ⊡ — 41 | top border | Amber (Or any of the tubular bead colors from the second row and thunderbird) | Glass Indian |
| 49 | neck and armholes | | |
| 4 | ties | | |
| ‾94 | | | |
| ◢ — 440-460 | thunderbird | Pearlized white | Tubular squaw |
| ◩ — 367 | second row and thunderbird | Green | Tubular squaw |
| ⊡(o) — 186 | second row and thunderbird | Red | Tubular squaw |
| ◈ — 54 | second row and thunderbird | Blue | Tubular squaw |
| ◈ — 6 | | | |
| ‾60 | eye of the bird | | |
| ⊡(■) — 24 | thunderbird | Black | Tubular squaw |

To make the thunderbird design for adults, add enough beading to make another row, plus extra to allow for more fringes and the larger area to be beaded around the neck and armholes. And don't forget that you can use squaw beads or plastic imitation Indian beads instead of glass Indian beads. As a rule, the tubular squaw beads should be used at the top and bottom of each section of the beading design on each row (see Fig. N-10) — not only for the great contrasting effect, but also for the very practical reason that these beads have smaller holes, thereby fitting snugly onto the fringing and helping the beading maintain its original planned position in the design.

I am being very explicit about the number of beads required because this is the way you should work out your beading plans, allowing yourself to adjust the colors to what you desire. But don't use too many dark colors in beading, or you will lose the effect. Try to use beads of contrasting color next to each other so the design will really stand out. You might want to use different combinations of beading around the neck and armholes. Or you might want to keep the squaw beads and change only the color of the glass beads. In any case, you can make any other changes you want once you know exactly how many beads are needed for which area.

Once all the planning is done, start your beading by edge-bead stitching around the neck and armholes. There are two types of stitches you can use: either a diagonal or a form of the connected cross-edge stitch.

The heavier cross-stitch is a good idea for edge-stitching if you want to give your edges a heavier rolled look. This stitch strengthens the edges and protects against wear, and I like it for single thickness on rougher garments. For beaded edges, this stitch holds the beads in place correctly. If a diagonal bead stitch is not done really well, your beads can tend to slip around to the outside edge or even to the inside, rather than staying positioned on the edge. If done properly, edge beading should sit between the hole and a little beyond or exactly on the edge on the right side of the garment.

You will need two different-colored beads taken from the pattern on the fringing. These are usually one color from the top border row and the other the predominant color bead in the pattern. I have listed how many beads of each color

are needed for my pattern, but your number may vary according to the size commercial pattern used. To figure out how many you will need for yours, count the number of holes punched around the neck and armholes and divide by two. The result will be the number of each color you will need — alternated around the neck and armholes.

If you decide to bead with a connected cross-back edge-bead stitch (see Fig. N-11), bring your first stitch from the right side to the wrong side. Take the loose end on the right side and flip it over the edge to the wrong side — not sewn, just flipped over. Now glue this tab to the wrong side between the first and second holes so that the end is secured on the wrong side. Now take your long lacing and whip it from the wrong side over the edge into the next (second) hole. Thread your first bead onto the lacing, bring the lacing back over the edge to the right side, and stitch once again into the first hole, bringing the lacing back to the wrong side. Now bring the lacing over the edge to the right side and stitch it into the next empty hole (the third hole), bringing it through to the wrong side. Then thread another bead — your second color — onto the lacing, and backstitch the lacing over the edge into the previous (second) hole in the row. Keep repeating this sequence until the edge beading is

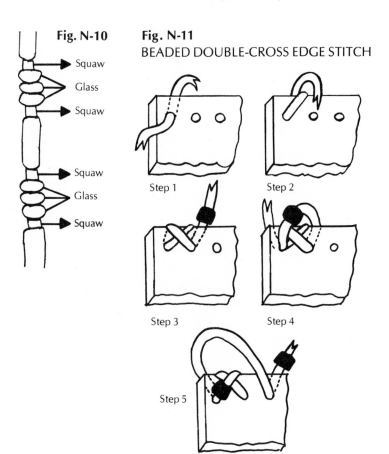

Fig. N-10

→ Squaw
→ Glass
→ Squaw

→ Squaw
→ Glass
→ Squaw

Fig. N-11
BEADED DOUBLE-CROSS EDGE STITCH

Step 1          Step 2

Step 3          Step 4

Step 5

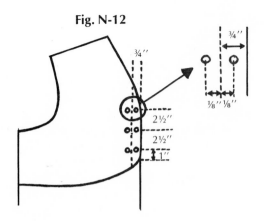

Fig. N-12

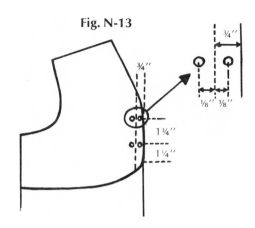

Fig. N-13

completed. Join the lacings by either stitching or gluing them tightly together, or backstitch into a few holes. This stitch is not good for ordinary stitching without beads, since it is a heavy stitch and not the easiest to do.

If all this seems too complicated, then substitute a diagonal edge stitch. If done tightly and properly, the diagonal should work out well and is a good idea for very soft leathers and smaller beads as it lies flatter. Simply stitch through the first hole from the wrong side to the right, thread on a bead, whip the lacing over the edge into the next hole, and through the wrong side again. Repeat using alternating colors until the beading is completed. Tuck the first tab at the beginning of the lacing under the first stitch and glue it down to secure it. To join, either backstitch into a few holes and beads or sew the lacings together. To finish it, tuck the end tab under a stitch and glue.

Once the beading is completed around the armholes and neckline, put your ties on the front of the vest. These are basically decoration here, but are functional in other places and are a good means of fastening leather clothing. They add a casual touch and are an easy way of making machine garments appear handmade. On the inside of the front unfringed section, mark and punch the holes for the ties. Punch three pairs of holes on either side for an adult's vest (see Fig. N-12) and two for a child's (see Fig. N-13). These pairs of holes should start on the adult's 1 inch up from the beginning of the fringing. There should be a 2½ inch distance between the first and second pairs of holes and a 2½ inch distance between the second and third pairs of holes. For the child's vest the measurements are 1¼ inches from the fringing and 1¾ inches between the first and second pairs of

holes. The holes on both vests should be ⅛ inch on either side of an imaginary line ¾ inch from the edge, so that one is ⅝ inch and the other is ⅞ inch from the edge. (All the above measurements are either center hole to center hole or center hole to edge). Take your lacings — six 42 inch lacings for the adult's vest and four 34 inch lacings for the child's — and trim both ends to a point. Bring the ends through both holes, starting from the wrong side (see Fig. L-11). Pull the lacing taut so that both ends are even. If you constructed the lacing from two connected pieces, then the join will be hidden on the inside between the two holes.

Now thread both lacings through the hole in the bead, and push the bead all the way up to the hole (see Fig. M-5). This will hold the two lacings together and prevent them from pulling out. (If you don't use a bead, simply tie a knot and it will do the same thing.) Use the same color beads here as you used for edge-bead stitching, and alternate. For the child's you will need four beads, all the same color, and all of the glass-bead type that you used for the top border; for the adult's, four of one color and two of the other. Now if you want to use the ties for fastening the garment, tie the adjacent lacings on either side of the front together.

## BEADED-FRINGE VEST

To bead your fringes with your design is a little trickier than putting it on the poncho, since you cannot draw the exact positions of the beads, but the final effect is really super.

You can't hang the vest from a cord, as it will twist and move, and if it starts moving about you won't be able to really judge when the beading is level and the design is correct. It should be braced solid so that you can easily handle it. When beading fringes I put my garment on a hanger and hook the hanger over one of the side hinges of a stepladder so that the area to be beaded is at a level where I can easily see what I am doing when sitting down. The garment can't wobble around and the ladder can be moved to different areas so that I am not confined to one spot. You can use a large hook on the wall or any other place that will hold the garment steady so that the fringes are free to be worked on.

In the end, it is pretty much up to you to judge the spacing of the beads on fringes. Just keep the beading to correspond to the look of your original design. Judge how far down on the fringes a particular line or design starts (a quarter of the way down? an eighth of the way down? halfway?), then transfer this estimate to the design on the fringes. You can use my spacing as a guide, but when measuring, remember that this is bead-per-square rather than bead-per-inch. The diamond has open spacing within the actual design, whereas the thunderbird has solid rows of beads and is therefore easier. Just try to keep the beads in each consecutive row aligned with your other rows, as shown in the pattern. Always start with the center row on the back of the vest and work out toward either side; for the front always work from the front to the side. This way, if there is adjusting to do that you did not count on, you will be able to make it on the side rather than right in the center back or front. You can push and pull to adjust the placement of the beads; when all the beading is finished, go back and check to make sure all is correct and adjust what isn't. However, all this pushing and pulling and threading will cause a certain amount of stretch on the fringes. So when you have finished beading and all has been adjusted to correspond to your original concept, trim the ends of the fringes to the desired shape again.

In Fig. N-14 you will find the pattern for the tubular squaw-beaded thunderbird. This pattern is for the child's vest, but can just as easily be used for an adult's. It can be enlarged for filling larger areas, or left as is. The enlarged design is the same as for the large beaded eagle of the jacket shown in Fig. P-24. Simply substitute squaw beads for the glass beads.

The diamond pattern shown in Fig. M-2 is planned for an adult's size but can also be made with tubular beads and placed on the child's vest. No matter which pattern you decide upon, however, remember to always start with the center fringe and work out to either side and to be sure to follow the pattern carefully. (Use the paper to cover each row on the pattern as you finish it to make things easier.)

The main parts of the design should be placed so that they fall above the area that will get a lot of pull when you are sitting. Be sure to keep as close to the original design as possible when beading, and then make the final adjustments after you have finished to be sure all is okay. The line extending from the main center back pattern to the front may have to be adjusted to fit the number of fringes you have, but try to keep to the original pattern as much as possible to avoid mistakes. Therefore, start from the front and the back so that the design meets under the arms where you can adjust it. The patterns shown will of course have the correct number of fringes so that all will work out perfectly. (For the adult's, sixty-seven on the back and thirty-four on each side of the front; for the child's, fifty-nine on the back and thirty-one on each side of the front.) But change it if necessary to fit your number of fringes.

For the adult's vest, first do either variation of the top border row shown in Fig. N-15 or N-19, then the second row (see Fig. N-16). Then do the center back pattern (see Fig. M-2) which extends around to the front, forming a third row of beading in the pattern (see Fig. N-17). The child's vest has only two rows of beading; either top border row (see Fig. N-18 or N-15), and a second row extending from a center back pattern (see Fig. N-14) around to the front of the vest (see Fig. N-19). On all vests always do the top border row, then the middle row (if there is one), and then the center back pattern, starting from the center fringe and working out to the sides under the arms.

The fronts require that you start from either side of the front and use the center front beading shown in the patterns. All the rows must match up on either end and across so that all the beading on each row is exactly even with the other side. (You have a mirror image of the pattern on either side of the front.) If it needs adjusting, try

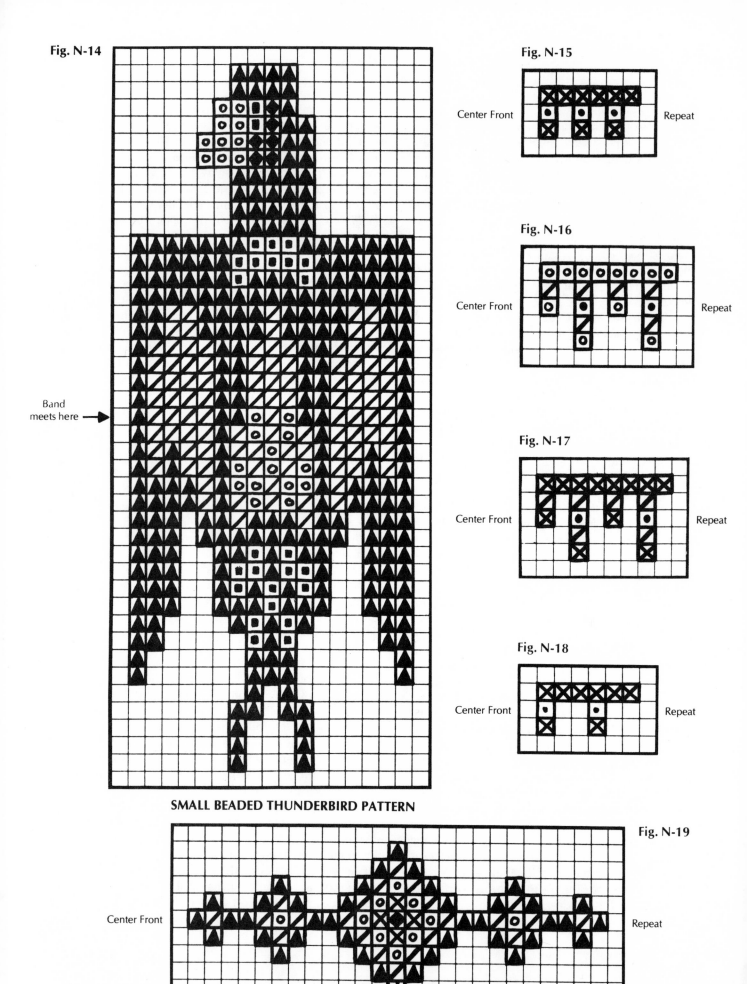

**Fig. N-14**

Band meets here →

**SMALL BEADED THUNDERBIRD PATTERN**

**Fig. N-15**

Center Front — Repeat

**Fig. N-16**

Center Front — Repeat

**Fig. N-17**

Center Front — Repeat

**Fig. N-18**

Center Front — Repeat

**Fig. N-19**

Center Front — Repeat

to make it as inconspicuous as possible. (For instance, to adjust for one or two beads, do it under the arms.) However, if there is a big discrepancy, add another single bead row to every place or every other place wherever the single-beaded rows fall.

An example of this adjustment is shown in the patterns for the top borders. You will notice that there is either an alternation of two colors, an alternation of a row of three beads with a row with a single bead, or an alternation of a row of three beads with two rows with single beads. So count the number of fringes and adjust accordingly. The back center main pattern always remains as it is in the original, however.

The top border of the beading follows the scalloped line formed by the top of the fringing. The main center pattern should fall so that it is high enough to avoid being sat on. And the second row — if there is one — falls evenly between the bottom of the top border row and the top of the center back main design. Therefore it is very difficult to give definite distances from the top to the beading on each fringe, as you have to adjust the distances to fit different needs. Your fringes may be shorter than the ones I cut because you are shorter, or longer because you are taller, or simply adjusted according to how you want to wear them. But on the center front, all rows of beading must match up on either edge *and* across the entire front so that they form mirror images. On the back, the top of the main beaded pattern must be at least two-thirds of the way up from the bottom.

If the vest is hung up properly and evenly balanced, you shouldn't have any difficulty beading everything evenly and accurately. Follow the patterns; and if you are using the ones in this book, check with the photos to be sure all is well. Try to be as accurate as possible while beading so that you won't have to make too many adjustments when you finish. (You will notice that in the adult's vest the lines are not as straight and geometric-looking as the child's.) Do whichever design you want, but I suggest that for the diamond you follow in opposition the scalloped curves of the top fringe line in the front, and in the back you follow the same curves as the top fringing line. But for the thunderbird, use

the straight lines to fit in with the feeling of the beading.

For my designs, the adult's long-fringed vest takes three rows of beading whether I use the thunderbird or the diamond pattern. The child's is very much smaller and does not require as much beading to fill in the space. And if you make a short adult's size — say to the waist — then you don't need the middle band of beading.

## LAST THOUGHTS ABOUT VESTS

Your decoration doesn't have to be fringing with a beaded design. You can eliminate the fringing and sew up all the seams to make a solid leather vest and go from there.

For instance, you could edge-stitch completely around the edges of the vest with a contrasting-colored lacing. Then punch holes for your patterns and weave in the design with the same contrasting lacing color used on the edges.

To edge-bead stitch and bead-weave in the design, you must adjust your pattern so that the leather of the garment acts as a replacement for some of the beads in the design, allowing you to anchor the lacing. This adjustment is especially important on designs like the thunderbird motif with its long solid rows of beading that would hang loose from the garment and could easily be ripped. You must decide the best way to adjust the pattern so that the lacings are tightly secured. The outside holes for weaving should be placed at the top and bottom, outside of the design.

Another possibility for decoration is to fill in the designs with plain studs, rhinestone studs, or rhinestones. Each stud would replace one bead in the design. You can even follow the same color scheme as in my design. For very delicate leathers and suedes used for dress wear, use rhinestones; but for heavier leathers use rhinestone studs. (If you can't find these locally, see the mail-order section in the back of this book.) Be sure to get studs of approximately the same size as the beads, since studs come in numerous different sizes. If you want to use different-size studs, adjust the entire placement to be sure the design fits properly into the area allotted it.

## TOOLS NEEDED

**MASKING TAPE**
**SCISSORS**
**BROWN PAPER**
**DRESSMAKER'S RULER**
**FELT-TIPPED PEN**
**MUSLIN**
**PINS**

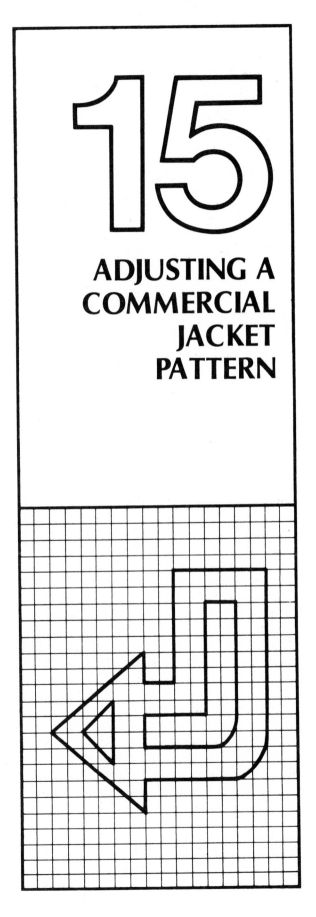

# 15

## ADJUSTING A COMMERCIAL JACKET PATTERN

In this section you will learn the basics of adjusting a commercial jacket pattern to fit the special needs of leather. Once you know how to sew in sleeves, put on collars, and make the garment fit your body perfectly, you can make shirts, coats, dresses, or anything that is fitted or requires sleeves, collars, and closures.

Check the dimensions given with the patterns to see which comes closest to your measurements. Commercial patterns make life simple if you know how to adjust them to fit the special needs of suede and leather. Don't even think you must restrict yourself to doing just what the pattern says.

We discussed pattern adjustments briefly in the last section and by now you should have some idea of how to handle measurements on leather. Here you simply add to what you already know about pattern making and adjusting. So buy your commercial patterns and fix them to your needs.

When you buy the pattern, check the back of the package to see what fabrics are recommended. Use this as your guide when purchasing your leather, and try to find a leather or suede with somewhat the same qualities (or feel) as the recommended fabric. Try to buy skins that are suited to your pattern pieces. Often, you will find that the texture or type of leather you want comes in skin sizes that aren't right for your pattern pieces. If the skins are small, you may have to adjust the pattern to fit into them. To do this, you must divide the pattern pieces into smaller sections, then make new seam lines and allowances so you can join these sections together.

Before making any changes on the pattern, draw a rough sketch of the garment. (If you are extremely meticulous, trace it from the pattern package.) Play around with the possible changes. Make a seam across the body (especially if you have one continuous pattern piece from neck to hem), the sleeve, or — for a complete suit — the pants leg.

Once you decide on the pattern changes, you must adjust your pattern accordingly. Draw the new lines on the pattern pieces.

Remember that with a curved hem, any new seams should follow the curve of the hem. Try to avoid making intersecting seams, as they cause bulk and you want everything to lie as flat as possible. For heavy leathers, try to avoid darts, as they can also cause bulk.

Cut the pattern apart along these new lines.

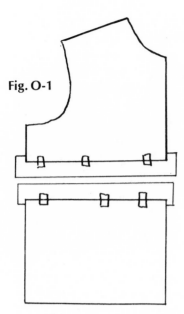

Fig. O-1

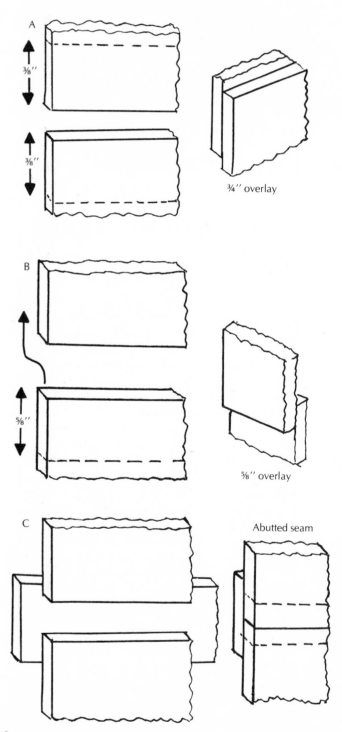

Fig. O-2
DIFFERENT SEAM ADJUSTMENTS

A

3/8''

3/8''

3/4'' overlay

B

5/8''

5/8'' overlay

C

Abutted seam

Now you must add seam allowances so you can join the pieces together. To do this, tape strips of paper about 2 to 3 inches wide (depending on whether you are adding length) along the cut edges. Draw in the seam allowances for the type of seam you are planning (see Fig. 0-1).

Don't forget that leather does not fray, so you can leave raw edges. This means you can use overlapped or abutted seams. In fact, if you are hand sewing, all seams *must* be overlapped or abutted. But even if you are using a machine, you can use this type of seam, even combining overlapped and regular seams in the same project. For example, if you have to add length to or divide the pattern pieces of a jacket or pants, why make just a straight seam? With overlapping seams, you can make the seam line a design element by making it a scalloped edge, band and triangle such as those on my appliquéd dungarees, or even a more complicated motif.

There are three different types of seams you can use (see Fig. O-2) — two versions of the overlapped seam, and the abutted seam. Choose the one you feel is best-suited to your purpose. All can be used for hand or machine sewing.

To make overlapped seams trim all seam allowances to 3/8 inch, overlap, glue, and sew. When this seam is overlapped, seam line will fall on top of seam line, and the center of the overlap will therefore be in the same place as the original seamline. This seam should be overlapped toward the back, and the complete overlap will measure 6/8 or 3/4 inch (see A. Fig. O-2). All hand stitching should ideally be done on the overlapped side of the raw edge, so that the center of the stitching falls directly on what would be the normal seam line. Of course you can stitch across the edge if you wish.

Another way to make an overlapped seam and the one I use most frequently, is to eliminate one seam allowance completely — generally the front seam, since you usually overlap toward the back. Place the trimmed seam edge over the untrimmed edge, keeping the trimmed edge along the original seam line, glue and stitch. In this version of the lapped seam, the raw edge falls exactly on the original seam line, and the complete overlap should measure ⅝ inch (see B, Fig. 0-2). In hand stitching, the lacing should extend across the raw edge that corresponds exactly to the original seam line, and should be where the center of the stitching falls. However, if it is more convenient you can stitch only to the overlapped side of the edge.

For the abutted (or slot) seams, eliminate seam allowances completely from both seams to be joined and cut a strip of leather ¾ to 1 inch wide. Glue each seam edge halfway over the strip so that they meet at the center, and sew (see C, Fig. 0-2). The strips used to back the seam can be short lengths of leather which you simply glue or sew together to form the required length of stripping.

There are variations on these seams which I like to use for very lightweight leathers I want to strengthen. These seams are first constructed as regular concealed seams and then topstitched either by machine or hand. But they cannot be used for applique-design-edged overlaps. For these seams you must add a ⅝-inch allowance on both edges. (Instructions for working these seams are given in the section on machine sew-

ing leather.) Just remember that if you feel you might need to reinforce seams, add the full ⅝-inch seam allowance.

If you are going to use overlapping seams on all the seams in your project, adjust the allowances on your pattern *now* . In addition, you can also eliminate all seam allowances around such outer edges as facings, pockets, cuffs, armholes, neck edges, and hems.

If you are using a fragile type of leather, add a little extra for "give" at heavy-wearing points such as around the hips and across the upper back. And with *all* leather types always add an extra inch to the bottom of the pants legs and to sleeves. Leather tends to crease and after a few wearings, this crease will become permanent at the elbow and knee, pulling the bottom up about an inch.

Most leathers (except for the very soft) aren't good for easing (fitting an extra amount of fabric into a smaller area), so you must take the ease out of fitted sleeves — a technique I explain later in this section. Raglan, kimono, and dropped sleeves are no problem with leather; but if you choose the right leather for your pattern you shouldn't have too much trouble in this respect anyway.

For pattern pieces such as a sleeve that needs reversed duplication (because you have two arms, each a mirror image of the other), it might be a good idea to make another pattern piece, this time reversing the original on brown paper. This way you will avoid making mistakes, and will be able to lay all your pattern pieces out on the leather at the same time so you can see exactly where each fits best. I like to make reversed duplicate patterns for either side of the front, front facing, sleeves (with redone cap and dart), and the collar. To make these reversed duplicate patterns for the front, front facings, and

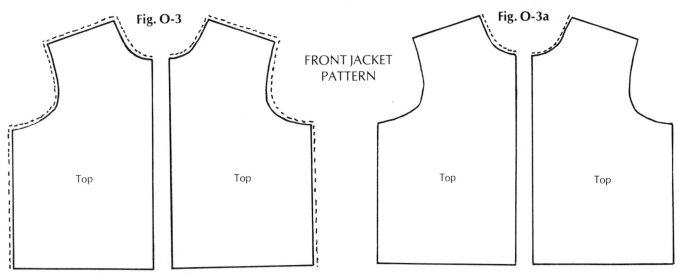

Fig. O-3

Fig. O-3a

FRONT JACKET PATTERN

Top      Top

Top      Top

Allowances for traditional seams

Allowances for overlapped seams

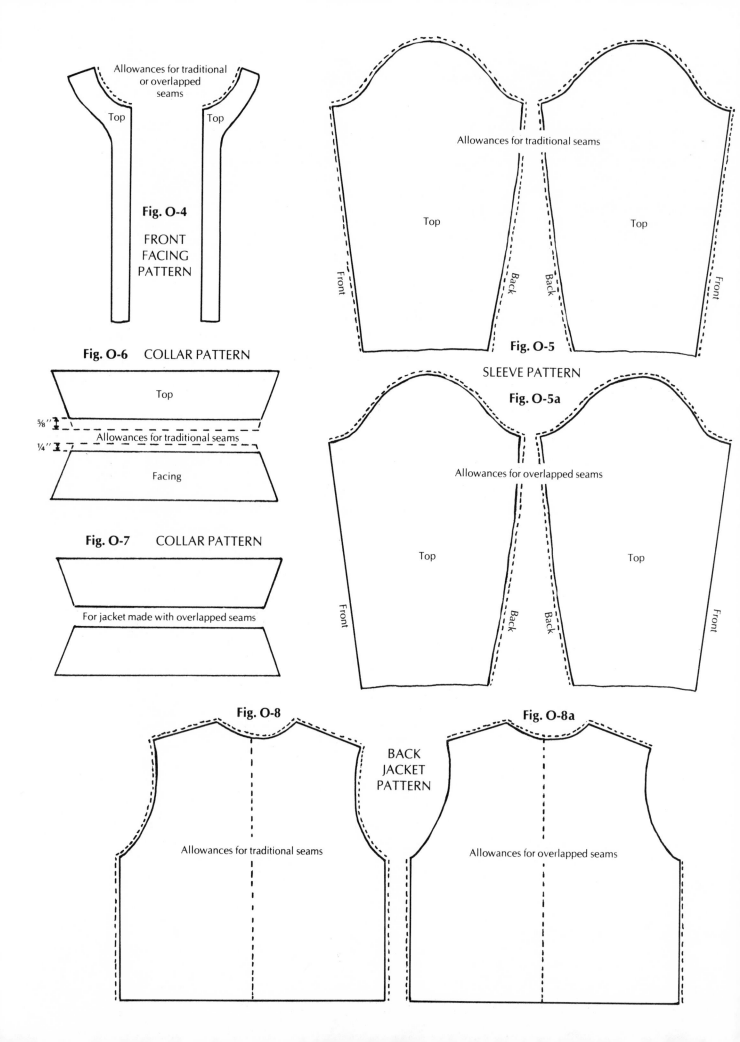

Allowances for traditional or overlapped seams

Top    Top

**Fig. O-4**

FRONT FACING PATTERN

Allowances for traditional seams

Top    Top

Front    Back    Back    Front

**Fig. O-5**

SLEEVE PATTERN

**Fig. O-5a**

**Fig. O-6**   COLLAR PATTERN

Top

⅝″

Allowances for traditional seams

¼″

Facing

**Fig. O-7**   COLLAR PATTERN

For jacket made with overlapped seams

Allowances for overlapped seams

Top    Top

Front    Back    Back    Front

**Fig. O-8**

BACK JACKET PATTERN

**Fig. O-8a**

Allowances for traditional seams

Allowances for overlapped seams

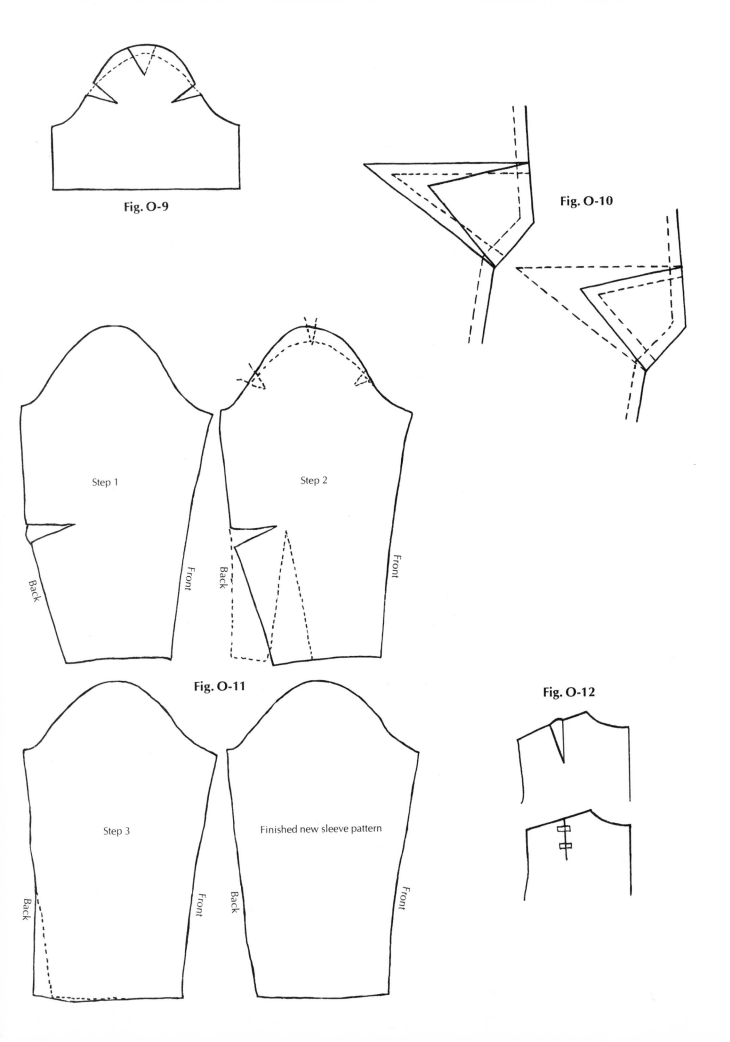

**Fig. O-9**

**Fig. O-10**

Step 1

Back

Front

Step 2

Back

Front

**Fig. O-11**

**Fig. O-12**

Step 3

Back

Front

Finished new sleeve pattern

Back

Front

sleeves, simply place the originals face down on brown paper, trace around them, cut them out — and mark the top of each so that you can be doubly sure (see Figs. O-3, O-3a, O-4, O-5, and O-5a).

To make a duplicate collar, use your original as the basic pattern. If you are edge-stitching around the outside and machine stitching the internal seaming, then eliminate ⅜ to ½ inch from the neckline edge (the shorter edge) on the piece that is going to act as the back facing for the collar. This means making up another brown paper pattern for the collar. Tape your original with its eliminated outer seam allowances to the brown paper and trace around it. Now mark the neckline on this brown paper pattern. Eliminate ¼ to ⅜ inch of the seam allowance on your original. Now either make another brown paper pattern and mark it as back facing, or mark the original back facing and use that (see Fig. O-6).

You should now have a pattern for the collar and a pattern for the collar facing. If you are sewing by hand, make an exact duplicate of the original with all its seam allowances removed (see Fig. O-7).

For the same reason you make reversed duplicates of certain pattern pieces, I also suggest that you make one whole pattern piece from the back so that there is no fold line (see Figs. O-8 and O-8a). Any pattern piece that needs to be placed on a fold should have a complete pattern made up for it, since you should never fold leather. Also, you should be able to lay the full pattern out to better judge your leather usage. There are two ways to do this. Either place the pattern piece on paper, trace around it, cut it out, and then tape the new half-pattern to the original pattern piece along the fold line. Or if you prefer, you can use the same method here as you used for the vest and make an entirely new single piece. To do this, lay the pattern on paper. Trace around it (including the fold line). Then flip the pattern original over, match it up against the fold line, and trace it again. Now you will have an entirely new solid pattern piece.

On commercial patterns, the sleeve cap — the top of the sleeve that is inserted in the shoulders of the jacket body — should most definitely be adjusted. Except for really soft types, such as chamois, leather doesn't have other fabrics' ability to ease and fit into the shoulder seam of the

jacket. The way to make it fit nicely is to shorten the sleeve cap (see Fig. O-9). Take the sleeve pattern, and cut in about 2½ to 3 inches at the center of the cap. Then overlap the two edges of the clipped piece about 1½ to 2 inches (or more) and tape them together. Now clip in about 1½ to 2 inches at the end of the ease as indicated on the pattern. This will cause the pattern to lie flat: The slits at the ends of the ease will open into a triangular shape and thus eliminate the excess material ease. Draw in a new cutting line on the pattern 1½ to 2 inches down from the original cutting line on the sleeve cap just to the end slits, and cut the pattern to this line. If you are fringing it is also advisable to shorten (or eliminate) the dart on the elbow, as the dart will interfere with the fringing. To make the elbow dart shorter, just bring the point in a little closer (¾ to 1 inch) to the edge. Keep the base of the dart the same and draw in new dart lines (see Fig. O-10). This method doesn't work if you try to shorten the dart too much, but in most cases you can shorten it a small amount with no problem. To eliminate the dart completely, you must cut out the dart, abut and tape the edges of the dart together, and snip in on the cuff right up to the point of the dart, thus letting out ease and giving you a new bottom line for the sleeve (see Step 1 of Fig. O-11). Now draw a new line from the extended sleeve bottom to above the dart (see Step 2 of Fig. O-11).

Once these adjustments are made on the original sleeve pattern, you are ready to make a new one with all the adjustments included. Tape your original over a piece of brown paper and trace around it, making a new pattern. If you eliminated the dart and made a new extended bottom, draw a new joining-seam line on the dart side from the extended sleeve bottom to above the dart, curving it slightly (see Step 3, Fig. O-11).

These adjustments might sound complicated, but if you do them step by step, they're really a snap. If a puffed-sleeve look is what you are after, use the original pattern without adjustments. However, I adjust the sleeve caps for normal set-in sleeves on most clothing, as I find most caps have too much fullness and don't follow the natural curve of the shoulders.

Another adjustment you may have to make on the pattern is on the jacket shoulder back —

you may need to eliminate the shoulder dart to eliminate bulk and avoid interference with the punching of holes for the fringing. Cut out the dart, abut the edges, and tape together. This will leave a slight fullness in the back, but ignore it. Straighten out the seam line (see Fig. O-12). This is not absolutely necessary; if you leave it, shorten it slightly and simply sew it up as you would the sleeve dart.

At this point — before you decide that these new adjusted pattern pieces are right for cutting out your leather — be sure they are correct. Unless you have used this pattern company before and know that their patterns fit you at least fairly accurately, you should make up a muslin of the jacket to be sure — a rough version of the bare outlines of the jacket on which you can make any necessary changes and transfer them to the final brown paper patterns. It is great to have a sleeve pattern that is a perfect fit, a jacket whose shoulders slope the way yours do, and a perfect fit across the back. And this is far easier to get if you make a muslin first.

A muslin takes only an hour or so to make, and can be used again and again. Cut out all the required pieces on muslin — the front, both sides, the back and the sleeves (the new pattern and its reverse). Now, following the instructions given with the pattern, join the pieces with a long basting stitch. Use either traditional concealed or overlapped and machine-topstitched seams; whatever variety you are going to use on the final jacket.

Don't worry — it doesn't have to be neat, just a perfect fit when finished. Once it is sewn, put it on inside out. Tear out seaming where it is too tight, take in where loose, and repin to fit. Now machine sew this again to where pinned. Put it on again and check to be sure it is right. (It would be a good idea to get a friend to help you pin and adjust it on you.) When you feel sure that it is right, take off the muslin. Run a felt-tipped pen along all the new seam lines and around the armholes to mark the placement of the new sewing lines.

Now rip open the seams. Pull it all apart and mark ½ to ⅝-inch seam allowances out from these new seam lines to indicate the cutting line. Use a dressmaker's ruler, and place the ½ to ⅝-inch line on the ruler over the felt-tipped-pen marking of the new seam lines so that the edge of the ruler is on the outside. Then draw lines indicating the new cutting line. Now recut the muslin to these new cutting lines.

These muslin pieces will serve as your pattern. You can either use them as is or make up brown paper duplicates. I like to use brown paper as I find the paper is faster, easier, and more accurate to work with. Muslin tends to fray at the edges, twist, and stretch unless it is cut on the grain, and this is hard to be sure of when you are working this way. But making a muslin is really a well-worthwhile investment as it can be adjusted to different types of jackets and insures an excellent fit.

## TOOLS NEEDED

HEAVY BROWN PAPER
GRAPH PAPER (SMALL SIZE)
CLEAR DRESSMAKER'S RULER
RUBBER OR LEATHER CEMENT AND
    BRUSHES
SNAPS AND SNAP SETTER
SHEARS AND SMALL SCISSORS
DRIVE PUNCH
HARDWOOD BOARD
MALLET
LACING
GLOVER'S NEEDLE FOR BOTH HAND AND
    MACHINE SEWING

### OPTIONAL

DRESSMAKER'S WHEEL AND TRACING
    PAPER
AWL
LARGE-EYED EMBROIDERY NEEDLE
MASKING TAPE

• MACHINE SEWING ONLY

EVEN-FEED OR WALKING FOOT
    (OPTIONAL BUT HIGHLY
    RECOMMENDED)
HEAVY MERCERIZED THREAD
TISSUE PAPER (OPTIONAL)

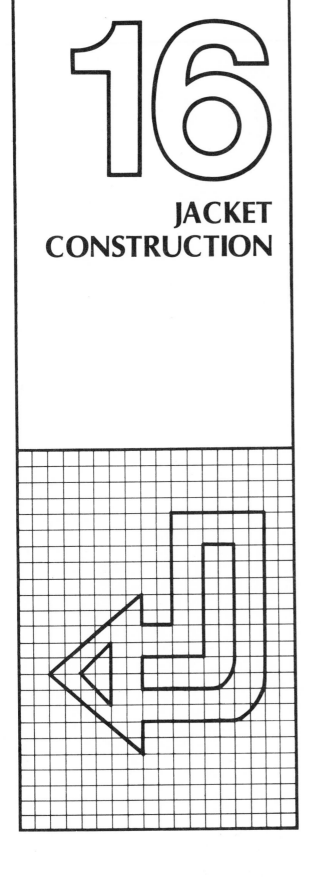

# 16
# JACKET CONSTRUCTION

The jackets shown in the color photos combine weaving, bead-weaving, fringing, and beading on fringing with a semifitted jacket with collar, front closures, and set-in sleeves. However, no jacket you make *has* to have fringing, let alone beading. The solid base of a jacket is complete in itself. (For instructions on a crazy-quilt jacket, see the end of this section.) If you do use fringes, they are not sewn in but rather weaved on. The fringes on my jacket are long, but a nice look is fringing about 10 inches long all the way across for an adult's jacket (and of course shorter for a child's).

My jacket has traditional concealed seams, but it could have overlapped hand-sewn seams, or even machine-sewn and then hand-stitched for decoration. All the outer edges are edge-stitched with a diagonal stitch to give it a nice, clean, tidy look. It has snap fasteners on the front, but you can use tie fasteners also. I have given the jacket a collar, but you could make a V-neck or rounded collarless jacket with short fringes and a top row of bead-weaving (see Fig. P-1). But no matter what decoration you add, the basic construction and fit must be accurate. So work from the inside out, perfecting the basic fit of the jacket first and then adding your decoration.

Before actual execution, you must plan ahead and mentally run through the complete construction. In fact, make a list of all the various steps and tick them off as you do them. I won't give you a pattern for this jacket, since it's best to buy a commercial pattern to your size. For adjusting, follow the steps in Section 15.

If you want fringe, your patterns should be for a box-type jacket with a collar — not a shirt-type collar, but one that fits straight onto the neckline of the main jacket body — front-fastening with a small overlap, set-in straight sleeves, and a jacket body that reaches to about

**Fig. P-1**

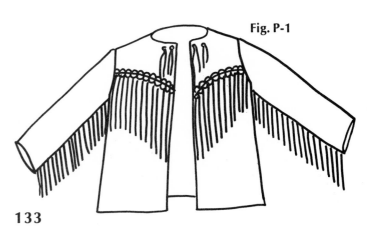

133

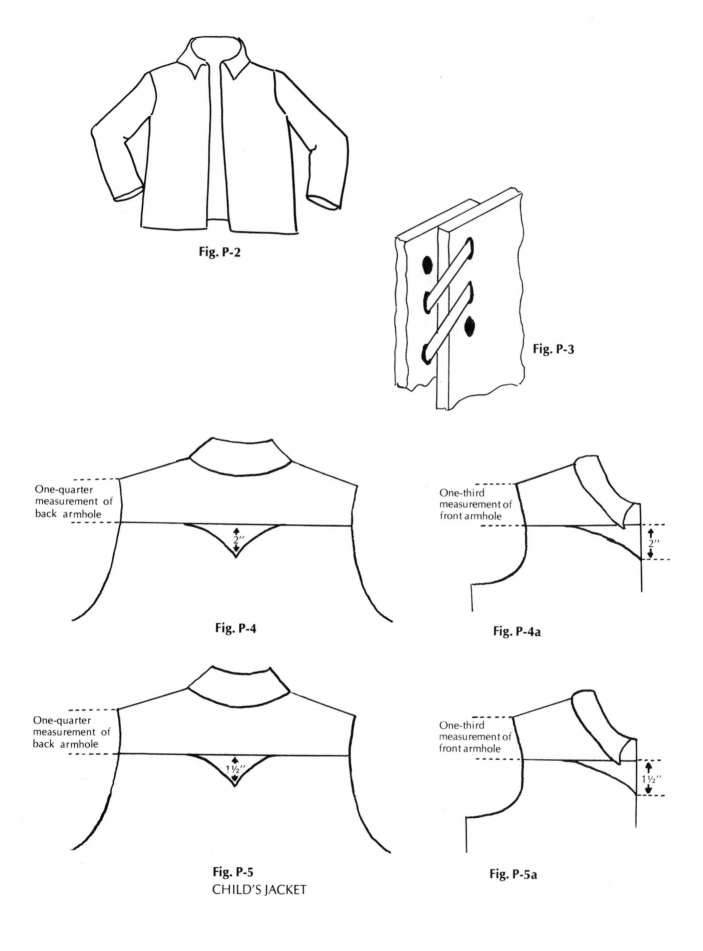

**Fig. P-2**

**Fig. P-3**

One-quarter
measurement of
back armhole

2″

**Fig. P-4**

One-third
measurement of
front armhole

2″

**Fig. P-4a**

One-quarter
measurement of
back armhole

1½″

**Fig. P-5**
CHILD'S JACKET

One-third
measurement of
front armhole

1½″

**Fig. P-5a**

4 inches below the waistline (see Fig. P-2). The fringing covers the jacket so that any shaping is covered and is not seen. For your first attempt at making a jacket, aim for a looser fit, which is easier to do.

If you don't want fringing, just a plain leather jacket, then choose a design you really like, whether fitted or not. But whether in cloth or leather, be sure it has fairly simple lines or you may run into a problem sewing unless you are already pretty good at making clothing from patterns. On your first jacket, let added touches such as edge-stitching lend a special effect.

If you are making a child's jacket, simply use a child's pattern size and adjust in the same manner as outlined for the adult's in Section 15 — only changing the measurements to fit, of course.

In order to prepare the edges to be top-stitched, I have eliminated (cut off) all the seam allowances around the outer edges of the jacket. This means around the three outer edges of the collar, down the center edges of the front of the jacket, down the straight edges of the front facing, and — if you choose — even around the hem of the jacket bottom. If you want to eliminate the collar and use a simple round or V-neck, then you will need to use the back facing that comes with the commercial pattern. And if you are hand sewing or topstitching with a machine, you will have to eliminate the seam allowance from both the neck edge of the jacket body and from the front and back facings. But if you are going to use a collar, *leave* the seam allowances around the neckline of the jacket back, jacket front, and front facings. And if you are machine stitching, do not remove the seam allowances of the neckline edge of the collar.

If you haven't bothered to make up new patterns for commercial pattern pieces with fold lines or which require reverse duplicates, you will need to do so now. To use a pattern piece with a fold line, first trace around the pattern to the fold line. Then flip the pattern piece over, line it up on the other side of the fold line, and trace around again. For sleeves and the opposite sides of the front, I first trace around them with the printed side up, then flip them over and trace again. For further information refer to Section 15.

You may have to make adjustments to other seams in your pattern depending on the type of internal seaming you plan to use. If you are machine stitching, or hand and machine stitching for decoration, leave the seam allowances as is and sew accordingly with your traditional concealed seams. But if you are sewing only by hand, you must adjust your seam allowances to make them suitable for overlapped seams. There are two different types of overlapped seams you can do (as you saw in Section 15), but I recommend you cut off the seam allowances of the front side seams, the armholes (both front and back), the neckline edge of both collar and collar back, the front shoulder seams, and the front sleeve seams. This allows you to cover the raw edges with a tight diagonal stitch that has the same look as the edge-stitching (see Fig. P-3). But whatever you decide, test it out on scraps to be sure.

Once your pattern is final, transfer all relevant markings from the original patterns and mark the placement of the fringing yoke so that you can easily transfer these markings to the leather when it is cut out. The fringing-yoke markings will, in addition, make it simple for you to make up the patterns for the pieces of leather from which your fringe will be cut.

The top scalloped shape of the fringing yoke is the exact opposite shape that it was on the vest top, so that the point in the center turns down rather than up. It is also much higher up than on the vest, starting not below the armhole but way up on the armhole in both the back and front. From the back it continues down the arms.

To figure out the fringing-line placement on the back (see Figs. P-4 and P-5), measure the circumference of the *back* armhole and divide by four. The answer will indicate how far down from the shoulder the fringing should go. (In other words, one-quarter of the back armhole measurement is the point down the back armhole at which the fringing begins.) Now draw a line and connect the points on both armholes, and measure down 2 inches (1½ inches for a child's jacket) from the exact center of this back line. Connect these two points on either side of the back to form a scallop-shaped yoke. For the front (see Figs. P-4a and P-5a), measure the front armhole — shoulder to underarm — and divide by three. The answer is the distance down the armhole where the fringing is to begin (in other words, one-third of the front armhole). Then draw a line from this point to meet the center front edge at right angles. Mark down 2 inches from this point on the center front

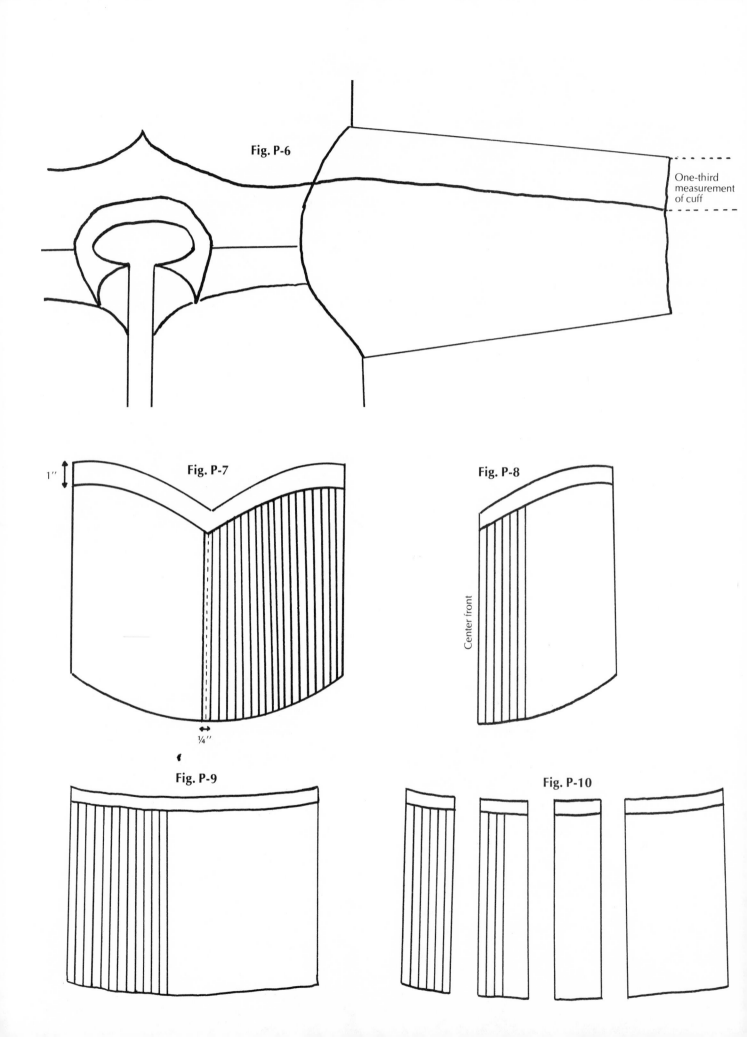

Fig. P-6

One-third measurement of cuff

Fig. P-7

1″

¼″

Fig. P-8

Center front

Fig. P-9

Fig. P-10

and join the points here and the point on the armhole edge with the appropriate scalloped shape. There is no fringing on the front of the sleeve, only on the back (see Fig. P-6). This row (or line, for now) runs from where it meets the other point on the back — or three-quarters up the sleeve cap (without seam allowance of course), measuring from the underarm up in back of the sleeve cap. It curves to follow the shape of the sleeve until it hits a point on the sleeve cuff equal to one-third the size of the cuff.

Once these are drawn in correctly on your pattern pieces, you can make up the patterns for the leather pieces — a total of five — from which your fringes will be cut: one for the back fringes, two for the front (one the reverse of the other), and two for the sleeves (one the reverse of the other). The back fringing pattern (see Fig. P-7) will be the width and shape of the top scalloped yoke line, indicating where fringing is to be added to the jacket. Its length will be the length from the scalloped line to the bottom of the jacket plus 5 inches (1 inch for the top inner border and 4 inches added extra length on the bottom). The bottom of the back fringing pattern is a straight line, and is shaped after it is on the jacket and everything else is finished. The *front fringing pattern* (see Fig. P-8) is measured in exactly the same way, only using the front jacket pattern as the model. Here you must make a reverse duplicate for the other side of the front to be sure you cut right. The width of the *sleeve fringing pattern* (see Fig. P-9) is the sleeve length as measured along the line marking the fringing, and the length is the same as that for the back pattern. This sleeve fringing can also be made by simply cutting pieces of the exact required length till there is enough for the needed amount of arm fringing for both sleeves (see Fig. P-10). This method may also enable you to use up spare leather. If necessary, you could cut the back and front in sections also. For the short-fringed jacket, just adjust the length to 10 to 12 inches — 5 to 6 inches for a child's jacket — or whatever you want, and figure out the amount needed.

The leather I recommend you use on this jacket is garment cowhide or any soft, yet firm, leather that is finished on both sides and is of the same approximate weight and texture. (I always like a leather that is finished on both sides so you don't have to bother to line it, and can use either side.)

For this jacket you must use large workable skins, since the pattern pieces call for fairly large flaw-free areas. Therefore you must work out the square footage required for each piece in order to get areas of flawless skin to accommodate the amount needed. Don't buy your leather until all adjustments and new pattern pieces are made, or your measurements will be off.

For an approximate idea of the amount of leather you'll need, the formula outlined in Section 1 works when converting from the yardage requirements on the back of the pattern envelope to the required square footage. If you are fringing, however, you will need more than what is indicated on the pattern, so add the square footage of the fringing to the amount required for the jacket. When buying your leather, tell the salesperson the approximate amount of footage you require. Check the skins for flaws and lay out your pattern on them to see if it fits. Don't feel you are being a pest — it's your right to get what you are paying for, so check to be sure it is exactly what you want. You can get away with some flaws in the solid underneath part of the jacket if you are going to cover it with fringing, but don't accept any really obvious or bad flaws.

(Once all the patterns for the fringing are made, you can lay out all your pattern pieces at once and thus discover the best arrangement for cutting. In fact, don't buy your leather until your patterns are made up so that you can lay out, or send, your pattern and thus buy an accurate amount.)

After your pattern is all adjusted and your pattern pieces ready and marked with all relevant information (including direction of the grain as indicated on the original pattern), cut out your leather. If you made duplicates and a solid pattern for the back, then lay out all the pattern pieces at the same time to find the best possible fit. Try to keep along the right grain of the leather so that you don't twist the seams.

Tape the pattern pieces down and trace around them. Don't forget to always cut your leather exactly on the *inside* of the line so that the line marked around them when tracing is left on the scraps and not on the pattern piece. Out of the leather be sure you cut one back, two sleeves (reverse duplicates), two sides for the front (reverse duplicates), two front facings (reverse duplicates), two collars (if you are machine

137

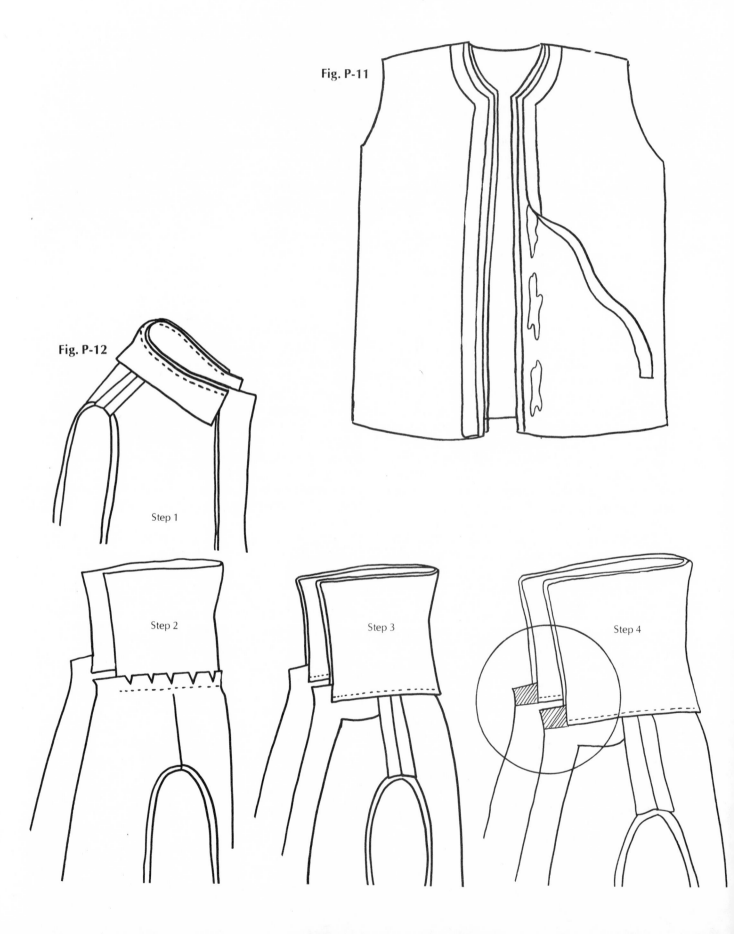

Fig. P-11

Fig. P-12

Step 1

Step 2

Step 3

Step 4

sewing, be sure you use the two different patterns for the collar and have no seam allowances on it if you are overlapping the seams and sewing by hand. The patterns illustrated in Section 15 are exactly what is needed here. If you are fringing, also cut one back-fringing piece, two front-fringing pieces (reverse duplicates) and two sleeve-fringing pieces (reverse duplicates).

Be sure to transfer all relevant markings and information from your patterns to the wrong side of the leather. Make sure the scalloped line is right by measuring on the armholes and center back and front and then lining up the scalloped top of the pattern pieces from the fringing for front and back. Indicate the seam allowances on the wrong side of the overlapping seams (the side that has the seam allowances removed) to make it easier to put these seams together. When constructing, just line up the raw edge with this mark, glue, measure, mark, punch holes, sew, and it's done. Mark the traditional seam allowances on both sides of the seam. Measure here as you have always done by taking your dressmaker's ruler and placing the ½ to ⅝-inch line in the ruler over the raw edge so that the ruler's edge is on the inside over the leather, and draw lines indicating the seam lines. If you are using darts, mark them and indicate the placement of the collar on the neckline.

I have used a front facing and a hem facing. The sleeve has a self-faced hem. Making facings is a snap. For the two front facings, use the facing pattern that comes with the commercial pattern. Eliminate the seam allowances down the front-edge seams, as I did with my jacket. For the bottom hem facing you'll need a 1½ to 2-inch-wide strip, or several strips which when combined go all the way around the bottom of the jacket. To cut these strips, take your dressmaker's ruler and draw a straight line the desired length for a strip. Then line up the appropriate red line in the ruler (1½ to 2 inches) over the line you just made. Draw another line parallel to it. You will now have two parallel lines 1½ to 2 inches apart. Again measure the length to be sure, and join the two lines together at the ends to form a strip. Cut this out. Try to always make the best possible use of your leather, so use scraps that can be joined to make the required length. Simply align these pieces wrong side to wrong side with the raw edges of the jacket, glue them

down, then measure, mark, and punch holes, then edge-stitch. The sleeves will usually have a self-facing hem allowance to give plenty of space for their self facing if that is the way you are doing them.

Once this is done, assemble the jacket pieces. First sew up the shoulder seams, either by hand or machine. Then take your front facings and glue them wrong side to wrong side on the inside of either side of the front, making sure the edges are properly aligned (see Fig. P-11). Now, if you are machine stitching, take the collar and sew it to the neckline within the marked area, with the right side of the collar against the wrong side of the jacket body (see Step 1, Fig. P-12) to form the top of the collar. Then glue the seam allowance for the collar on the jacket body up against the wrong side of the front to the collar. Clip out little V-shaped notches about every ½ inch to make it fit, and take out the excess material around the curve (see Step 2, Fig. P-12). Glue the back of the collar, wrong side to wrong side, to the already-attached front collar, aligning all the outside edges. If you are machine stitching, the neckline edge of your back collar should cover the front stitch line. Now simply topstitch this down to the jacket just below or on the stitching line of the front, ¼ inch in from the neckline edge of the back collar (see Step 3, Fig. P-12). If you have an excess of seam allowance on the neck edge from the collar to the center front edge (see Step 4, Fig. P-12), clip at the end of the collar down to the end of the seam allowance, and cut it off all the way to the front edge. This seam allowance to be eliminated will include neckline seam allowance from the jacket body and the front facing. This means part of the neckline seam allowance of the front facing will be glued or sewn to the inside of the collar, along with the neckline seam allowance of the jacket body.

If you are sewing by hand, clip V-shaped notches to take out the excess (see Step 1, Fig. P-13) as described above, and simply glue the neckline seam allowance to the wrong side of the collar. Both neckline edges of the front and back collars will fall at an equal point on opposite sides of the jacket body neckline. Stitch the collar to the jacket body by punching a double row of holes, one on either side of the raw edge of the collar (see Step 2, Fig. P-13), and

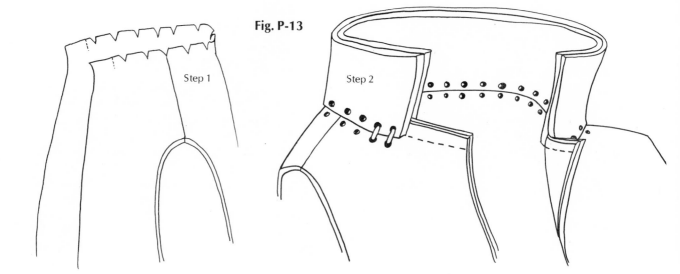

Fig. P-13

Step 1

Step 2

sew the collar to the jacket with a close diagonal stitch. Cut off any excess seam allowances extending from the collar to center front edge (see Step 4, Fig. P-12).

If you were making a plain jacket, at this point you would sew up the seam lines and then set in the sleeves. But for hand-stitching, fringed or otherwise decorated jackets, you should sew the sleeves first, and sew the seams later. Many people say this is a sign of a poorly made garment, but I feel that it is often the only way to deal with leather, which is not as flexible as a lot of fabrics and is difficult to fit into the armhole of the jacket body. So be sure that you adjusted the sleeve cap and took out the excess ease.

To prepare your sleeve, sew up the dart if there is one. For machine sewing a dart, simply sew as indicated in the pattern. If you are sewing by hand, cut out the dart completely, including the seam allowances. Abut the edges and glue a 1 inch wide strip to the wrong side of the dart so that the abutted edges meet at the center of the strip. Then punch your holes and sew. Now, if you are sewing by machine with traditional concealed seams, line up the sleeve cap to the shoulder seam — right side to right side — and sew, being sure to ease in any fullness left in the cap (see Fig. P-14). If you are sewing by hand with overlapped seams, overlap the shoulder of the jacket body over the sleeve cap to the appropriate overlap distance and glue, being sure to ease in the fullness (see Fig. P-15). Now mark, punch, and sew. I recommend a close diagonal stitch such as for the collar.

Before you punch the holes for your fringing, put this partially made jacket over your shoulders, and measure the correct sleeve length. In fact make it ¾ to 1 inch longer than needed, as leather tends to pull up at the elbows to form a permanent crease that raises the cuff and makes the sleeve shorter.

Once this is measured and marked, you are ready to punch your holes in preparation for the fringing. The markings for the scalloped yoke line should already have been transferred to the leather, ready for you to work on. You will need to punch three rows of holes altogether to do the bead-weaving fringe (see Fig. P-16), but only two for just beading. The holes in each row should be ¼ inch apart. The top row of the punching is the line already drawn indicating the top of the yoke. The second is ½ inch down from that, and the third row is ¼ inch down from the second. (These measurements are center hole to center hole.) Use your drive punch here as it is the easiest: Just lay the jacket out flat and punch. Your markings should be kept as light as possible to blend in with the color of the leather when finished. Mark and punch from the inside directly over the mark indicating the hole position.

Once these holes are punched completely, cut your fringes. First take your fringing pieces and draw a line 1 inch down from the top to mark the point to which your fringes will be cut (see Figs. P-7, P-8, P-9, and P-10). Then mark the center of the back, being sure the line is at right angles to the bottom of the jacket. Starting from the center back, measure ⅛ inch on either side

140

of this center line and cut your first fringe. Then work out toward the sides measuring, marking, and cutting three to four fringes at a time. Use sharp shears and cut with smooth, even strokes, keeping the cuts as straight as possible. On the front, measure and cut, starting from the center front and working toward the sides. Measure and cut the sleeve fringes by working from the center out toward the sides. If you are using many pieces for the sleeve fringing, then cut as you feel best.

To attach the fringing to the jacket, pull one of the fringed strips through each of the holes in the top row and pull it taut. Then starting from the center back and the center fronts, thread alternate-colored beads onto each lace and push them up against the jacket body. Thread each lace back into the second row of holes designated for each fringe. Pull tight so that the beads

alternate, one up and one down, to form a zig-zag row (see Fig. P-17). Otherwise the beads won't fit side by side as they are too wide.

Now take the fringes and pull each one through the third row of holes allowed for each fringe. This will bring it through to the right side to fall on the outside of the jacket. Make sure that all is pulled through properly and neatly, with the beading arranged as indicated. The fringing will now be all uneven because of all the pulling, but leave this until all else is finsihed. If you are using double fringing, simply glue the two top borders of the fringing together and lace two fringes (one for each piece) on the jacket. (The fringes on the beige eagle beaded jacket are double, since it is fairly soft leather. The purple has only one layer of fringing.)

In certain designs where the leather is very soft and pliable, where there are a great many

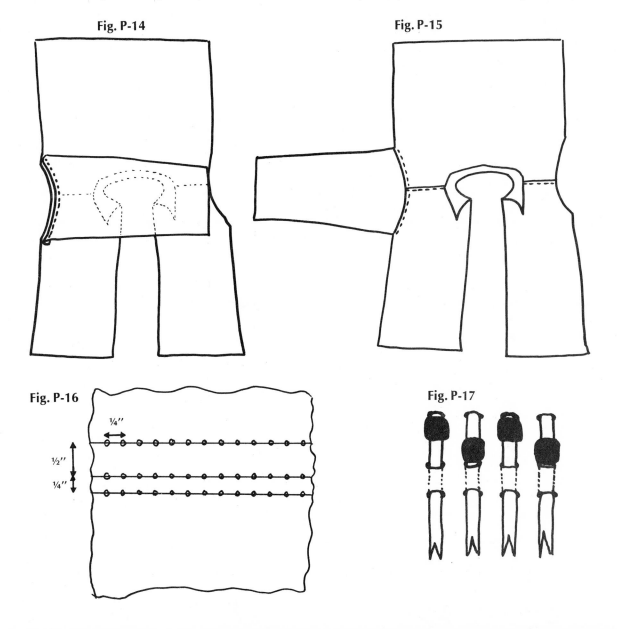

Fig. P-14    Fig. P-15

Fig. P-16    Fig. P-17

¼''

½''

¼''

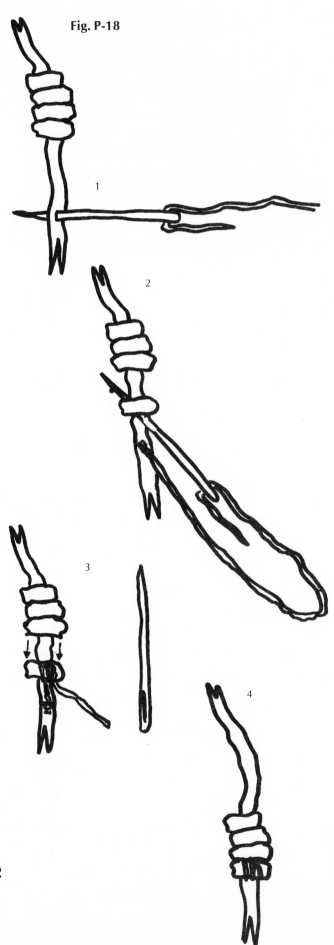

**Fig. P-18**

heavy beads on one fringe, or for rows where you don't have a squaw bead on the bottom for security, you must sew the last bead in every section on each row down to the leather fringe (see Fig. P-18). (The patterns for the vest do not require this, but some on the eagle jacket do.) To do this take a needle and thread the same color as your bead and knot the end of the thread. Now push the bead to be sewn down a little higher up on the fringe than it would be on the finished fringe — the equivalent of about one bead higher. Bring the needle and thread straight through on the fringe, and loop — sew the thread around the bead a couple of times. Then sew it back through the fringe where you first brought it through and knot the end. Now cut the thread and pull the bead back down to cover where you stitched through the fringe, and it will be perfect.

After the fringing is attached, baste (glue or tape) the seams together, put on the jacket, and adjust the seams if necessary. Now sew up the seams. This can be a rather awkward maneuver because of the fringes, but can be done nicely if you are careful. Just make sure you don't sew any fringes into the seam. To get them out of the way, I take the sleeve fringing and pull it to the cuff end. I put a rubber band around the back fringes, bunching it like a pony tail, and do the same for the front fringes.

If you are sewing by machine with traditional concealed seams, simply baste the seams and sew, taking in the appropriate seam allowances. Then glue the seams open and flat. If you are hand-stitching, the procedure is a little different. You can simply overlap the side seams of the jacket body and then measure, punch holes, and sew. But the tight area of the sleeve (or pants legs, if you are making trousers) won't allow you to do this. For the sleeves you can get around this problem by measuring and punching the holes on each side of the sleeve seam line separately. Then align the holes and glue and sew a small section of the sleeve seam at a time (see Fig. P-19). This method works fine if you punch accurately. Another way to do it is to take a very narrow strip of wood (2 inches wide) and place it exactly under the seam. Avoiding the beads on the other side of the sleeves, glue, measure, mark, punch, and sew in small sections at a time (see Fig. P-20). Or you can do the same

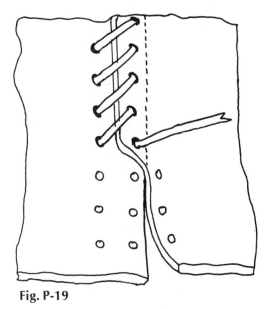

Fig. P-19

Fig. P-20

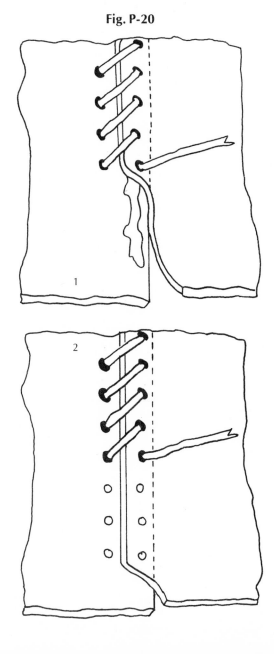

thing only using a rotary punch and gluing about 6 inches of the overlapped sleeve seam down at a time, sewing as you go along. If you use the rotary punch, be sure you don't accidentally bunch the leather up and make a hole through two or more layers.

Once all the seams are sewn, put on the jacket and measure the correct length of the sleeves and body. (Have a friend help you if possible.) If you find there are too many fringes on the sleeve, then undo until they are the right length. Turn up the self facing on the sleeves and glue it down. Trim the bottom hem of the jacket so that it is a nice, even length. Now glue the separate facing of the hem down around the jacket bottom, wrong side to wrong side, making sure that the edges are lined up evenly.

Punch the holes for your edge-stitching around the entire outer edges of the body. The holes here should be ¼ inch from the edge and ½ inch apart. The places to be punched are the collar, the remaining neckline, the front edges, the hem of the jacket, and the sleeve cuffs. Edgestitch diagonally; starting, joining, and finishing as described previously.

Once this is done, mark where you want your ties or fasteners to be on the front. Leather lacing ties look best if you use short fringing, hand sewing, or feel you want a hand-sewn look. Punch two holes ⅛ inch on either side of a line parallel to and ½ to ¾ inches from the front edge as you did with the vest. Now thread your lacing in and tie a knot to secure it. Trim the bottom of the ties so they don't hang below the fringing or the bottom of the jacket. Lacing ties can take the same spacing as snaps, or you can adjust it so that the bottom ties aren't quite as low as snaps would be. Three inches up from the bottom and 4-inch spacing between the ties might be better measurements.

## SNAPS

Snaps are one of the most useful of closures for leather, as well as one of the easiest and fastest to apply. They come in various sizes and colors and are thus useful for all types of leather. Snaps are readily available in most fabric and hobby stores. (However, if you can't find them, check the mail-order listings in this book.)

To apply snaps, use a specially designed pliers to assemble the metal parts (see Fig. P-21); or else use a standard snap setter with an anvil (see Fig. P-22). I prefer the latter tool, as it can be used for heavier leathers. You can get one to accept several different-sized snaps or one that accepts only one size, and since you hit the snap setter with a hammer, it doesn't hurt your hands.

A snap has four parts (see Fig. P-23): two, A and B, from the top, and two more, C and D, from the bottom. To set snaps, first mark where the snap is to go on both sides of the front closure. For the top snap, punch a hole right over your mark, to correspond to the size of B on the overlapping side of the front, and another the size of D on the underlap. If you are using a snap setter, place B on the largest part of the setter (if it is a multiple setter place on the section that fits) and put the leather wrong side down, so that the hole punched for B on the overlap falls on top of B. Place the cap A over B where it comes through the leather. Then place the concave cylinder of the snap setter over cap A and hit it with your rawhide mallet, attaching A to B to form the top part of the snap.

To set the bottom half of the snap, be sure you have punched a hole the size of D on the underlap of the closure (The underside of the jacket front). Place D on the smaller peg of the setter (for multiple-size setter, place where it fits). Place the leather wrong side down over D. Put C on top of D and atop the leather so the leather is sandwiched between C on top and D on the bottom. Take the smaller end of the cylinder setter and place it atop C. Firmly tap down with the rawhide mallet to set the bottom of the snap.

If you are using pliers, place the snap pieces on the appropriate side of the plier head after punching your hole, with the right side of the leather always up over the peg. Close the pliers hard to apply the snap. This plier setter is best for softer leathers, since I find it a little awkward to control.

For snaps, I suggest starting 1 to 1½ inches from the top and putting the bottom one 1½ inches from the bottom of the jacket. The spacing between the snaps should be about 3 inches, and each should be ⅝ to ¾ inch from the edge. (This is center to center and edge to center.) You will, therefore, need the appropriate number of snaps to fill the length of your jacket front.

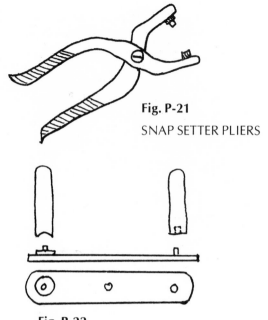

Fig. P-21

SNAP SETTER PLIERS

Fig. P-22

STANDARD SNAP SETTER

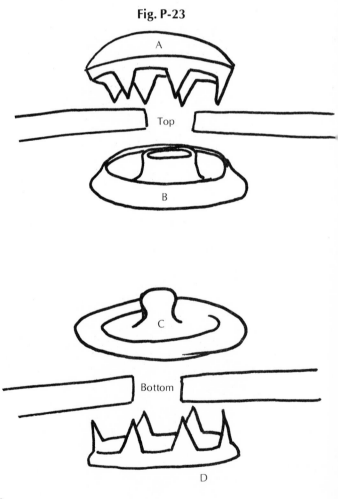

Fig. P-23

A

Top

B

C

Bottom

D

**Beading Color Key**

⊠ — Translucent light blue or aqua glass beads

⊡ — Translucent orange/red glass beads

◤▲ — Translucent dark purple glass beads

⧄ — Opaque smoky-white glass beads

◉ — Black tubular squaw beads

◆ — Translucent dark blue glass beads

**Fig. P-24**

LARGE THUNDERBIRD BEADING PATTERN

Now attach your snaps to the jacket. These snaps come in various sizes amd colors, so you could even match them to your beading. Use the placement mark to indicate the center of each snap and put them through both the jacket and its facing.

Now hang up the jacket for beading as you would any other fringed garment, only this time take a pole such as a broomstick and push it through both sleeves of the jacket so that it looks like a scarecrow. Now all is set up for you to be able to bead properly. If you are not beading, trim the fringes to the correct shape as shown in the photos.

When beading, follow your patterns carefully. Work from the center fringe out toward the sides on the back and then continue down the sleeves. For the front, work from the center fringe of either side out toward the sleeve and center front simultaneously. Follow carefully the diagrams given for the beading. The beading for the thunderbird (see Fig. P-24) looks long and narrow here, but don't worry — the fringing is pulled apart and thus

causes the design to spread open and look wider. Many people find glass beading a little heavy, and if you wish you can substitute squaw or even the plastic beads rather than glass.

The star beading for the sleeves (see Fig. P-25) is separate from the back and should be treated and beaded separately. The stars on the sleeves are placed along three lines. However, as you can see, these lines are not three complete rows. They would form only one solid row when pushed together, but the way they are spaced gives the impression of three lines when in fact there is only one zigzag line. So watch your spacing carefully. The designs for the front (see Fig. P-26) are duplicated on either side and form Maltese-cross-type designs surrounded by stars forming what appears to be a circular shape.

If you are making a child's jacket, take your beading design from the thunderbird vest pattern, and use the large diamond pattern from the band around the same vest for the front designs (see Figs. N-15 and N-20). Be sure to use squaw tubular beads here. In order to use the star circle around the bird,

**Fig. P-25**    STAR SLEEVE-BEADING PATTERN

4½-5″  To top of fringing

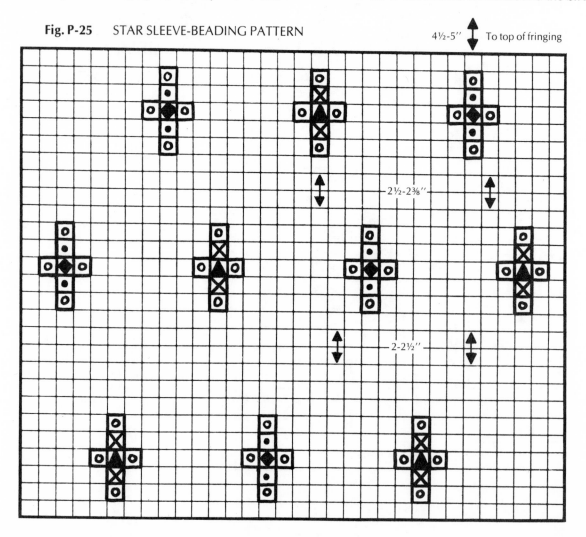

Center Front

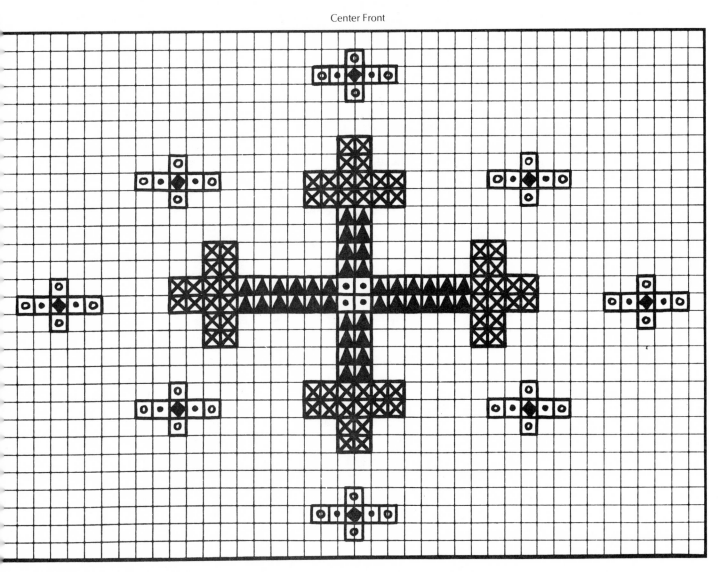

**Fig. P-26**
MALTESE CROSS BEADING PATTERN

you must adjust it. The number of the stars in the circle is determined strictly by the number of fringes used for the eagle, plus enough on either side to make a good circle. To make a pattern, sketch the bird design on graph paper and draw a circle or circular shape around it. That line will mark the approximate center bead of each star. Adjust the circular shape slightly to fit the fringes of the jacket; look at the diagram for the adult's to get an idea of how it is done.

If you are using a very soft leather or if your beading is mostly done with large glass beads, you may well have to secure the beads to the fringes. This means sewing the bottom bead at the end of a section of beading on each row to the fringe. On the center back fringe, for instance, you must sew down three beads — the bottom bead of the top star, the bottom bead of the eagle, and again the bottom bead on the bottom star on that fringe (see Fig. P-27). Be sure the beading is all even and matches your pattern.

Then take a needle and thread the same color as your bead, and sew as described previously.

Once all the beading is done and the beads are sewn down where necessary, you must trim the bottom of the fringes to match the shape shown in the photos. Measure down 4 inches below the bottom of the jacket body in the center back and trim the central five fringes to this length. Using them as your guide, cut the rest of the fringes into the shape shown in Fig. P-28, remembering that the center back is the longest point.

## CRAZY-QUILT JACKET

If you don't want to make a fringed or beaded-fringed jacket, you can decorate your jacket with contrasting lacing, studs, appliqués, bead-weaving, weaving, or whatever you want. You can make it multicolored and even employ a crazy-quilt pattern. A crazy-quilt jacket is a fantastically effective garment to make (but not for

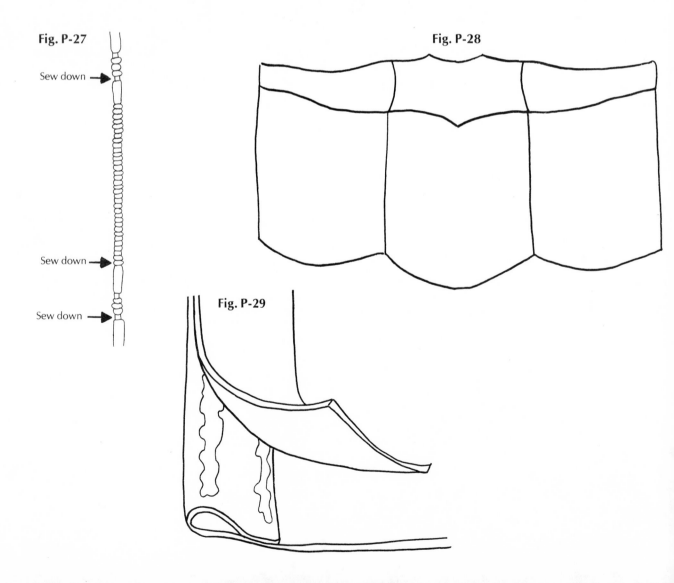

**Fig. P-27**

Sew down →

Sew down →

Sew down →

**Fig. P-28**

**Fig. P-29**

pants, as I feel patchwork, unless of very soft leather, makes them a little bulky).

To make a crazy-quilt jacket, overlap your scraps, trim, and glue with a ½ inch overlap as you did with the cushions. You will need to construct areas large enough to cover the pattern pieces. Lay your adjusted pattern piece on the wrong side of the leather scraps, trace around it, and cut. Put in your markings. Now sew the pieces of scraps together. If you are machine sewing, first sew a basting line around the outer edge of the cut-out pattern piece to stop possible stretching. Sew ¼ inch from the edge of each piece, using concealed seams for regular internal seams and darts, and machine topstitching around the facings and collar of outside edges. (Another method for machine sewing is to eliminate the outer seam allowances as you would normally do on the facings, but not on the gar-

ment pieces. Then when sewing fold over the seam allowances and glue down. Take your facing without seam allowances and glue it to wrong side to wrong side along the outer edges, then topstitch (see Fig. P-29). This cuts down on bulk and gives a much neater look than raw edges.)

If you are sewing by hand, first cut out the darts completely at the sewing edge. Abut the edges together and put a strip under them, punch holes, and sew with a fine lacing. Then sew down all the leather scraps using a fine lacing, overlap the seams, and edge-stitch around the outer edges. For either machine- or hand-sewn garments, put on snaps or insert a zipper as previously described for pillows and later for an appliqué dress. If you are going to insert a zipper, however, you must eliminate the overlap allowance on the front of the jacket.

**149**

## TOOLS NEEDED

GRAPH PAPER, BOTH THE SMALL AND
    THE 1-INCH SIZE
HEAVY BROWN PAPER
WATERPROOF FELT-TIPPED PEN
SHEARS
SMALL SCISSORS
MUSLIN
RUBBER OR LEATHER CEMENT AND
    BRUSHES
STUD SETTER (OPTIONAL BUT HIGHLY
    RECOMMENDED)

- IF YOU DON'T USE THE STUD SETTER

AWL OR VERY SMALL DRIVE PUNCH
HARDWOOD BOARD
MALLET
PLIERS

    OPTIONAL

PERMANENT CEMENT
MASKING TAPE
SNAP SETTER

- FOR MACHINE SEWING

EVEN-FEED OR WALKING FOOT
    (OPTIONAL BUT HIGHLY
    RECOMMENDED)
HEAVY MERCERIZED THREAD
TISSUE PAPER (OPTIONAL)
GLOVER'S NEEDLES FOR BOTH MACHINE
    AND HAND SEWING

- FOR HAND SEWING

AWL, SMALL DRIVE PUNCH, OR SEWING
    MACHINE FOR MAKING HOLES
BOTTONHOLE TWIST
LARGE-EYED GLOVER'S NEEDLE
HARDWOOD BOARD
MALLET

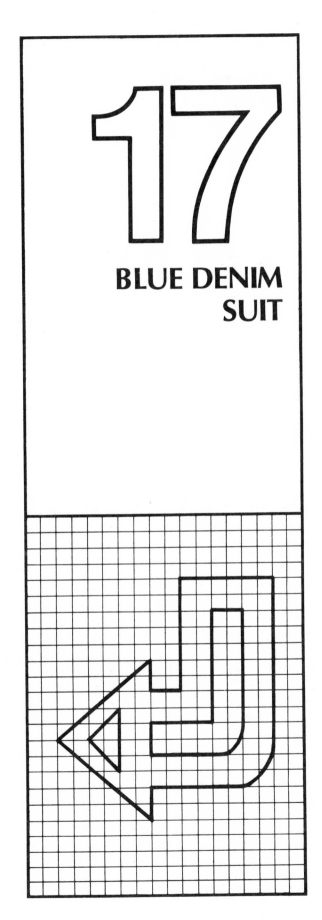

# 17
# BLUE DENIM SUIT

In this section you will learn the basics of copying from an existing garment and how to stud leather garments.

The blue denim suit shown in the color section has studded leather overlaid on the yoke, the front facing, the waistband, the sleeve cuffs, the V-shaped inset below the jacket pockets, the back pants pockets, and a triangular-shaped gusset on the bottom of the pants on the outer side of each leg.

To make up the pattern pieces for these overlays, you will have to use the denim suit as the basis for some of the patterns. To insure perfect fit, you will need to make a muslin pattern first and make a paper pattern from that. However, for the cuffs, waistband, and the V-shaped gusset, you can make your pattern directly on brown paper.

Purchase a traditional dungaree suit in the required size. Wash it to get rid of that new dungaree stiffness, and to allow it to do its normal amount of shrinkage. After this put it on to see if the fit is really good. If not, take it in where necessary, using traditional seams. Don't take out the seams that are already there, but sew right over them.

If you want to lighten the dungarees, do so now. But be careful when bleaching — if you don't dilute the bleach properly, it will eat right through the material, or weaken it so that it may rip after you have put time and effort into decorating the suit. You can bleach out dungarees in a washing machine, but I like to do it in the bathtub. I put 4½ cups of bleach into a bathtub one-third full of very hot water, stirring to be sure it is well mixed. I then lay my pants or jacket flat down on one side — front or back — in the tub. I keep pressing them down with a wooden hanger, using it like a plunger, to make sure they stay covered with water at all times to get an even, bleached-out tone. After about twenty-five to thirty minutes, depending on the tone wanted, I turn them on the other side and do the same there. They won't yet look as if they are bleached out, but take them out anyway. When washed and dried they will be perfect. For the other half of the suit, do the same thing for the same amount of time. (If the water is cold, let some of it out and add another ½ cup of bleach. Refill with hot water to one-third full.) Wash them out immediately after bleaching.

If there are snaps, or if you wish to replace the buttons with snaps after you have applied leather to the waistband, yoke, and cuffs, cut lit-

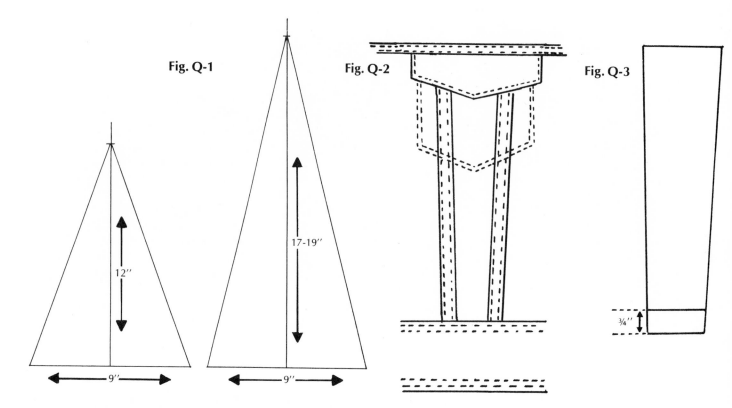

Fig. Q-1          Fig. Q-2          Fig. Q-3

12"

17-19"

9"          9"

¾"

tle squares around the buttons or snaps in these areas, thus removing a piece of the denim jacket along with the snap or button. Then glue a piece of denim or similar material over the hole. Later cover it with leather and add a snap. I recommend removing both snaps and buttons and replacing later, since it is difficult to use buttons and buttonholes with the excess bulk the leather creates.

Now you're ready to make up the patterns for your leather appliqués. For the waistband you will need a strip of leather the width — usually 2 inches — and length of the waistband, plus 2 to 2½ inches on either end if you removed the snaps or buttons, or ½ inch on one end and 2½ inches on the other if you left the buttons on. For the cuffs you will need two strips the width and length of the cuffs plus 2 to 2½ inches on either end, or ½ inch and 2½ inches per the waistband pattern.

To make the pattern for these cuffs and the bottom waistband, make strips or patterns the way you did for the facings on the jacket. Take your dressmaker's ruler and draw a straight line the length of the cuff, plus 1¼ inches if you left the buttons on and 4 to 5 inches if you removed the snaps or buttons. Then take the ruler and draw a straight line the length of the waistband plus 2 ⅔ inches if the buttons are left on and

5½ to 6 inches if removed. Now line up your dressmaker's ruler at the appropriate line in the ruler or edge of the ruler on the line drawn and draw another line parallel to it at the required width — usually 2 inches. Now take the ruler and join the ends across the width at the correct length. This is the pattern for the leather appliqué for the cuffs and waistband.

You must remove the back pants pockets if you want to stud a pattern on them and still leave them useable. The pockets themselves will then act as the pattern for the leather — just lay them on the leather and trace around them.

You will also need a pattern for the triangular gussets to be added to the bottom of the pants on the outer side of each leg (see Fig. Q-1). This should measure 9 inches along the base, and 12 inches from the base to the point if you are using flared-bottom pants and 17 to 19 inches if you are using straight-legged pants. (For a child's size, use a base of 7 inches and a height of 8 to 10 inches.) To make these pattern pieces, use brown paper. With your ruler, draw a straight line and mark to the desired length on the base — 9 inches. Then mark the center of this line and draw a second straight line at right angles to the base from this point. Mark on this second line the desired height of the V-shaped gusset (12 or 17 to 19 inches). Connect the

152

points on the base marking the width, with the mark on the center line marking the height. Now cut out your pattern.

Your other pattern pieces take their shape directly from the denim suit. Therefore, they must be made in muslin and then transferred to brown paper. To make a pattern for the V shape running from beneath the pocket lapel on the jacket to the jacket waistband (see Fig. Q-2), take a piece of muslin and lay it flat against the jacket over the V-shaped inset under the jacket pockets. Pin it to the jacket on either side of the seams that form this shape, being sure both muslin and jacket are smoothed out flat. With a felt-tipped pen, trace along the outer edge of the seam line (not the inner) of this shape. You will easily be able to feel where this is. Now draw a straight line where it meets at the bottom band and another at the top of the pocket. Unpin the muslin and remove. Add an extra ¾ inch to the bottom (see Fig. Q-3), using your dressmaker's ruler to measure. You can use this muslin pattern as your final pattern, but I prefer to transfer it to brown paper, which is easier and better to work with. To transfer, tape the muslin to paper and trace around it.

You must now make the yoke pattern. Again, use your denim jacket as the direct basis for the making of the pattern. Take a piece of muslin at least as long as the shoulder width of the jacket and at least as wide as the height of the back yoke. Take one straight edge of the muslin and pin it along the edge of the bottom seam line of the yoke back. Place one hand on the inside of the jacket, smooth the muslin over the yoke, and pin it down. Keep adjusting the pins, smoothing and pinning the muslin until you

are sure that it fits as well as it can over the denim suit. Now pin the muslin along the outer edges of the yoke back, being sure to pin only to the center of the welt shoulder seam. Then take a felt-tipped pen and trace around the outer edges of all seams — the armhole, yoke bottom, and neckline — but only to the center of the welt shoulder seam.

Remove the muslin from the jacket and add a ½ to ⅝ inch seam allowance to the shoulder and neckline seams, but not to the outer edges of the yoke, since these will be overlaid. Cut out the pattern, being sure to cut just to the inside of the marked lines (see Fig. Q-4).

Take another piece of muslin a little larger than one side of the front jacket yoke. Pin the muslin to the jacket along the bottom seam line of the front yoke, leaving a slight overlap. Now smooth and pin, trying to keep the grain of the muslin and denim going in the same direction. Be sure to pin to the shoulder seam, neckline, armhole, and center front. With a pen, mark around the outer edges of the neckline, armhole, and center front, but only to the center of the welt shoulder seam. Remove the pins and add ½ to ⅝ inch seam allowances to the neckline, the shoulder seam, and the center front edge (see Fig. Q-4a). Cut around the edges along the inside of the outer lines. Now iron this muslin flat, and tape or pin it to another piece of muslin, being sure both are perfectly flat, and trace around it. Cut out the new pattern piece on the *inside* of the marked line.

You will now have three pattern pieces for the yoke. You can use these as is or make up brown paper patterns, being sure the fronts are marked as to which side should be up so that

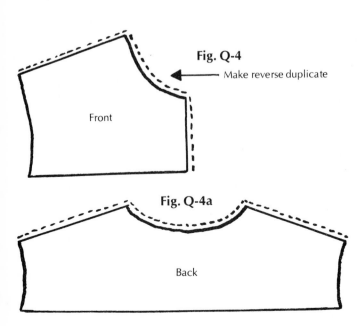

**Fig. Q-4**
Make reverse duplicate

Front

**Fig. Q-4a**

Back

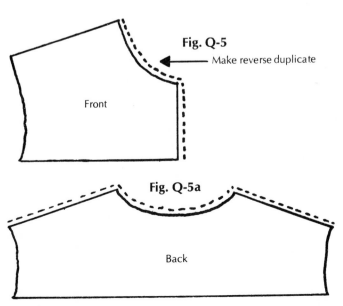

**Fig. Q-5**
Make reverse duplicate

Front

**Fig. Q-5a**

Back

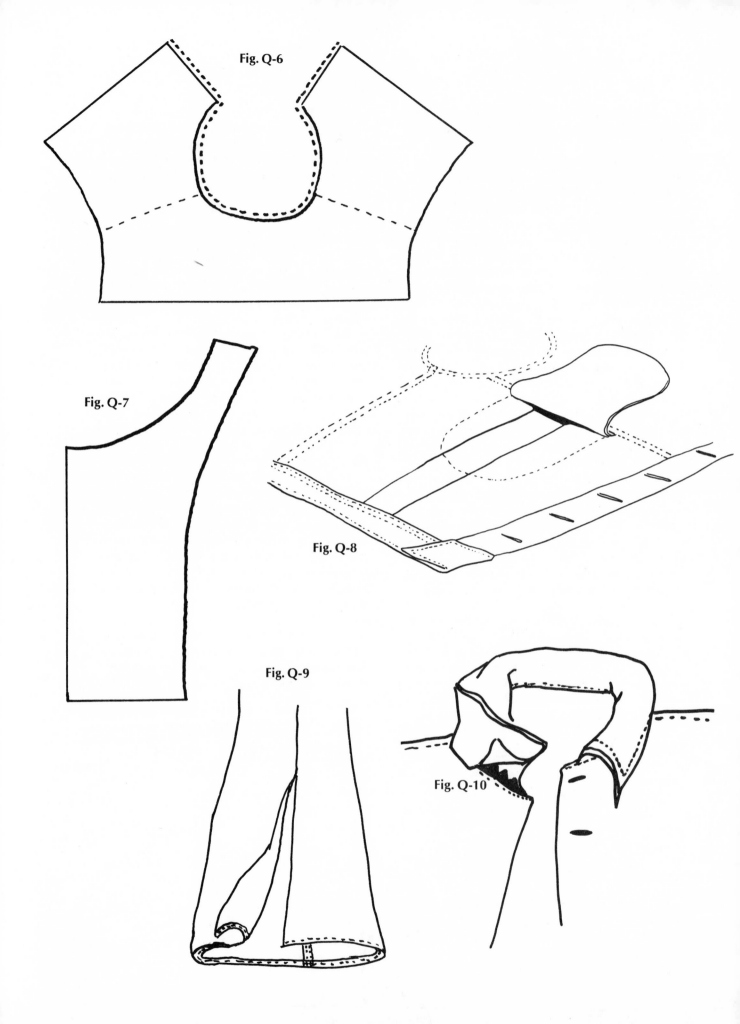

Fig. Q-6

Fig. Q-7

Fig. Q-8

Fig. Q-9

Fig. Q-10

you will have two reverse-duplicate pieces when the leather is cut. If you use the three pattern pieces to construct your yoke, you will have to make traditional concealed shoulder seams. If you want overlapped seams, eliminate the seam allowances on the back shoulder seam to overlap toward the front (see Fig. Q-5).

If you prefer, you can make one pattern for the entire yoke (see Fig. Q-6), which is what I did. Pin or sew the muslin pieces together at the shoulder seams with traditional seams, using the appropriate seam allowance as marked on the pattern. Now tape the entire muslin pattern against brown paper — being sure not to stretch the muslin by pulling too taut — trace around it and cut. Your pattern is done after you transfer all the relevant markings such as seam allowances.

You will also need to make a pattern for the front facings of the jacket (see Fig. Q-7). Pin and smooth muslin to the inside of the front, along the bottom of the yoke, the neckline, the edges of the existing front facing, and the center front edge. Mark around these edges with a felt-tipped pen. Remove the pins and cut it out, not adding any seam allowances. Make a copy of this pattern, or at least remember to reverse it once when cutting leather so that you end up with reverse duplicates.

Now prepare the jacket pockets for putting the leather in the inset beneath the pocket flap. You will find the pockets of most denim jackets are attached from the back. Undo the bottom and side seams so they lift up like flaps (see Fig. Q-8). This will leave the pockets open and useful. Of course, if you don't want to use the V inset under the flaps, or if you never use these pockets, don't bother to do this. You can sew through the pockets.

If there are press studs (snaps) on the suit rather than buttons, remove them by cutting out a small piece of denim around them wherever you are going to put leather. Glue a piece of denim over the hole. You will glue leather over this and put on new snaps later. (As previously mentioned, you can also remove buttons and replace later with snaps.)

To find the placement of the V-shaped gusset on the side of the leg, first measure the exact center of the leg side. Dungarees are cut rapidly in huge stacks of denim, and are often cut so

that the center of the pants — front and back — falls on the diagonal rather than on the straight grain of the fabric. When this happens, you may not notice that the cut is really off until you wash the dungarees. When the fabric softens, it will fall so that the straight grain hangs straight down, twisting the seams forward or backward. When trying on dungarees I advise you to check the bottoms to see how the seam falls there. Most people don't bother to look at that part of the fit. If the seam comes forward or backward quite a bit, try on another pair. However, no matter how carefully you check, you cannot be absolutely sure that it is right, so always measure the exact center of the side. Put on the pants and mark the center of the sides by placing a pin where the pants fall at the exact center side. Get a friend to help if you can. Once pinned, walk around the house, then check in a mirror to see if it stayed the same. If it moved forward or backward, adjust it. Now take another pin and pin it about 17 to 19 inches up the leg if they are straight-legged pants, about 11½ inches for slightly flared legs. Remove the jeans. Mark the pins' position with a pen, then remove them.

Now take a ruler and check the distance from the top mark to the bottom. Adjust to the above measurements, then draw a straight line connecting the points. If it is a straight leg, slash up the line only 14 to 16 inches (see Fig. Q-9), so that you can flare the bottom of the pants slightly.

You will have to wait to buy the leather until after you make up the patterns for your leather appliqués, so that you can lay out your pattern when buying to be sure of amounts. For an adult's suit, however, you will usually need one small skin or half of a small garment cowhide. Get any type leather that is soft and pliable. Again, I recommend leather with qualities similar to garment cowhide. You can use either the suede or the leather side out, but I prefer leather for this type of look with studs.

As usual, you should lay all your pattern pieces on the the leather at the same time to get the best possible use. Trace around each piece and then cut out. Transfer all relevant markings such as the center of the gusset onto the leather.

Now prepare the suit for adding the leather. If you are using neckline seam allowances, undo the back collar seam and about ¾ to 1 inch up on the side seams of the collar (see Fig. Q-10), so that you can glue the leather down easily and neatly.

Once the pattern pieces are cut out and the suit prepared, attach your leather, gluing all the pieces to the suit before sewing or studding. On the pockets put the studding pattern on the leather before sewing the leather to the fabric or studding them back to the pants — see the technique later in this chapter. (On the others you sew the appliqués down before studding. But most of the studding here is as utilitarian as it is decorative, since you can just stud leather to the denim without any sewing.)

Before attaching the yoke, first cut a square equal to the seam allowances at the top corner where the center front and neckline seam allowances meet, or simply cut off the corner with a diagonal cut (see Fig. Q-11). This will eliminate bulk and give you a nice clean finish where the center edge meets the neckline. Now glue the entire yoke down using a brush and cement, spreading it smoothly and evenly. First glue down the back, then around the neckline, and then the front, smoothing the leather as you did when pinning the muslin, and carefully aligning the edges of the yoke. If you are leaving the metal buttons on, glue no closer than ½ inch to them in order to get around them. Now cut in a slit on the front to just beyond the center of each button (see Fig. Q-12). Glue the leather down around the button, being sure to abut the edges of the slit tightly on the other side of the button — wrap the seam allowance around the front edge. Glue down around the neck seam allow-

ance, clipping little V-shaped notches out of the neckline seam allowance just around the collar edge, and ease to fit. Then clip the neckline seam allowance of the leather yoke at the collar edge, and wrap the rest of it over the jacket edge. After the yoke is on, glue the front facings down, wrong side to wrong side on the inside of the jacket, so that the edges are aligned and the leather falls exactly over the original front facing of the denim jacket.

Attach the V-shaped inset under the pocket flaps on the jacket front. Glue the leather down, aligning the outer edges of the seams forming the inset. Be sure that the pockets on the back are undone (see Fig. Q-8). When gluing, cut straight in over the button to just a little more than half way over it, as you did in the yoke, or remove the snaps or buttons completely.

Now put the leather pieces on the sleeve cuffs and around the waistband. Glue them down, aligning the edges and underlap allowances on the ends of the bands. If you left the buttons on, then wrap the ⅝-inch allowance around the buttonhole end, being sure you don't glue any allowance over the buttonholes, and treat the buttons as on the yoke. If you removed the buttons or snaps, simply wrap the allowances over the ends. If you are one of the many people who always roll up their cuffs and wear them permanently that way, then put the leather and studding on the inside of the cuffs (see Fig. Q-13) as you would if it were the outside.

Now apply the pants gussets. If the pants bottoms flare slightly into a bell shape, take the leather triangle and brush glue along the line

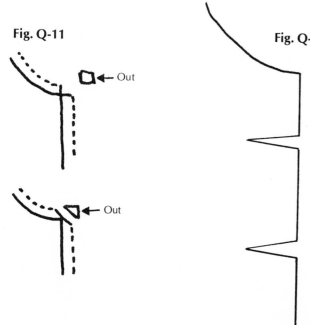

**Fig. Q-11**

Out

Out

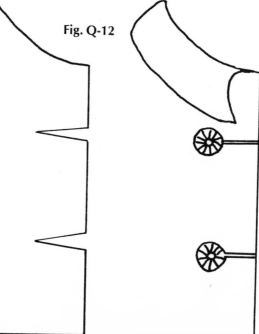

**Fig. Q-12**

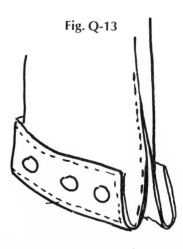

**Fig. Q-13**

marking its center. Now press this center line down along the line marking the center of the side of the pants. Brush glue on the rest of the leather and glue down flat. Trim the leather if any falls below the bottom of the pants. If you are using straight-legged pants, you should have already cut up along the marked line. Mark 2½ inches on either side of the center line on the wrong side of the leather gusset. Lay out the pants so that the bottom of the slit spreads open forming a V-shape measuring 5 inches at the base. Align the bottom edges of the slit with the marks you just made 2½ inches on either side of the center line and glue the leather to the denim at these points. Allow the V to open up by itself and glue the rest of the leather to the denim, thus forming a gusset inset. Cut any excess from the bottom, trimming the leather into a shape to match the shape of the inside-seam side. Check to be sure it is right and all ready to be sewn or studded. To add body to the inset gusset here, glue a 1-inch strip to the bottom of the leather.

For your back pockets, brush cement evenly and smoothly over the leather pieces and glue them flat down on the denim pockets. Do not attach them to the pants until after they have been studded.

If you are sewing, sew your leather-appliquéd yoke to the jacket by edge-stitching about ⅛ inch from the edge up the center front, around the neckline, down the other center front, along the bottom of one side of the front yoke, up around the armhole, across the bottom of the back yoke, around the other armhole, across the other side of the front yoke and up the other side of the center front. Then sew the collar back down to the jacket in the same way it was originally sewn. Do another line of stitching ¼ inch from the first line, around the armholes and the bottom of the yoke both back and front, but not around the neckline. If you are adding studs, do another row of stitching ¾ inch in from the first or either side of the center front. Then do a third row of stitching following the outer edge of the facing.

Do this stitching as explained in Section 3, by sewing with a zipper or zigzag foot such as on the even-feed or walking foot. Your first row should be ⅛ inch, either set the zipper foot ⅛ inch from the edge or use a zigzag foot and

check through its large hole to maintain the ⅛-inch distance. If you are using a zipper foot, align it at what looks like the right distance — ¼ inch — from the first row, and sew. If you are using a zigzag foot, align it with the first row itself, and you will get a perfectly spaced second row.

If you don't want to sew or find that your machine has difficulty sewing through the heavy denim seams, you can sew around only the center front edges and around the neckline. Then stud a single row of small studding around the bottom of the yoke and armholes to attach the leather appliqué to the jacket. (You could also stud around the front edges and neckline if you wish.)

In fact, if you have any question as to your ability to sew these appliqués by machine, I recommend punching holes in the leather with the machine (no thread), then sewing by hand with buttonhole twist or a heavy thread. If this doesn't work I punch holes with an awl and then sew by hand. Whenever I have any difficulty sewing through leather, I find that the thread is usually the main problem, as it breaks easily. However, if you sew at a slow, steady speed, and use an even-feed or walking foot and a glover's needle, generally you should have no problems.

For the V-shaped inset beneath the pocket flaps, double stitch along the seam lines and across the upper pocket slit. If you prefer, you can sew across the pocket slit and stud the sides to the jacket.

On the pants gusset, sew a double row of stitching on the outer edges around the entire triangle. Edge-stitch the cuffs and waistband with the usual double row of stitching around the outer edges. If you find that you can't stitch two rows here because the buttons are too close to the edge, do a single row or use a glover's needle and sew by hand. If you are adding snaps, do your second row of stitching ¾ inch in from the first on either end of the cuffs and band where you will be placing the snaps. However, if you glued properly and stitched through both layers of leather, one on either side of the denim, you don't have to worry at all about the leather coming loose.

Sew the leather on the pockets to the top of the fabric pocket using a double row of stitching,

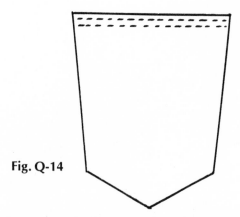

**Fig. Q-14**

but not on the bottom or the sides (see Fig. Q-14). You cannot sew or stud the pockets back onto the pants until you have studded the design on their center. Then sew or stud the pockets back down onto the pants in the exact place from which you removed them using the usual double row of stitching or single row of studding.

For sewing, use the same color thread as leather. The stitching used here is a double row, first sewing ⅛ inch from the edge and then ¼ inch in from that line — or the equivalent of the size of the stud being used. Follow the method described in Section 3, or hand-sew by using an awl to punch the holes and buttonhole twist to sew with.

## STUD SETTER AND STUDS

No fabric takes the application of studs like leather. It is one of the oldest decorations known and has been used for centuries.

Studs come in any number of sizes, shapes, and colors. You can get stars, diamonds, circles — even rhinestone studs consisting of a metal ring with prongs attached, around a rhinestone core. They maintain all the solid strength of studs while capturing the color and sparkle of rhinestones. Simple rhinestones can be applied to soft, soft, leather, but for heavy leather I prefer studs.

Studs are generally a decorative feature, but they can also be used to attach two pieces of leather — or leather and fabric — together. If you are using many layers of leather or fabric, then I recommend you get the studs with the extra-long prongs.

There is a relatively inexpensive machine for both studding and rhinestoning (see Fig. Q-15) which makes the process simple, and I advise anyone who plans on really getting into studding to get one.

I don't want to advertise any one product, but I don't know any other machine that does the job as easily. You may find these machines in hobby or sewing departments of department stores; if not, write to the address in the mail-order section in the back of this book.

To stud, first mark the exact center of the stud's placement on the wrong side of the leather, as you would if you were punching holes. If you are using the machine, place the stud, prongs up, in the anvil holder in the bottom of the machine. Place the leather wrong side up with the placement mark centered on the stud in the anvil, and push the plunger. This automatically pushes the prongs through the leather and bends them in, pressing the points toward the stud's center, thus attaching it to the leather.

When studding with this machine you will find a somewhat similar problem as with the rotary punch—you have to ease the leather into a confined space, especially if you are doing a long seam. So be careful and stud only where you want. If you are using many layers of leather or fabric, then get the studs with extra-long prongs. The same company that manufactures the machine also sells studs and can send you information about price and sizes. Interchangeable heads that accept different-size studs, rhinestones, and rhinestone studs can be obtained for this machine, so you can combine different sizes in a design. (I personally like size-15 and -30 studs, and just the small size 15 rhinestones.)

Another way to apply studs is to punch tiny holes in the leather the equivalent size and position of the prongs on the studs. (Use the two-pronged studs for this method, since they are easier.) Place your stud over the center of the mark for it and press down, thus leaving marks indicating where the prong holes must be punched. Then punch out small holes with an awl or a punch. Push the prongs through these holes with the studs on the right side of the leather. Take a pair of pliers and press these prongs into the center of the studs. Be sure to press the points *inward,* as they can hurt if they stick into you when you're wearing the garment.

To decorate this denim outfit you will need about 410 size-15 studs, and 55 to 60 size-30 studs. These are very cheap and are usually sold in packets of 100.

If you are studding the leather appliqués to

the denim suit you must still sew on the yoke up the center front edges, around the neckline, and then sew the collar back down. On all other places where you would normally do a double row of stitching, do a row of studding. Use small studs here — size 15 or ⅜ inch. The studs should be ¼ inch from the edge and ½ inch apart — this is center stud to center stud and edge to center stud. If you are studding purely for decoration, make sure all the leather appliqués are sewn to the suit. But do not attach the pocket yet — wait until the center studding design on it is done.

The pattern for the studding design on the pocket is in Fig. Q-16, and should be reversed for the opposite pocket. Follow the pattern, using the intersecting point of the two lines to mark the placement of the first stud. You should allow ½ inch between the small studs and place the large one in the corner formed by the intersecting lines. To find the placement of these two lines along which the studs will be placed, first draw a line straight across the pocket about 2¼ inches from the bottom point. Then draw another line intersecting the first at right angles, about 1¼

inches in from the outside edge of the pocket. Stud along these lines, making the point of intersection the placement of your first stud. Follow the given pattern so that only two studs extend beyond the intersecting point on both lines.

It is very important to do these lines properly. (If you followed the lines of the pockets, you would get diagonal rather than straight lines and thus destroy the exact linear geometric quality of the design.) Once this pocket studding is done, stud or sew the pocket back down on the pants in the exact place it was removed from. Sew with a double row of stitching; or stud ¼ inch from the edge, leaving ½ inch between the studs.

The studding pattern for the yoke back is shown in Fig. Q -17. To find the lines for this design, draw — on the back of the *inside* of the jacket — two rows straight across the yoke back. The first should be 1½ inches up from and parallel to the bottom of the yoke back, and the second 1½ inches up from the first row. On either end draw another line intersecting these first two at right angles so that the measurement at the bottom of the line where the armhole and yoke

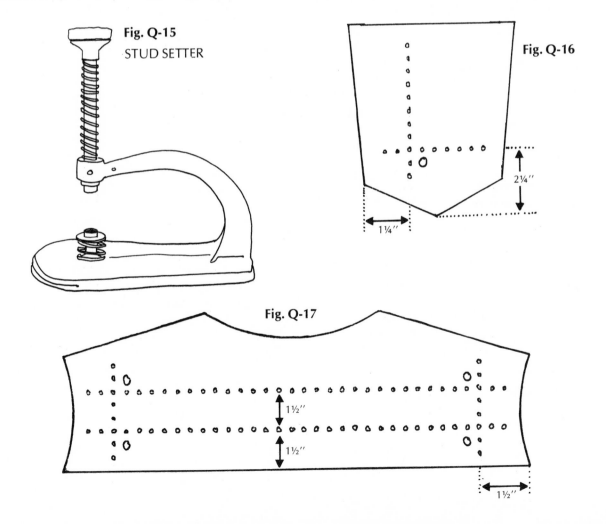

**Fig. Q-15**
STUD SETTER

**Fig. Q-16**

2¼''

1¼''

**Fig. Q-17**

1½''

1½''

1½''

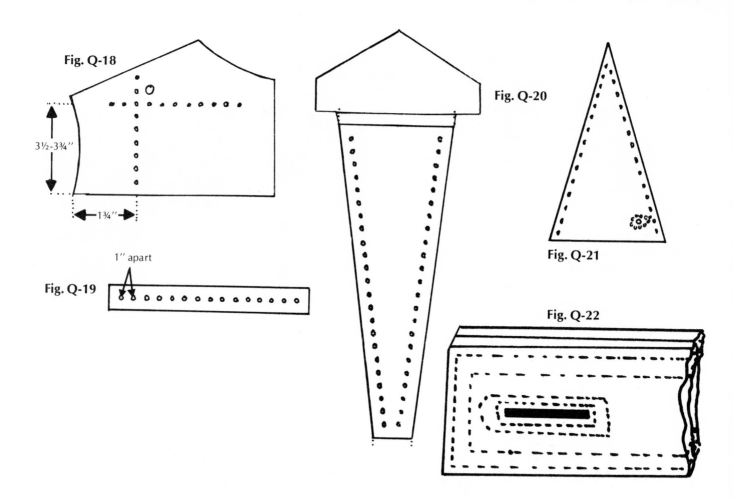

Fig. Q-18

3½-3¾"

1¾"

1" apart

Fig. Q-19

Fig. Q-20

Fig. Q-21

Fig. Q-22

bottom meet is 1½ inches, and gradually increase toward the top. This line should extend 1 inch above and below the top and bottom lines. Now stud along these lines following the pattern. Use the intersecting points as marks for the first studs, and measure from there. Space these small studs in rows ½ inch apart, and place large studs in the corners as shown in the studding pattern.

For the front yoke, the pattern is reversed on either side. On the inside of the jacket, draw a line at right angles to the bottom of the yoke straight up to the shoulder at 1¾ inches from the armhole, then intersect a line at right angles through the first line at 3½ to 3¾ inches from the bottom of the yoke line. Now stud in the manner shown in the diagram (see Fig. Q-18), making sure your first stud is at the intersecting point and leaving ½ inch between studs.

On the cuffs and waistband (again, on the inside) draw a line through the exact center of the width along the entire length. Stud along this line (see Fig. Q-19), using large (size-30) studs. There should be 1 inch from center stud to center stud, and ½ to ¾ inch from the button

and buttonhole, or from the place where the snaps will be placed on either end of the waistband and cuffs. The V inset under the jacket pocket and the pants gusset is decorated by studding along the edges (see Figs. Q-20 and Q-21). These studs should be ¼ inch from the edge of the inset and ½ inch apart — falling between the double row of saddle stitching.

As you can see, the graphic linear pattern is simple yet effective. But here, as everywhere, careful planning is essential.

Once all the studding is done, you should replace any snaps that were removed, placing them in the same positions, centered between two rows of stitching — one ⅛ inch from the edge and the other ¾ inch in from that. If you are keeping the buttons, then on the cuffs and waistband slit through where the buttonhole is and sew a row of stitching about ¼ inch from the edges of the buttonhole, or a double row — one at ⅛ inch from the edge and another ¼ inch from that (see Fig. Q-22). There is no point in making buttonholes on the yoke front unless you really use these buttons. If you do, slash and sew

160

around them as you did for the cuffs and waist-band.

In addition to these designs, you can transfer all the beading patterns given in this book to studding, since you work out studding patterns on graph paper in the same way you do with beading. To use the beading patterns already given, simply adjust the spacing to correspond to the size stud being used.

You can apply rhinestones to softer leather very effectively, but for heavy leather I prefer the rhinestone studs — metal rings with prongs attached, put around a rhinestone core. These are attached in the exact same way as studs. Therefore, you get all the sparkle of rhinestones with the more casual look and the strength of studs.

If you do use soft, soft leather then use rhinestones — but you will need the studding machine for applying them, as they are almost impossible to do by hand. In fact, if you really want to use rhinestones or studs, even for one big garment, I think the machine — really inexpensive — is a worthwhile investment.

But if you don't use a machine, don't forget to mark the placement of the prongs carefully and to always make small holes, even for really soft leathers. If you don't, you will tend to stretch the leather when pushing the prongs through.

To stud properly, you must mark the exact center of the stud. I like to make up my patterns on graph paper whose squares correspond approximately to the size of studs being used. I then take this pattern and tape it on the wrong side of the leather over the exact area of the garment to be studded, take a pen, and stick the point through the center of each square, being sure to mark right through to the leather. This will mark the center of each stud; otherwise you must use your dressmaker's ruler and measure each placement. Therefore, I advise making up your original graph pattern and then making up a copy for transferring to the leather.

## TOOLS NEEDED

GRAPH PAPER, BOTH THE SMALL AND
   THE 1-INCH SIZE
BROWN PAPER
CLEAR DRESSMAKER'S RULER
FELT-TIPPED PEN
SHEARS
SMALL SCISSORS
RUBBER OR LEATHER CEMENT AND
   BRUSHES

### OPTIONAL

PERMANENT CEMENT
SNAP SETTER

- MACHINE SEWING

EVEN-FEED OR WALKING FOOT
GLOVER'S NEEDLES FOR BOTH MACHINE
   AND HAND SEWING
HEAVY MERCERIZED THREAD
TISSUE PAPER (OPTIONAL)

- HAND SEWING

AWL, SMALL DRIVE PUNCH, OR SEWING
   MACHINE FOR MAKING HOLES
BUTTONHOLE TWIST THREAD
GLOVER'S NEEDLES
BEESWAX (OPTIONAL)

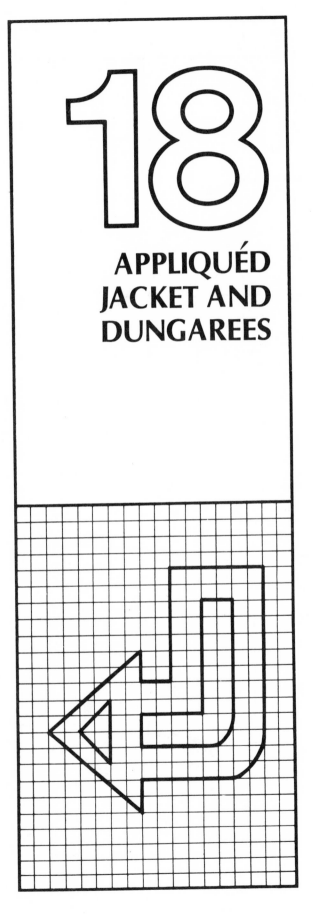

# 18
## APPLIQUÉD JACKET AND DUNGAREES

Appliqué — from the French word for "applied" — is basically the attachment of one material to another, usually by sewing. It's an art form used in both the so-called primitive reverse appliqué of the Cuna Indians of the Panamanian San Blas Islands, and the felt banners of such pop artists as Warhol and Lichtenstein. Appliqué can be used to decorate ready-made garments, or you can create an area such as a quilt to accommodate a special design.

Most of my appliqué is based on cartoon characters, but you could use anything you want as an appliqué design. Appliqués can be put on just about anything you want — leather cushions, denim pillows, quilts, or wall hangings. You can combine appliqué with studes, beads, embroidery, painting with magic markers, or anything else you can think of to achieve the effect you want. It looks great with denim jackets, pants, and skirts; or on leather coats, quilts, or pillows. Appliqué has practically limitless possibilities, and the really great thing about appliquéing with leather is that you can make great combinations of colors and textures to make beautiful and unusual designs.

I use appliqué on both leather and fabric bases — usually overlaid and/or overlapped pieces of leather built up to form a picture, and then attached to a solid base such as a denim suit or a leather coat or cushion. Since the leather edges can't fray, you can cut the appliqué into any shape and easily sew or glue it (with permanent cement) to the base.

To design an appliqué, first draw it out in full—either freehand or traced from an already complete picture. In fact, you can even trace an off-size motif you really like, and enlarge or reduce it to suit your purposes (see Fig. R-1). I always make my original appliqué sketches on graph paper to allow me the freedom of using each square as ½ inch, 1 inch, or 2 inches as I see fit. (The appliqués in this book are all intended to be raised to 1-inch graph paper, but you could just as well use a ½ or 2-inch scale if you like.)

Once your original design has been adjusted to the appropriate size, you then divide it into several pieces or layers which will later be reassembled to create your leather appliqué. When deciding upon the picture, therefore, be sure it is fairly simple and composed of definite, fairly large pieces that can be easily disassembled.

To reduce the design to layers or sections,

**163**

Fig. R-1

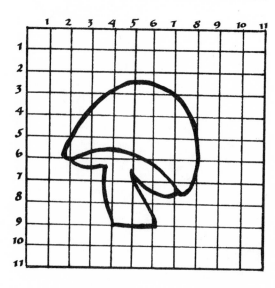

164

you must first decide which method is the most appropriate for the design — overlaid or overlapped. The overlaid technique — in which you work the pieces in layers — is used primarily for full-scale compositions or drawings made in layers such as cartoon characters. (Most comic-strip characters are simple outlines printed with overlays of color and are therefore easy to copy. In animated films, they are worked on clear acetate and each section is then overlaid on top of the section beneath. This way the artists can easily remove one layer such as the face, keeping the background the same, and then redraw the face with different expressions. Animated characters must be redrawn and photographed many times to make them appear to move and speak. If the artists had to redraw the background and the body each time, it would take forever.)

To make an overlay pattern, first trace around the outlines of the largest part, which underlays everything. Then trace around each piece which falls on top of it in the order in which you feel it is arranged, ending up with the fine details. For instance, if you are making an appliqué of a figure, first draw the body, then the clothing, then the face parts and fine details such as gloves or shoes. If any colors from the lower layers appear on the top, cut out the appropriate shape in the top and let it show through.

The owl appliqué is an example of overlay. Here I have taken the largest area — the circle — and laid all the other pieces such as the beak and eyes of top of it in order to build up the picture (see Fig. R-2).

You can't use this method if there are too many details, however, because there will be too many layers of leather. Instead, you must use the overlapping method: Make a pattern for each separate part of the design, add an underlap allowance in the appropriate places, and assemble. This way, the completed appliqué is no more than two layers thick in any one place.

To make an overlapped appliqué, first take tracing paper and trace around each of the more important parts of the design (such as the body, the tail, the head, the wing, the fins, or whatever), separating parts of the design into different sections. Each section will be a different color leather and each will either overlap or underlap. Decide which pieces of the design will underlap and which will overlap. Then, on your tracing paper, add a ¼ to ⅜-inch allowance on all the edges that must under-

lap another piece. You must add these underlap allowances or the final design will not be accurate. For instance, on the pattern for the fly motif, you will notice that extensions have been added to all the underlapping pieces so that they fit accurately under the body (see Fig. R-3). Be careful when pulling apart pictures for appliqués; always remember that for any two adjoining sections, one must have an underlap allowance added and the other must overlap that. The overlap method usually requires less leather than the overlaid method and enables you to use smaller scraps.

Once you have traced the pattern pieces and made the required adjustments for either overlaid or overlapped appliqués, number each pattern piece on the tracing paper and give the corresponding part on the original graph paper patterns the same number. Then place these on brown paper, trace around them, and remove. Transfer such relevant markings as the numbers and the underlap allowances.

Now cut out each pattern piece. If you did it right, the same side as the top on the original will be the numbered side. Now turn the piece over and mark the other side top. Each piece will now have one side with a number, and one side with a top label. When you cut out the leather, the right side must correspond to the original drawing. So place the right (numbered) side face down and the wrong (top) side up. This way the pattern piece will correspond to the way the leather is laid out when being marked ready for cutting — namely, wrong side up and right side down. Now trace around, number, and cut out the leather on the inside of the lines.

With the overlapped-appliqué method I carefully attach the pieces by gluing just along the underlap area and pressing the pieces together. Just underlap one under the other as indicated on the pattern pieces until you build up your design. This means using a brush and rubber cement, or permanent cement if you are not planning on sewing. But be very careful that no glue gets on the outer surface of the appliqué. You can construct each overlapped appliqué completely and, if you are sewing, sew down the smaller pieces such as the eyes and the mouth. Then attach them to your background. Or you can glue each piece directly onto the base, overlaying and underlapping where necessary, gluing and sewing as you proceed. This is the method I prefer for constructing smaller appliqués such as those on the denim pants.

**165**

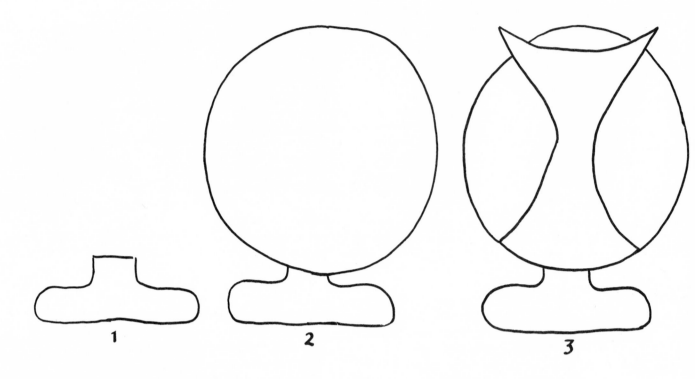

Fig. R-2

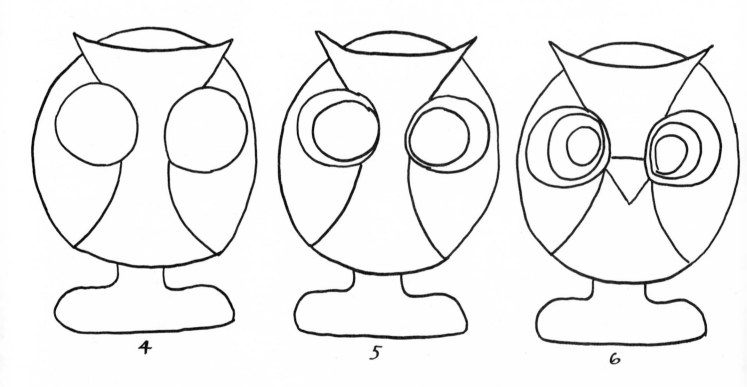

Fig. R-3

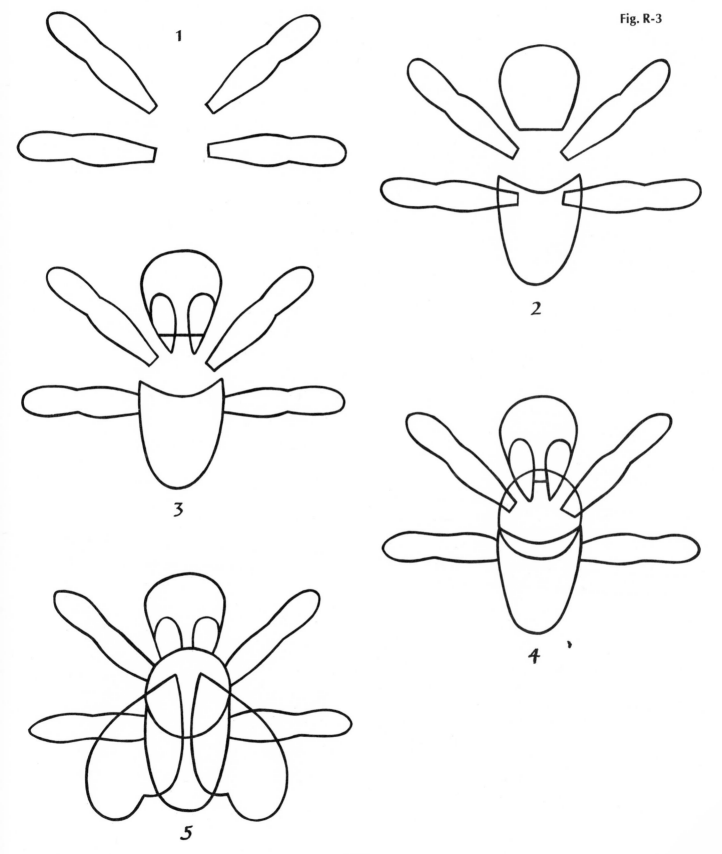

1

2

3

4

5

For the other method, which is primarily for full-scale compositions or larger overlaid pieces, start with the bottom layer and glue each section directly to the surface where it will be applied. Then, if you are sewing, sew each layer down as you go along. This means if you were constructing a clothed figure you would first lay down the body and sew it down, then lay on the clothing item and sew that, and continue until all the pieces are finally laid down as in the original design.

I like to sew around the edge of each and every piece of the design ⅛ inch from the edge. Then I sew in little details such as lines indicating the veins in the wings on the bug, the fins on a fish, or even to delineate fingers on a hand, using different-colored thread for each detail. You can, however, use permanent glue and draw in the details with magic markers. (Magic markers are great for painting or drawing on leather as they are permanent, waterproof, and extremely easy to use. But I wouldn't use them on the suede surfaces, that I often use for flat, textured areas like the hide on a cartoon buffalo.)

As you can see from the photos, I like to give eyes to my cartoon-type appliques. It adds a human quality to them, giving them interest and liveliness. They appear to be looking in different directions, at each other, at you, or even crosseyed. It gives each a unique character of its own.

## JACKETS

Denim jackets such as those shown in the color photos are great bases for appliqué work. For the seascape jacket, you will need to add a leather collar, cuffs, waistband, and pocket flaps. In addition you will need an appliqué fish, a snail, a starfish, a rock, and seaweed for the back of the jacket; an octopus and a seahorse for the front (see Figs. R-4, R-5, R-6, R-7, and R-8).

First prepare the jacket by washing, bleaching, and adjusting where necessary. If there are snaps, or if you want to replace the buttons with snaps after you have applied leather to the waistband and cuffs, follow the procedure described in Section 17. I recommend removing both snaps and buttons and replacing them later with snaps, as it is difficult to use buttons and buttonholes with the excess bulk the leather creates.

If you want you can remove the outer layer of denim fabric on the cuffs, waistband, and collar to eliminate any bulkiness that may be caused by adding a layer of leather to them. To do this remove the cuffs and waistband. Now measure ½ inch from the bottom edge on the outer layer of fabric, mark, and using this as your cutting line, cut off the outer layer (see Figs. R-9a and R-9b). For the collar, first remove the stitching from the inner collar where it is attached to the jacket body. Then, if it is two separate layers of material, simply undo the stitching around the outer edge and remove the top layer. (You can use this as your pattern for the leather collar.) If this is not possible since the collar is a self facing one, proceed as you would for the cuffs and waistband which are always self faced (see Fig. R-9c).

For the waistband you will need a strip of leather the width and length of the waistband, adding 2 to 2½ inches on either end if you removed the snaps; or adding ½ inch on one end and 2½ inches on the other if you left the buttons on. For the cuffs you will need two strips the width and length of the cuffs plus 2 to 2½ inches on either end or ½ inch and 2½ inches, per the waistband.

If you removed the top layer of denim from your collar, you can use that as the pattern. If it is a complete collar simply trace around it, but if it has ½ inch missing from the longest edge where you cut it off the original collar, trace around it and add ½ inch to that edge.

Or take the collar pattern from the denim jacket itself. Pin a piece of muslin to the base of the collar along the neckline edge. Smooth and pin the muslin flat over the collar, being sure it stays flat, then mark around the four sides of the collar. Be careful to mark exactly at the beginning of the collar's edge so that the pattern width will be right. Remove the muslin from the jacket, cut out the pattern, and make a paper pattern from it. Always cut on the inside marking lines each step of the way, or it won't work out right.

If you want to make flaps on the pockets you have two choices. The way to do it is to undo the bottom row of stitching on the welt seam on top of the pocket holding the flap to the jacket. Remove the pocket flap and then, if you want, remove the top layer of denim in the same way you would for the collar. Use the remaining bottom layer as your

**168**

**Fig. R-4**
FISH — PISES

**Fig. R-5**
SNAIL

**Fig. R-6**
STARFISH (PLAIN)

**Fig. R-7**
OCTOPUS

**Fig. R-8**
SEAHORSE

**Fig. R-4a**
FISH — PISCES

170

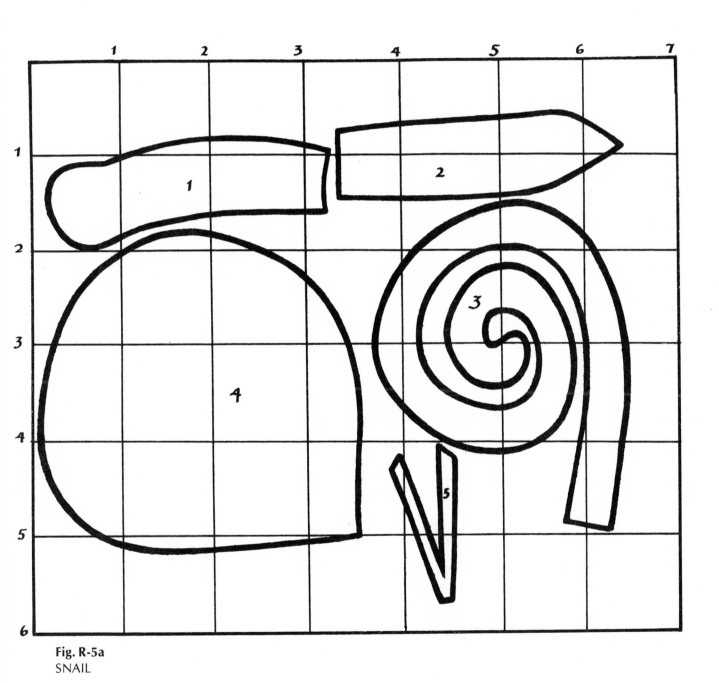

**Fig. R-5a**
SNAIL

171

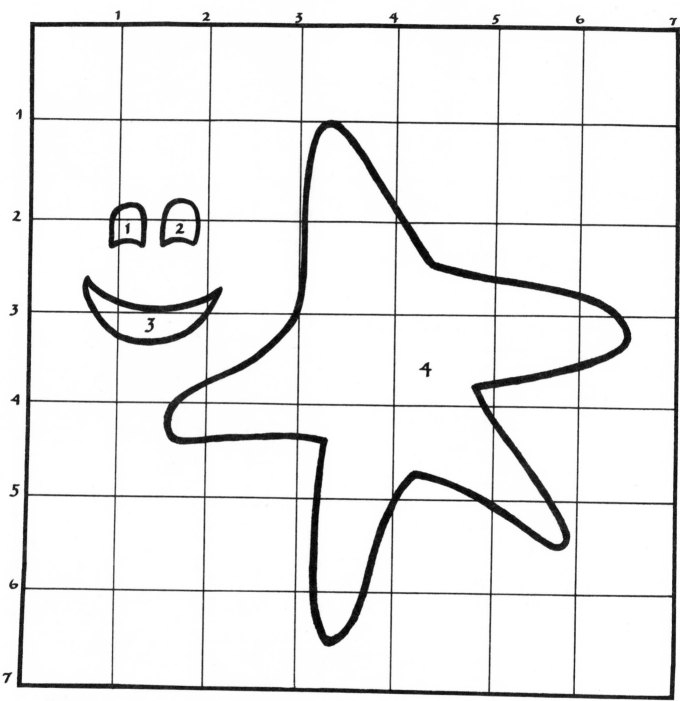

**Fig. R-6a**
STARFISH (PLAIN)

172

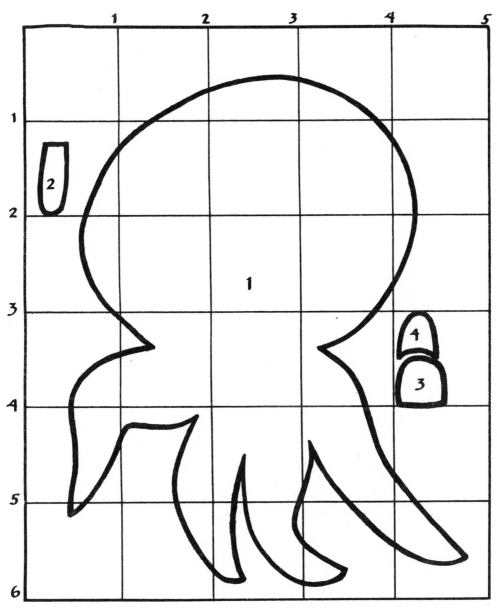

**Fig. R-7a**
OCTOPUS

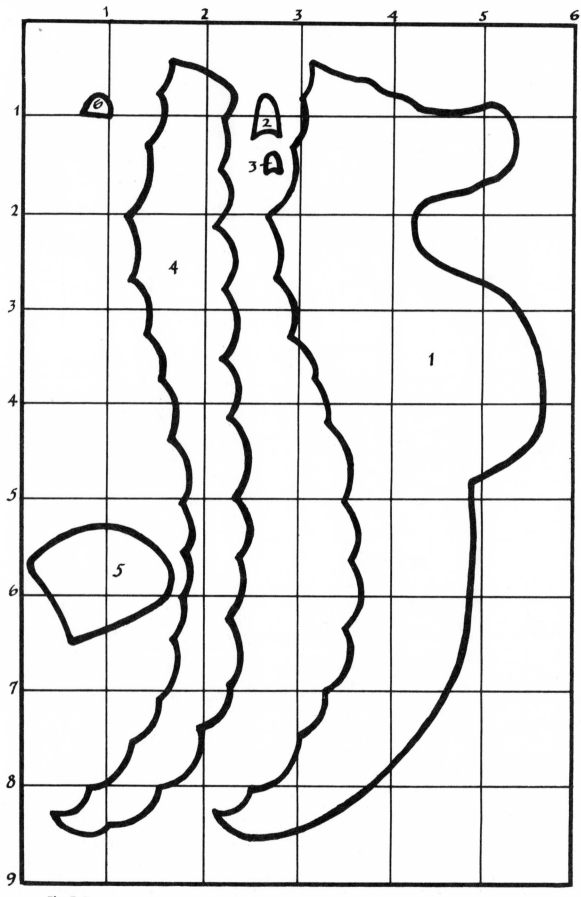

**Fig. R-8a**
SEAHORSE

Fig. R-9

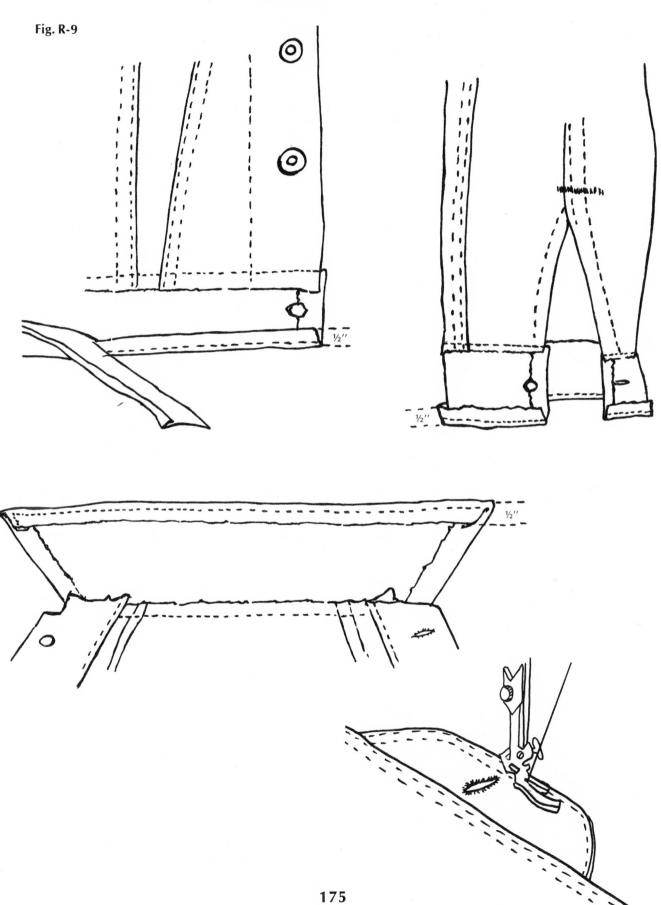

pattern. If you don't want to remove the pocket flaps, pin the muslin along the top line of the pocket flap, then smooth, flatten, and pin it across the entire surface of the flap. Mark around the edges, cut out the muslin, and make a brown paper pattern.

The graph patterns for the appliqués on the seascape jacket are provided in Figs. R-4a, R-5a, R-6a, R-7a, and R-8a. You must enlarge them onto 1-inch graph paper. Be very careful when enlarging; everything must be copied accurately in order for their ultimate size and shape to turn out right.

In order to enlarge designs, purchase large 1-inch graph paper. Or construct it yourself, drawing a grid of 1-inch squares with all corners at right angles to each other. (Your dressmaker's ruler will help here.) Then draw a box around the design on the original graph paper, and number the squares vertically and horizontally, as in Fig. R-1. Now draw a box around the equivalent number of squares on the large graph paper, numbering them horizontally and vertically as in the original. This makes it easier to transfer the design: You can easily find the exact location of each square in the design and transfer the markings correctly.

In each 1-inch square, draw the exact same pattern lines you see in the corresponding square on the smaller diagram. Don't think of it as a whole at first: deal with one square at a time and transfer the markings from one square to the other as accurately as possible. Once all the markings are transferred, your pattern will be enlarged to full size.

Once the large-grid paper design is completed, cut it out and mark the top. My pieces have already been reversed so the top actually is the top and not the bottom, as it would be with patterns you make up from scratch. Now number each piece to correspond to the number in the original design, and don't forget to indicate underlap allowances where necessary.

Lay the pattern pieces out top side up on the wrong side of the leather, and trace around them. Use my color combinations or your own if you wish. Cut out and number each piece. Then just overlap or overlay one piece over the other as indicated in the original pattern until you build up the design into a completed appliqué. In using my patterns the pieces are assembled so as to correspond to their matching sketches —

for example, the pieces of Fig. R-5a, are assembled to correspond to Fig. R-5.

If you are using permanent cement, leave the appliqué as is and put aside until later. Otherwise sew around the smaller sections of the appliqué such as the eyes, nose, and mouth so that you will have to sew around only the larger pieces when attaching it to the jacket later. Check the photos and sketches to see how each appliqué looks after assembly. (You don't really need a pattern for the seaweed. Just cut out wavy strips of leather about 9 to 12 inches long to correspond to those in the photo.)

Now attach the leather appliqués on the collar, waistband, cuffs, and — if you want — flaps of the pockets of the denim jacket. Align the edges of the denim and leather and glue down. Fold over the excess on the ends of the cuffs and waistband. If you left the buttons, be sure *not* to cover the buttonholes. Cut straight in over the button from the end of the strip to just beyond the center of the button. Wrap the slit leather around the button, abut the edges on the other side, and fold it over the edge (see Fig. Q-12).

Trim any excess leather on the edges so the denim and leather edges are exactly aligned with each other. Now, using your even-feed or walking foot and a glover's needle, topstitch with contrasting thread ⅛ inch from the edge around each piece and ¼ inch in from the first row around each and every piece except for the places where you will be adding snaps. In that case sew your second row ¾ inch from the first.

The only place where you might have a problem is on the pocket flap. If you removed the flaps, the leather should now be applied to them. So simply slip them under the welt seam on the jacket where they were removed from and sew the seam back up, thus replacing the flaps. If you didn't remove the flaps you can easily do the three free sides, but on the top, which is attached to the jacket, you might find it a little tight. Lay the flap out flat and sew all around the edges with the required double row of stitching (see Fig. R-9).

Once these leather cuffs, collar, waistband, and pocket flaps are attached, you can apply the snaps where necessary on the cuffs and waistband. (The technique for applying snaps is detailed in Sections 16 and 17.)

Once the basic pieces are down, lay the

jacket down so the right side of the back is flat up. Then, if you are doing the seascape jacket, for instance, lay out your seaweed on the back so that all fronds radiate from the center point at the bottom of the back, as in the photo. Glue them all down except the one that goes almost straight up the back. Glue just the bottom half of this one, leaving the top half free. If you are not using a permanent cement, sew each piece down ⅛ inch from the edge. Then take your rock and glue it over the bottom of all the seaweed pieces. If sewing, sew down. Now brush rubber cement evenly and smoothly over the back of your assembled fish, place it in the exact center of the back, and sew. Take the free piece of seaweed, glue it right down over the fish, and sew. Place your starfish on the bottom left of the jacket, just below the sleeve and overlapping the waistband. Put the snail on the other side of the bottom back. Place the seahorse on one side of the front and the octopus on the other, arranging them so they don't cover the pockets.

Don't lay all these appliqués straight up and down, but turn them on the diagonal to give a feeling of liveliness and interest. Remember it is not necessary to sew if you used permanent cement; but if you are sewing, sew around each piece of the appliqué including such small things as eyes, nose, or mouth. This adds a great finishing touch.

## CRAB JACKET

To make the crab jacket, prepare the cuffs, waistband, collar, and, if wanted, the pocket flaps as previously described. Cut out the crab using the pattern in Fig. R-10a, and assemble it according to the color photos of the jacket and its corresponding sketch in Fig. R-10, using the underlaps and overlaps as indicated in the pattern. If you are not using permanent cement, be sure to sew down any of the smaller details.

Now cut out a circle with 4½-inch radius (9-inch diameter) to act as the underpart of the

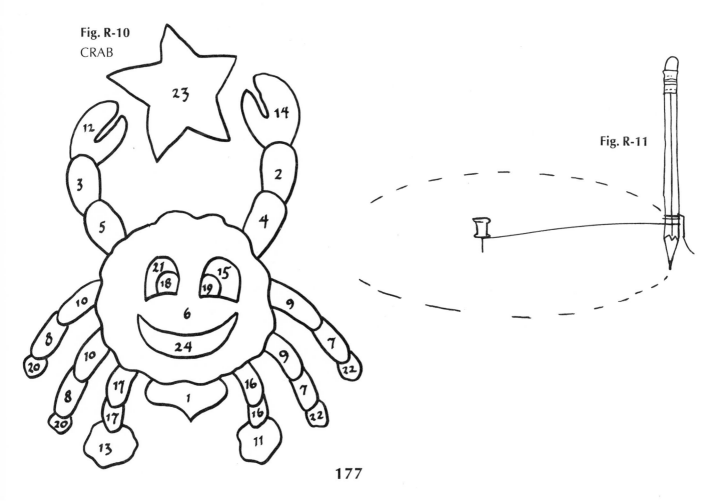

**Fig. R-10**
CRAB

**Fig. R-11**

177

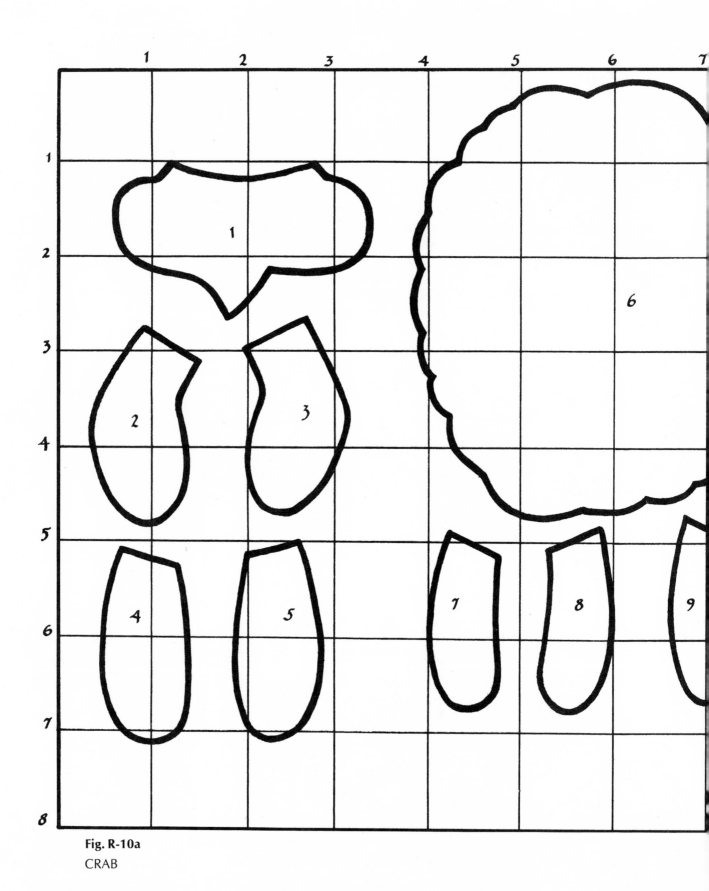

**Fig. R-10a**
CRAB

178

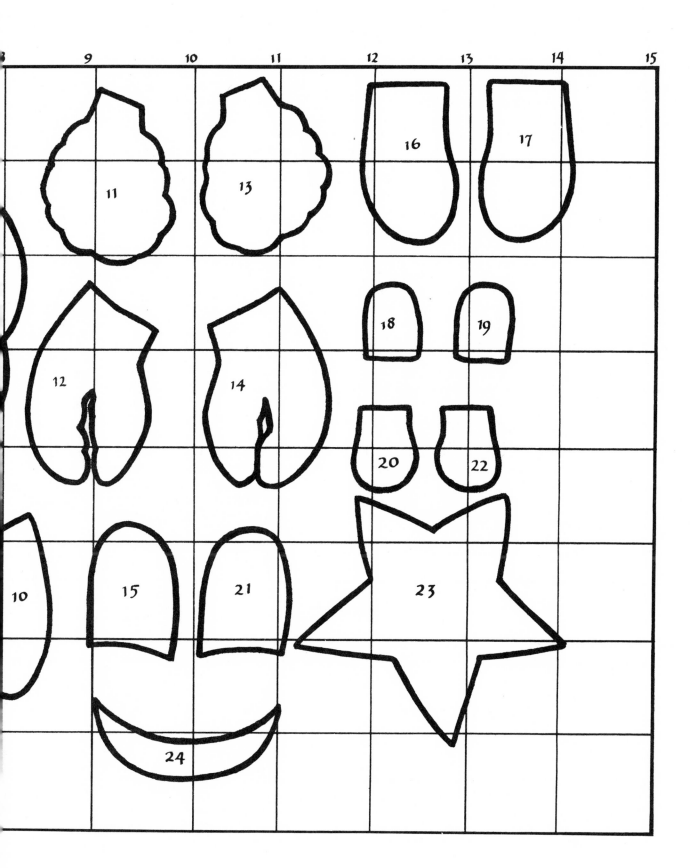

crab appliqué and show it to its best advantage. Use a compass or a dinner plate to insure a perfect circle. Or use the string-tied-to-a-pencil technique: Tie a thin string to a tack. Then tie the other end of the string to a pencil so that the string between tack and pencil measures 4½ inches, the radius of the desired circle. Stick the tack into a piece of brown paper, and, holding the pencil straight down, bring it in a circle around the tack keeping the string taut (see Fig. R-11). This will form your circle.

You will also need twelve stars — six of one color and six of another. Enlarge the star pattern given, or draw your own. (You will notice that mine isn't perfect — this should teach you not to worry too much, as a *little* irregularity doesn't show.)

Lay the large circle down on the center of the back, and place the twelve stars, alternating the two colors, around it. Unless you are using permanent cement, sew these down. Now glue the assembled crab down in the center of the circle. Sew the edges, if necessary, around each section.

You could use any appliqué design you want to replace the crab, of course. The decorated circle surrounded by stars is really an effective motif, but any of the appliqués shown here can be enlarged to fit into the circle.

## DUNGAREES

To make the appliquéd dungarees shown in the color photos you will need to make a "seat," cufflike bands for the leg bottoms, and V-shaped gussets for both outer sides of the legs, as well as several appliqué designs.

Depending on your taste, you can eliminate the seat, the cuffs, the gusset, or all of these, and simply appliqué the pants with motifs. I like the complete look, however, and will describe the construction of a pair decorated that way. The photos show both the back and the front of the dungarees to help you with the placement and coloring of appliques.

Prepare your dungarees by washing, bleaching, and making any necessary adjustments such as shortening or lengthening. Mark the exact center of the outside of the pants legs by following the directions outlined in Section 17 on making the studded denim suit. Put on the dungarees and place a pin on the center of the outside of the legs. Jeans don't always fall straight at the side but tend to fall forward toward the front or back. Now place another pin in the exact center of the other side of each leg, either 11½ inches or 14 to 15 inches up from the bottom depending on the size gusset being used — 12 inches for pre-flared pants or 15 to 17 inches on the straight legs to be flared. Walk around, make sure the sides are marked correctly and don't move after being worn. Mark the placement of the pins with a magic marker and draw a straight line connecting these points. Then take a pair of scissors and cut out small squares at the bottom of each leg seamline so that you eliminate the many layers of material accumulated here. This will make sewing easier.

Make the pattern for the gusset, following the

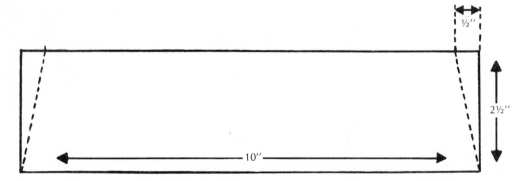

**Fig. R-12**

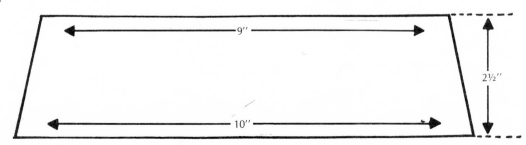

procedure for the studded suits. Make a triangle with a base of 9 inches and center height of 12 inches if you are using slightly flared pants, and a base of 9 inches and height of 15 to 17 inches for straight pants which you will be flaring slightly. Draw a straight line 9 inches long and mark either end. Mark the center of the line (4½ inches) and depending on the size gusset you are making, draw a line 12 inches or 15 to 17 inches long at right angles to the base at this mark. Now join the ends of these two lines to make a triangular pattern (see Fig. Q-1).

You can't just cut two straight strips for the cuffs, as they would not fit properly. Make a pattern by drawing two 10-inch lines parallel to each other and 2½ inches apart. Then shorten one line 1 inch by eliminating ½ inch from either end, and connect the ends of the short and long lines — 9 and 10 inches, respectively — together (see Fig. R-12). You will then have a strip 2½ inches wide and 10 inches long on one side and 9 inches long on the other. Cut out two of these strips for each leg. You must make your patterns this way, since you will be overlapping the ends of the two pieces in the appropriate amounts to conform to the shape of the dungaree legs. Belled pants flare out slightly, and are therefore, wider on the bottom than 2½ inches higher up the leg. If the pants are straight to begin with, you will be flaring them, so again you will have to compensate for the difference.

The method for making the pattern for the seat is the same as for copying any pattern from a garment. The seat is easy to do, but you can't just put a plain solid piece of leather over the seat area, since the seats of pants are curved to follow the lines of your body. It is necessary to make four pattern pieces which, when sewn together, form a shape resembling a well-rounded saddle.

There is no standard pattern for seats, and you must adjust them to fit each pair of dungarees — or at least each different size. Take a piece of muslin and pin it along the center back seam line, extending from the center crotch to 1¾ to 3 inches below the pants top, depending on the height of the rise (how high the waist is on the pants). Then start to smooth it out over the seat itself, pinning as you go. Keep one hand on the inside of the dungarees, and with the other smooth and pin the muslin over the outside. Now pin the muslin 4½ to 5½ inches

down the inner seam line of the leg extending from the crotch out. As you smooth and pin, you will find a fold may form around the seams. If this happens, remove the pins from the seam and adjust the muslin over it until it is smooth; again pin it in place. Keep running your hand over the muslin, pinning, repinning, and adjusting until you feel sure it is completely smooth and conforms to the shape of the seat. Now with a felt-tipped pen mark the seams on the muslin so that the center back seam runs from the crotch to 1¾ to 3 inches from the pants top and the inner seam line of the pants leg extends 4½ to 5½ inches out from the crotch. When the seam lines are marked, take your felt-tipped pen and connect the ends of these two seams with almost an inverted U shape, being sure the outer lines of the seat pattern always follows the shape of the inner center seam (see Fig. R-13). Remove the pins and take the muslin off.

For the front seat pattern pieces, pin the muslin from the crotch forward to just beneath the fly, and 4½ to 5½ inches — whichever you used on the back pattern — along the inner seam of the pants. Smooth it over the dungarees, adjust, and repin until the muslin fits right. With a felt-tipped pen, mark along the seam lines of the leg 4½ to 5½ inches. Now join the ends of the two seams with a shape resembling a quarter of an oblong (see Fig. R-14). Take the pins out and remove the muslin from the pants.

If you are using traditional concealed seams, add ½-inch seam allowances on the center back seam, center front seam, and all along the inner leg seam lines (see Fig. R-15). If you are using overlapping seams, add the ½-inch seam allow-

**Fig. R-13**

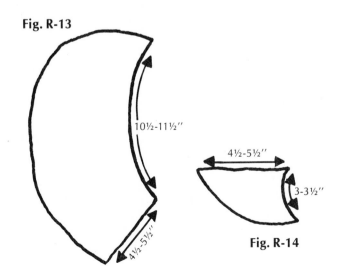

10½-11½''

4½-5½''

4½-5½''

3-3½''

**Fig. R-14**

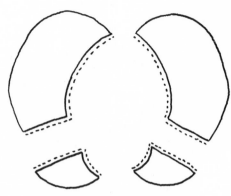

Fig. R-15

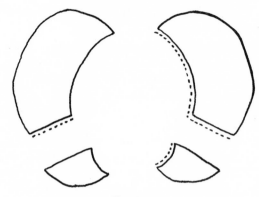

Fig. R-16

ance to only one side of each connecting seam (see Fig. R-16). Do not add seam allowances on the outer edges of the seat no matter what type of seams you are using.

Now cut out the muslin pattern, cutting on the inside of the lines that mark the outer edges of the seam allowances. Make up the brown paper patterns by taping the muslin to the brown paper, being sure not to stretch the muslin by pulling it too taut. Trace around each piece and cut out. Then make reverse duplicates of the front and back pieces and mark the tops so that you don't make mistakes when cutting.

You must now put the seat, cuffs, and gusset onto the pants. First assemble the four pieces of the seat. I prefer to use concealed seams, but you can use overlapped seams and topstitch. If you use overlapped seams, overlap in the order shown in Fig. R-16, and use thread the same color as the leather to maintain the feeling of the seat being one solid leather piece. Keep the contrasting thread for the outside seams of the seat. After sewing, if you are using traditional seams, glue them open flat.

Once the leather seat is assembled, first glue the leather seat to the dungarees along the seam lines of the center back and front, starting at the center crotch. Then brush glue evenly and smoothly over the inside of either the left or right side of the leather seat — you don't want bumps or unevenness here! Then carefully guide it so that its seam lines align with the leg seam line of the pants. Press the two seams together. With one hand on the inside of the pants and one on the outside of the leather, smooth over the appropriate areas on the dungarees so that the leather conforms to the shape of the pants underneath. After one side is done, do the other.

Now sew two rows of topstitching in con-

trasting colors all around the outside edges of the seat. Be sure you are always stitching through only one layer of dungaree pants. Do this stitching as previously explained in Section 3 and 7 by sewing with a zipper or zigzag foot such as on the even-feed or walking foot. Your first row should be ⅛ inch from the edge, and the second ¼ inch in from that.

For the gusset and the bottom cuffs, first, if you are using slightly flared pants, glue along the center of the outer leg to the center line of the gusset. If you are using straight-legged pants, slit up this line on the pants leg (see Fig. Q-9), and mark the seam allowances along the long edges of the leather triangle. Draw a line 2 inches long — from the bottom edge up — on the inner leg of the pants at a point exactly opposite the center line of the outer leg. This line marks the center of the overlapping ends of the cuffs. Make sure it doesn't fall along the seam line of the pants, or it will be hard to sew because of the many layers of accumulated fabric. To attach the cuffs, first put on the back strip. Place it so that the longer edge is on the bottom, one end overlaps the 2″ line on the inner leg by ½ to ¾ inch, and the bottom edges are aligned. Then attach the front strip, being sure the overlap of the ends is enough to compensate for the shape of the bottom of the pants so that the bottom edges of the cuffs and pants are aligned. Trim any excess from the bottom.

Now for flared pants glue the rest of the V-shaped gusset down, overlapping the ends of the cuffs. For the straight legged pants mark 2½ inches on either side of the center line on the leather gusset. Align the bottom edges of the slit with these marks and glue the denim and leather together at these points. Allow the V-shape to open by itself and glue the rest of the leather to the denim. Trim any excess from the bottom for

182

a smooth and even edge. Sew a double row of stitching first around the top edge of the cuff, then on the overlap of the inner leg, then on the two long sides of the triangle, and finally around the entire bottom of the pant. Backstitch a few stitches, sewing right into the holes already there, to finish up a seam in topstitching.

Now cut out and assemble the appliqués you are planning to use. If you are going to duplicate the pants shown in the photos, use any of the appliqué patterns given throughout this chapter to correspond to the ones I used. Use the photos as your guide for the specific appliqués used, the colors, and the completed appearance. Assemble the appliqués by gluing the pieces together, using the appropriate underlaps. If you are using permanent cement, leave as is; otherwise sew around the smaller sections of the appliqué such as the eyes, nose, or mouth so that when attaching to the dungarees you will have to sew around only the larger pieces. After the appliqués are completely assembled, place them on the dungarees, front and back, as shown in the color photo, or in the arrangement of your choice. Overlap the seats, gusset, and cuffs if necessary for effect, and place the appliqués on different axes to add variety. Then, if you are sewing, sew ⅛ inch in from the edges where necessary.

Don't put any appliqués around the narrow area of the knees, as it is an awkward spot to sew and tends to stretch out of shape easily. If you must put something in this area, make it not too complicated a design.

To machine sew these appliqués on dungarees, roll up the legs on the pants and ease the fabric into the machine under the needle, being sure only one layer goes through at a time. Now slowly and carefully sew around each appliqué, maneuvering the pants to follow the contours of the designs. This is really quite easily done; just try it. The only awkward spot is in tight areas such as around the knees. If you feel you can't do it, try sewing a scrap of leather to a pair of old dungarees before doing any work on the real ones. Try a few times until you get the hang of it. If you find it really impossible, then lay out all the appliqués where you want them and glue down only those that fall over the tight areas of the legs. Do not glue down any that might eventually overlap the seat, cuffs, or gusset. Open up the inside leg seam and sew the glued appliqués

to the dungarees. Sew the seams back up using traditional concealed seams, attach the seat, cuffs, and gusset as previously described, and then the rest of the appliqués.

You could of course attach the leather seat and simply indicate the areas which will be covered by the cuffs and gusset. Then glue down the appliqués, being sure not to infringe on the areas reserved for the cuffs and gusset or over the inner leg seams. Open up the inner leg seam just to 2 inches below the seat, and sew the appliqués down. Then resew the seam.

If you are not putting on the seat, gusset, or cuffs, simply lay the appliqués out where you want them and glue them down. The open up the inner leg seam lines and sew them down. And after they are sewn, resew the seams using traditional concealed seams.

## HANDSEWING

If you are sewing by hand, then you must use a very fine lacing — you can't punch really huge holes through the denim, or it will rip. Punch the holes so that the stitches always go through both the denim and leather and never through the denim alone. Use a running diagonal, or a close cross-stitch.

If you are hand-stitching, it is really best to sew with heavy thread or twine. Make your holes in the leather first, glue the leather to the denim, and then sew through these holes. Depending on the thickness of your lacing, either use a small punch to make these holes, or sew with your sewing machine without thread, making perfectly spaced holes. Use either a glover's needle or a big-eyed tapestry or embroidery needle, again depending on the size of your lacing or thread. Buttonhole twist is perfect here as it is strong and looks good. Wool, twine, or heavy embroidery threads are other possibilities.

Whenever there is any difficulty sewing through leather, I recommend punching the holes in the leather with your machine and sewing with buttonhole twist or a heavy thread. I find that it is usually the thread that is the main problem when sewing, as it breaks easily. However, if you sew at a slow, steady speed, use an even-feed foot and a glover's needle, you should have no problems.

**183**

# SOME ADDITIONAL APPLIQUÉ DESIGNS
## PATTERNS BEGIN ON PAGE 190

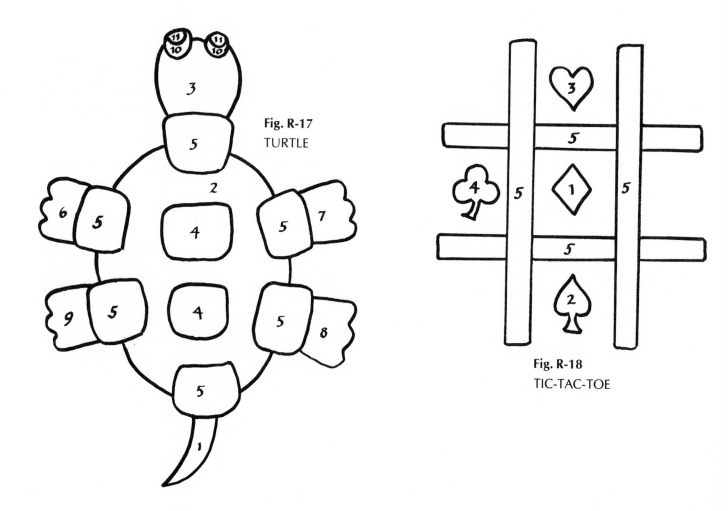

Fig. R-17
TURTLE

Fig. R-18
TIC-TAC-TOE

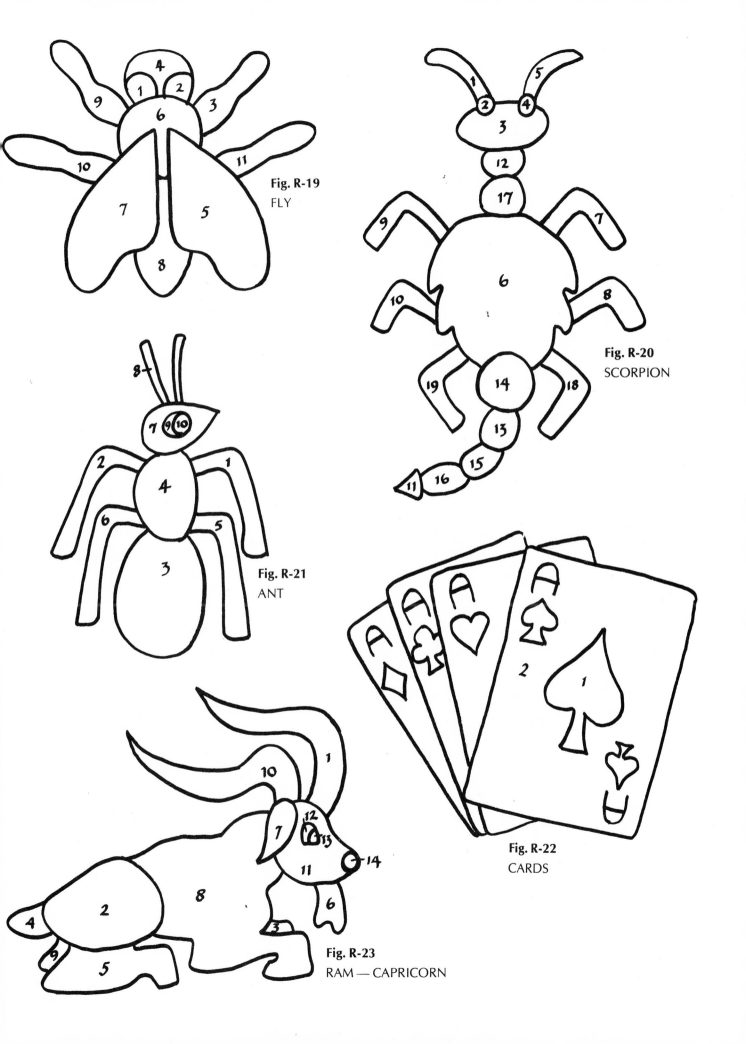

**Fig. R-19**
FLY

**Fig. R-20**
SCORPION

**Fig. R-21**
ANT

**Fig. R-22**
CARDS

**Fig. R-23**
RAM — CAPRICORN

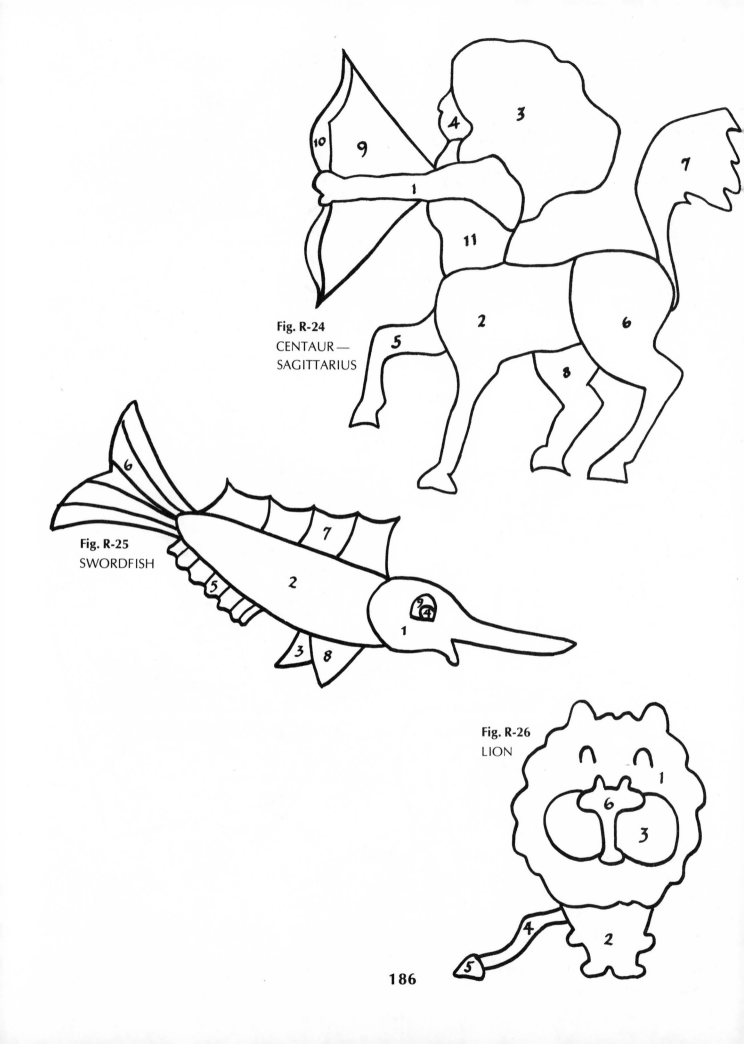

**Fig. R-24**
CENTAUR—
SAGITTARIUS

**Fig. R-25**
SWORDFISH

**Fig. R-26**
LION

186

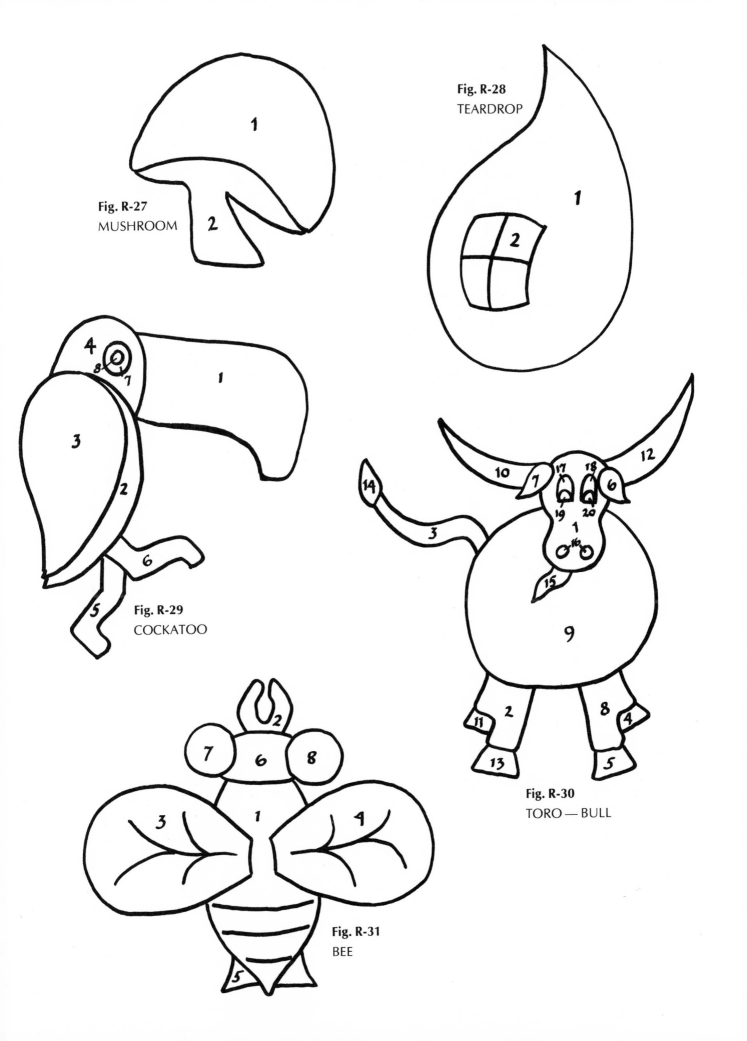

**Fig. R-27**
MUSHROOM

**Fig. R-28**
TEARDROP

**Fig. R-29**
COCKATOO

**Fig. R-30**
TORO — BULL

**Fig. R-31**
BEE

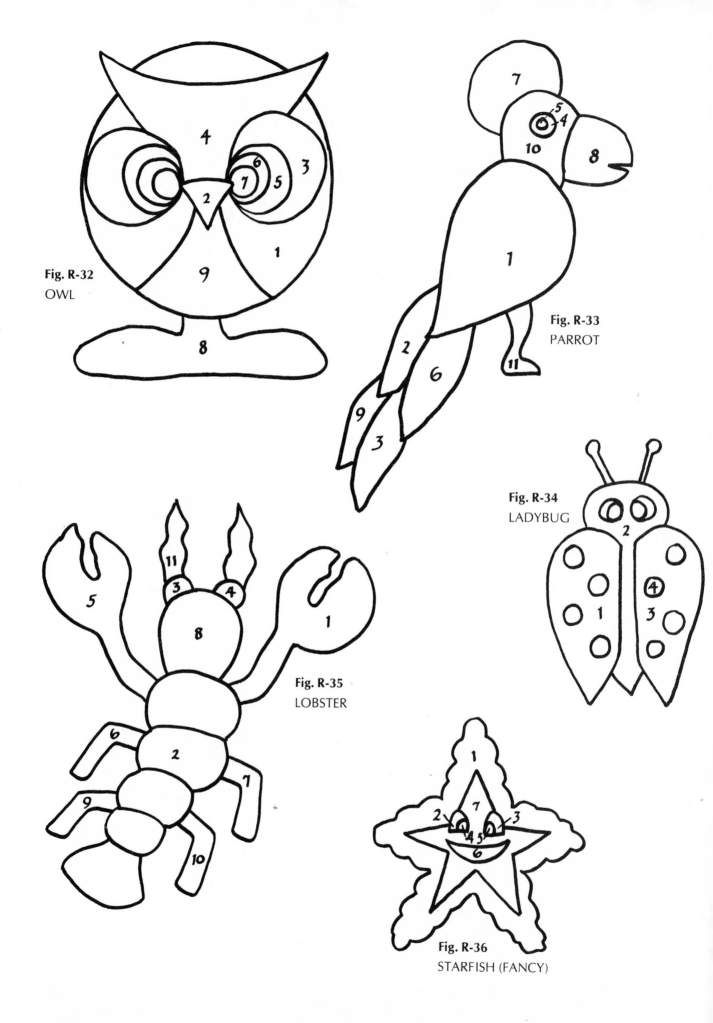

**Fig. R-32**
OWL

**Fig. R-33**
PARROT

**Fig. R-34**
LADYBUG

**Fig. R-35**
LOBSTER

**Fig. R-36**
STARFISH (FANCY)

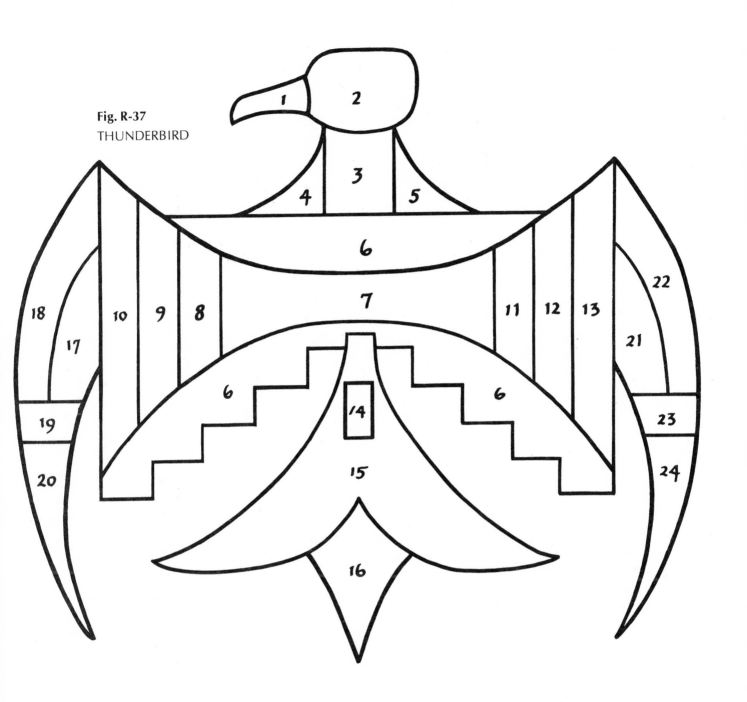

**Fig. R-37**
THUNDERBIRD

**Fig. R-38**
THUNDERBIRD BAND
PATTERN

189

**Fig. R-17a**
TURTLE

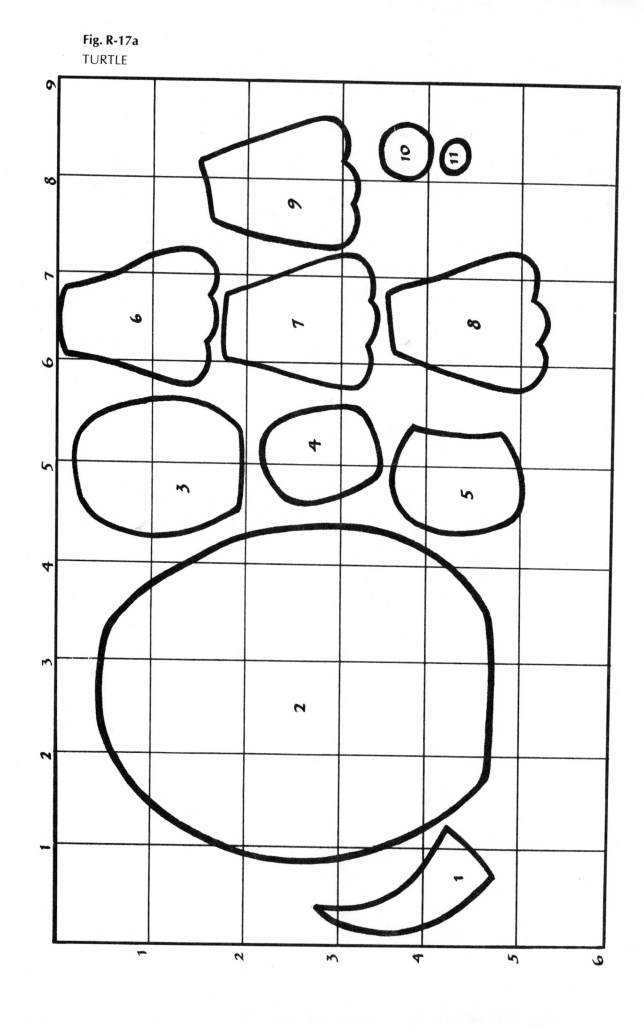

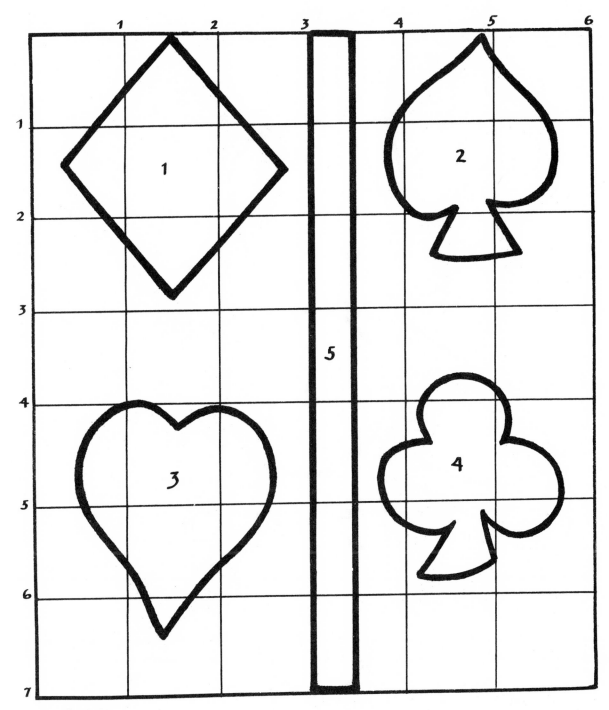

**Fig. R-18a**
TIC-TAC-TOE

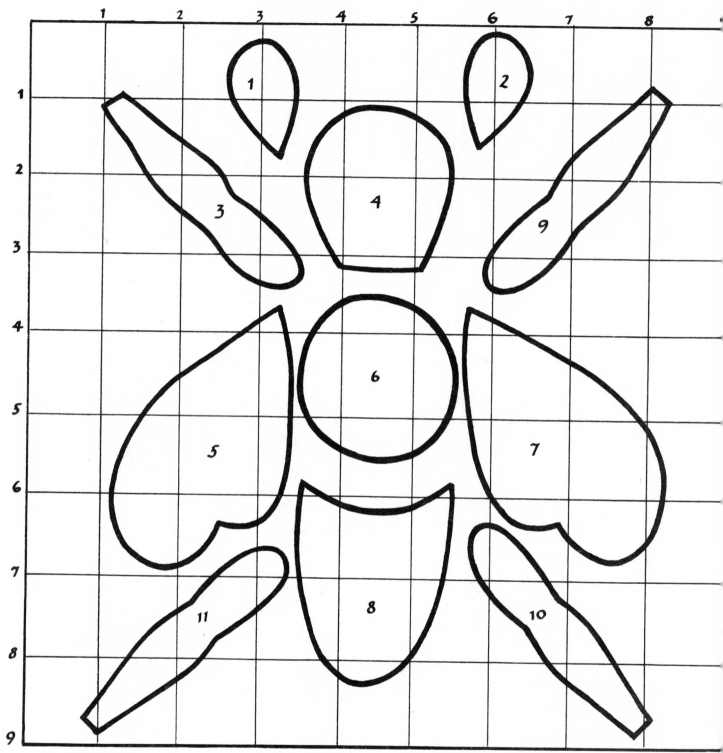

**Fig. R-19a**
FLY

192

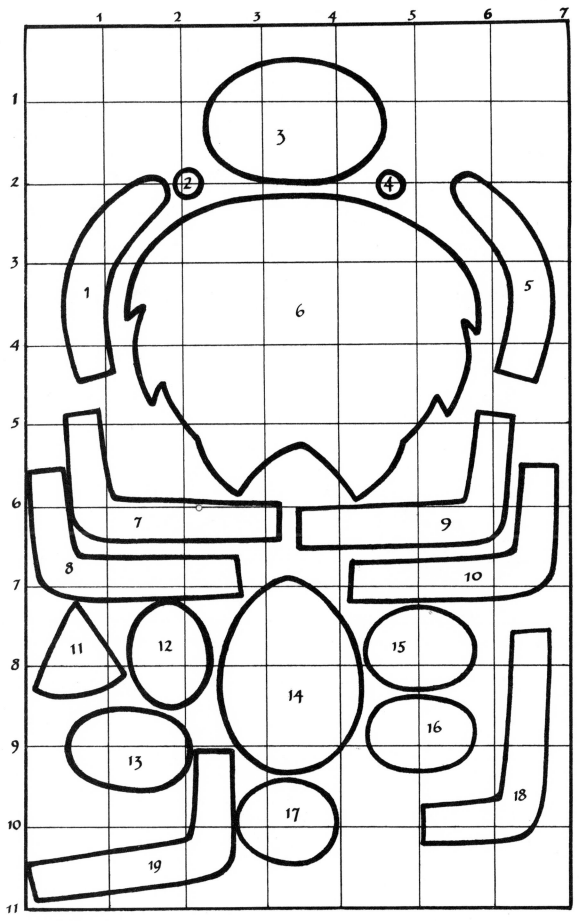

**Fig. R-20a**
SCORPION

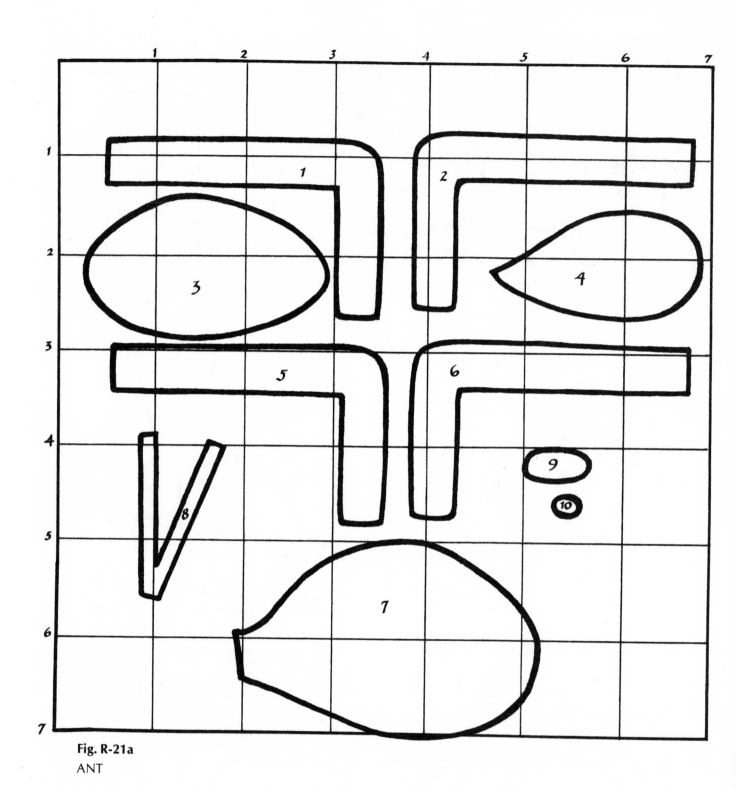

**Fig. R-21a**
ANT

194

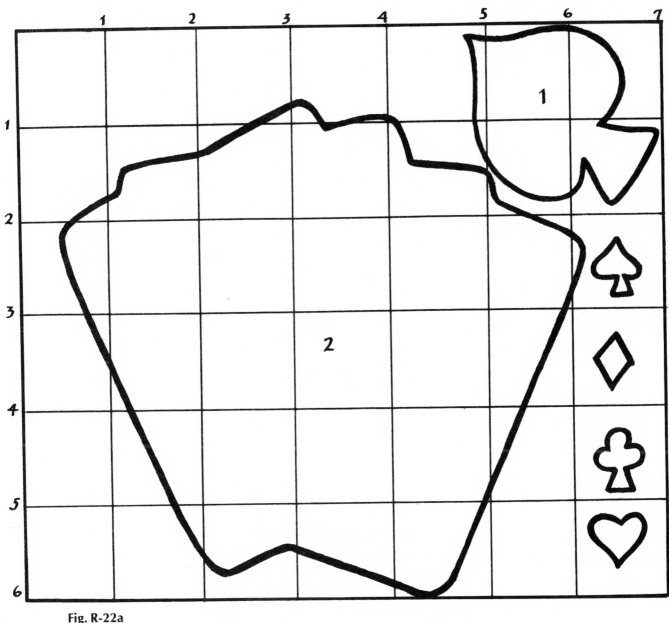

**Fig. R-22a**
CARDS

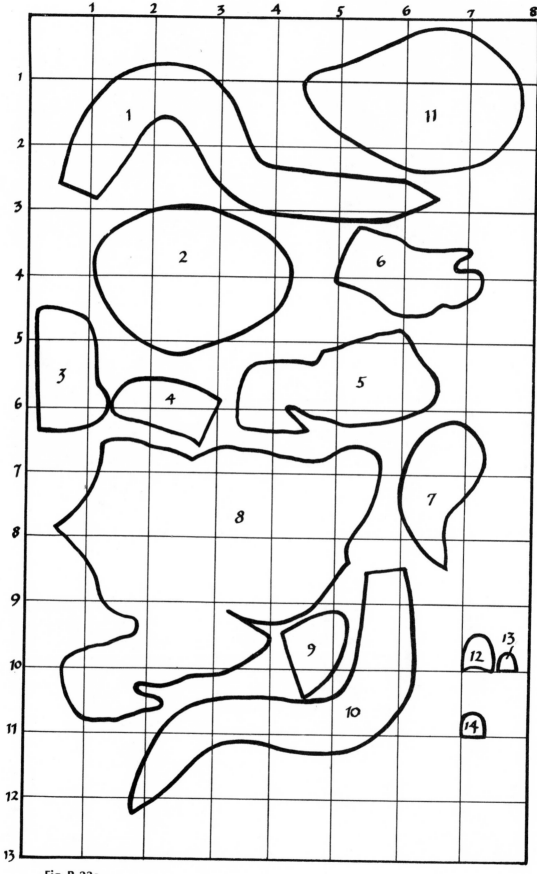

**Fig. R-23a**

RAM — CAPRICORN

**Fig. R-24a**

CENTAUR — SAGITTARIUS

197

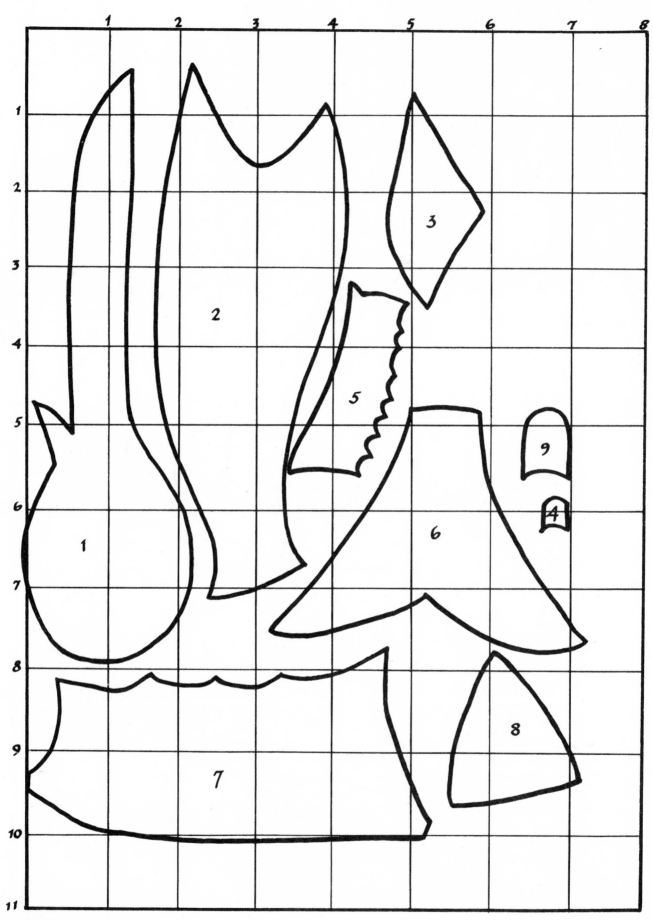

**Fig. R-25a**
SWORDFISH

198

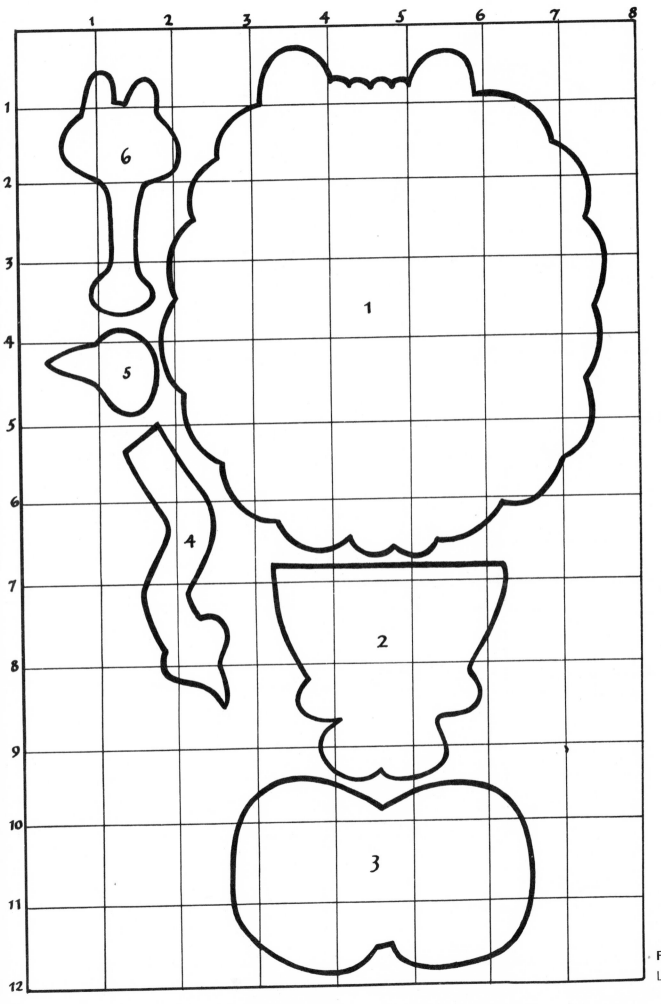

**Fig. R-26a**
LION

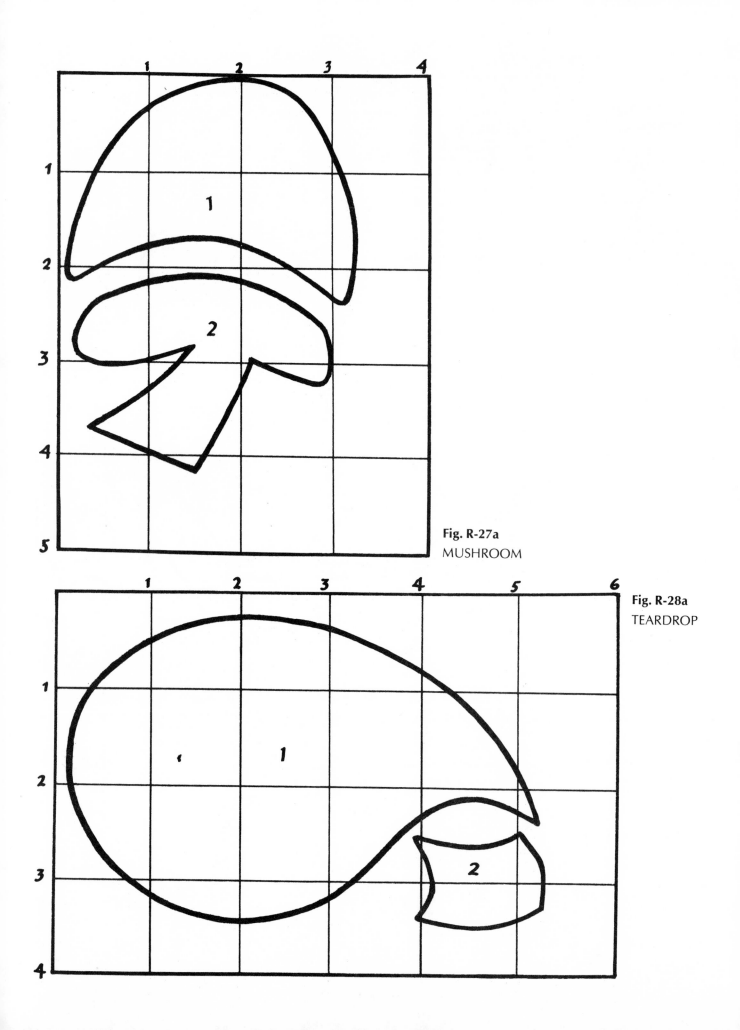

**Fig. R-27a**
MUSHROOM

**Fig. R-28a**
TEARDROP

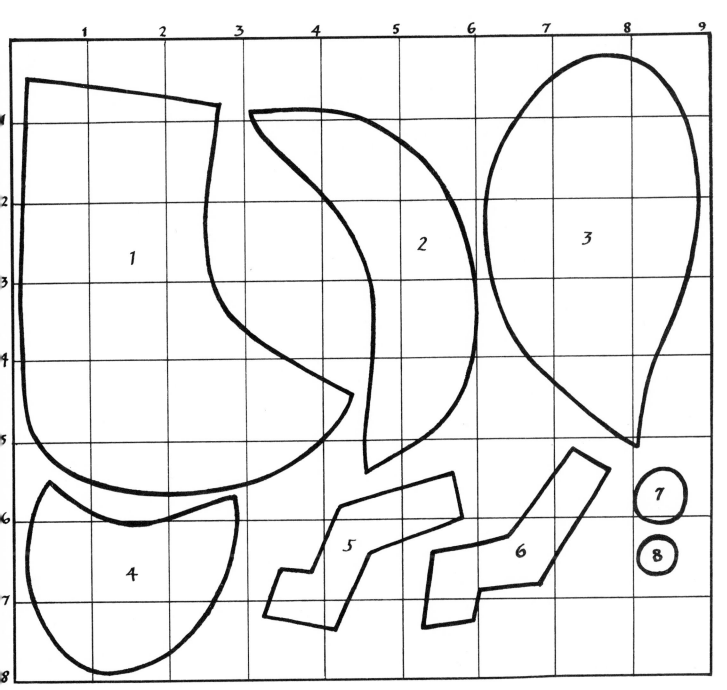

**Fig. 29a**
COCKATOO

201

**Fig. R-30a**

TORO — BULL

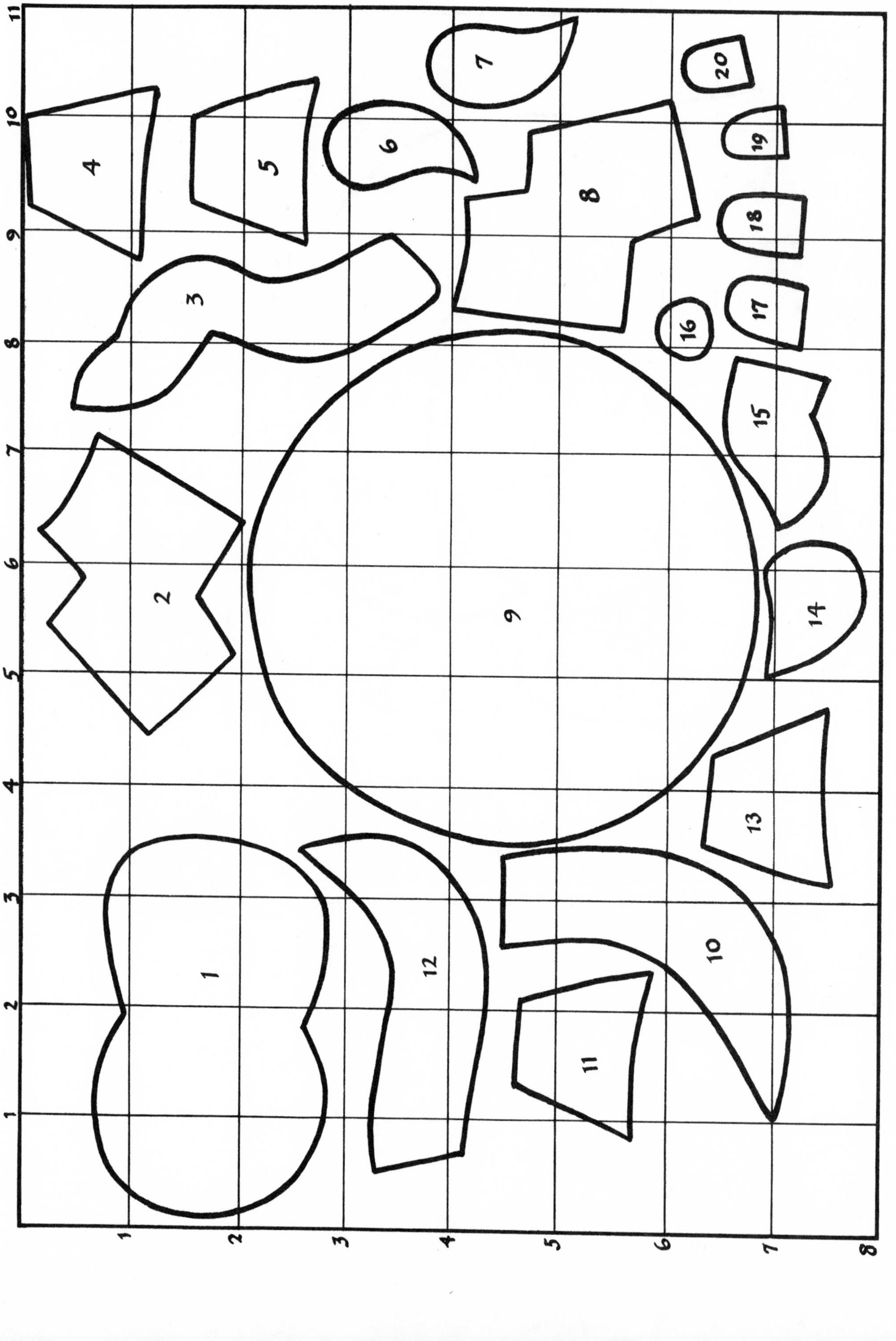

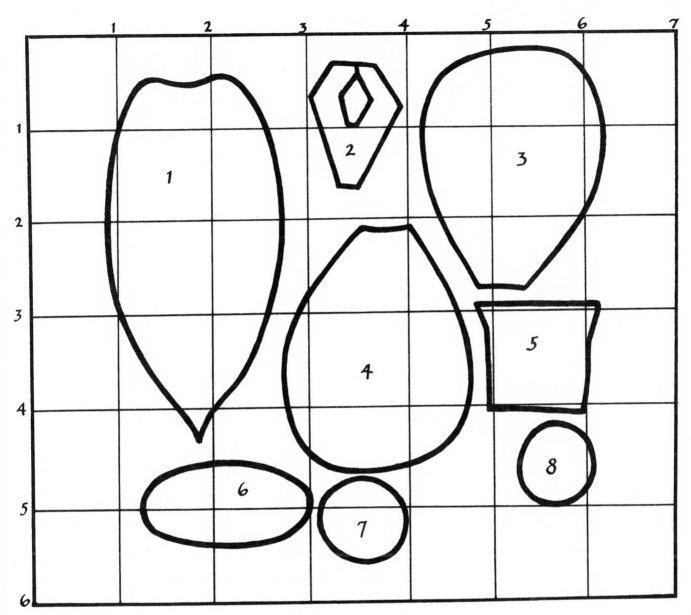

**Fig. R-31a**
BEE

203

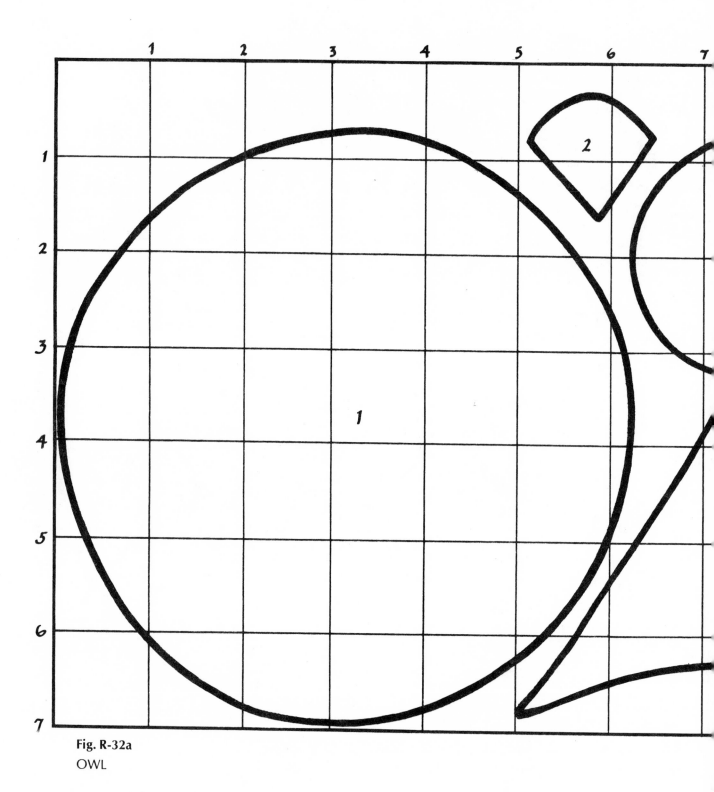

**Fig. R-32a**
OWL

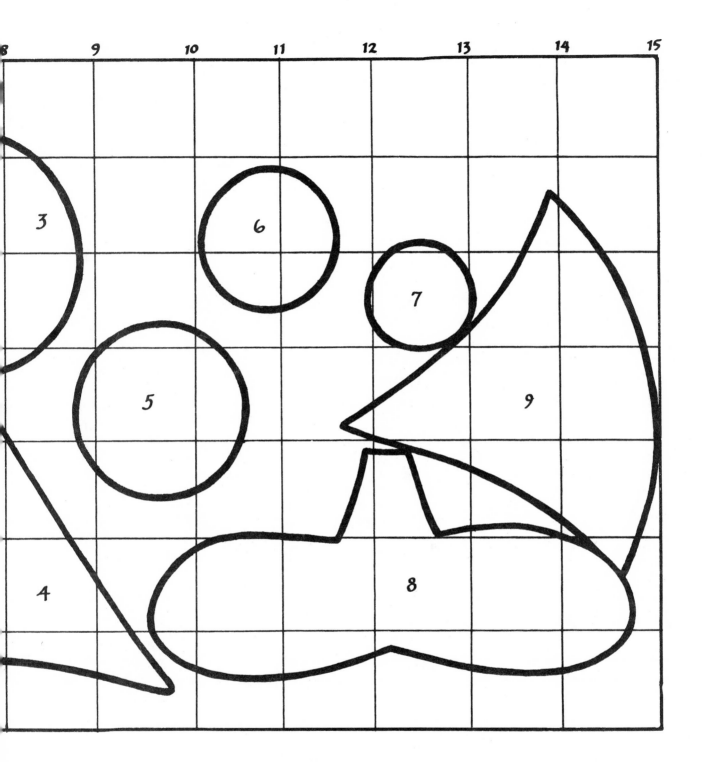

3

6

7

5

9

4

8

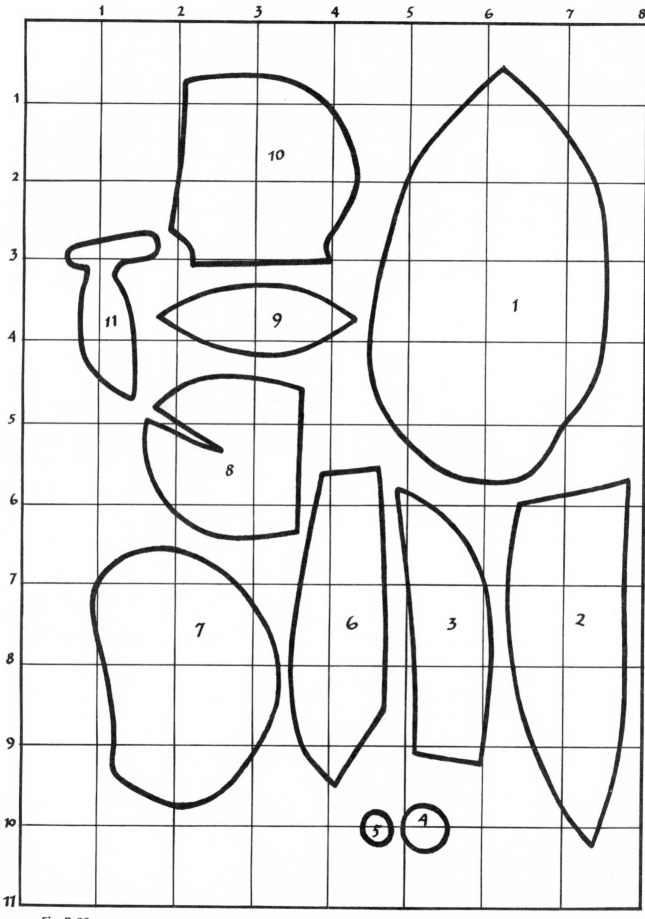

**Fig. R-33a**

PARROT

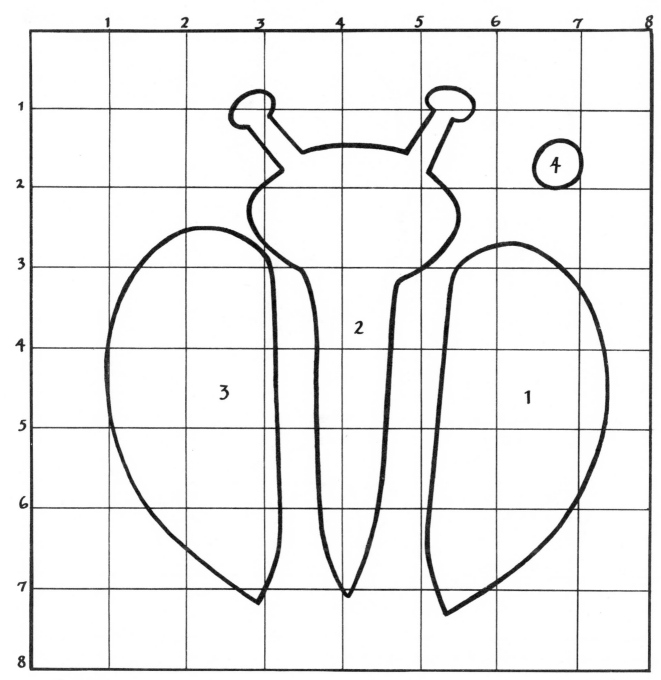

**Fig. R-34a**
LADYBUG

**Fig. R-35a**
LOBSTER

**Fig. R-36a**
STARFISH (FANCY)

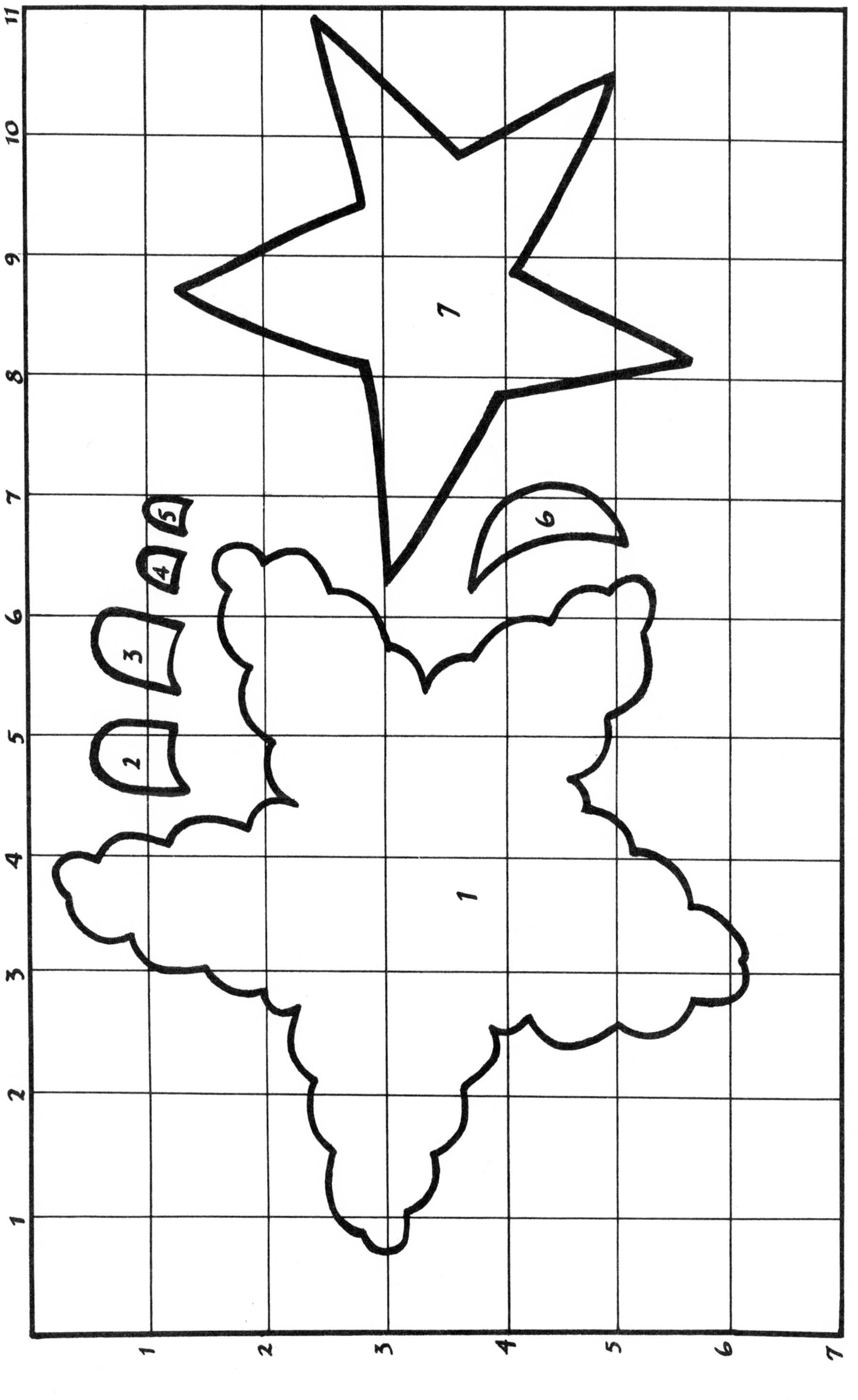

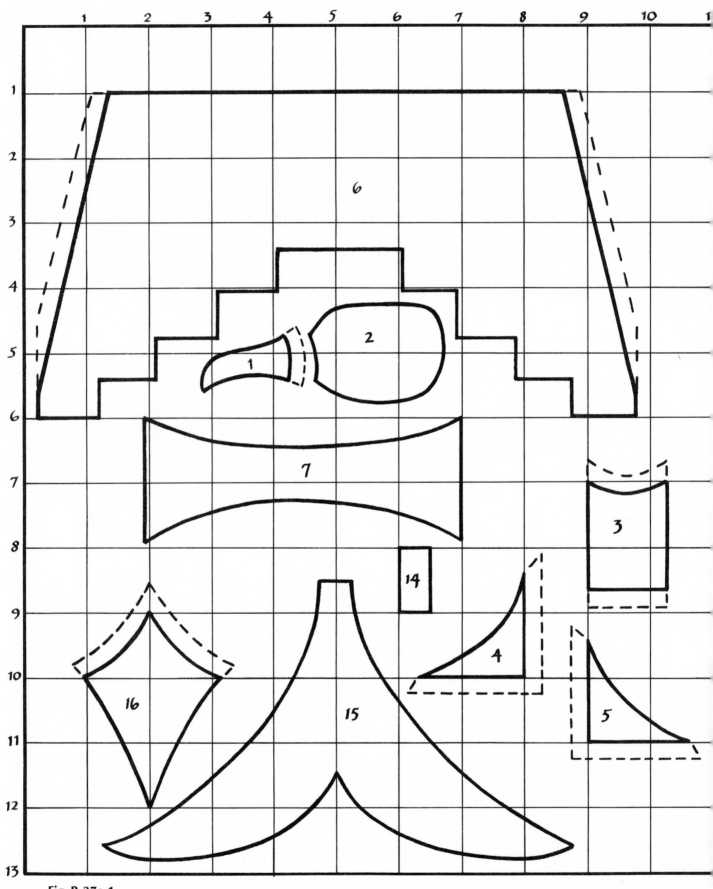

**Fig. R-37a-1**
THUNDERBIRD

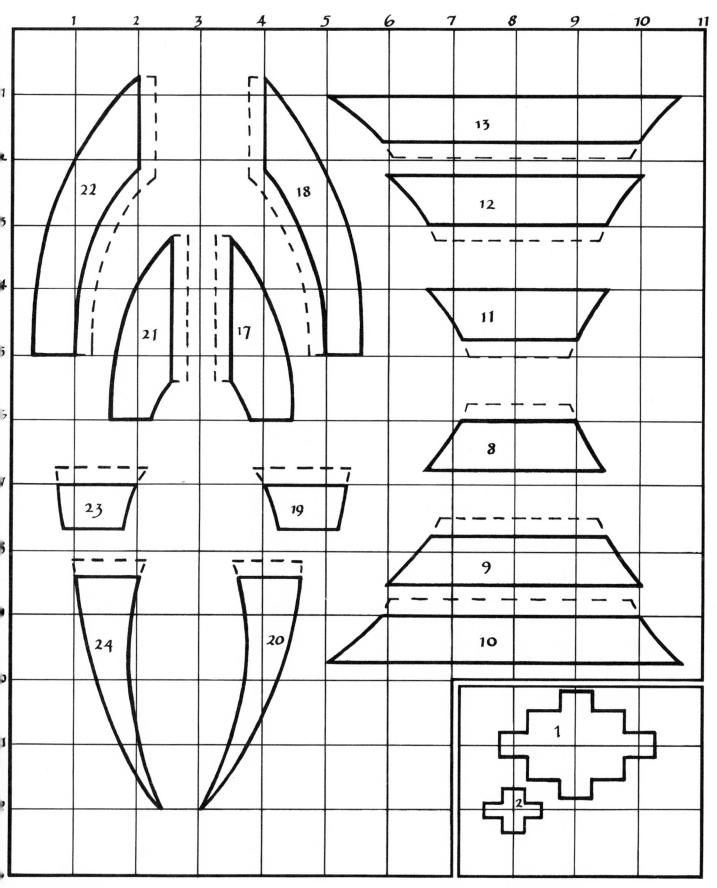

**Fig. R-37a-2**
THUNDERBIRD

**Fig. R-38a**
THUNDERBIRD BAND
PATTERN

## TOOLS NEEDED

GRAPH PAPER, BOTH SMALL AND THE
    1-INCH SIZE
BROWN PAPER
CLEAR DRESSMAKER'S RULER
WATERPROOF FELT-TIPPED PEN
RUBBER OR LEATHER CEMENT AND
    BRUSHES
PERMANENT CEMENT (OPTIONAL BUT
    HIGHLY RECOMMENDED)
SHEARS
SMALL SCISSORS
MASKING TAPE
RUFFER OR SANDPAPER (OPTIONAL)

- MACHINE SEWING

EVEN-FEED OR WALKING FOOT
GLOVER'S NEEDLES FOR BOTH MACHINE
    AND HAND SEWING
HEAVY MERCERIZED THREAD
TISSUE PAPER (OPTIONAL)

- HAND SEWING

DRIVE PUNCH OR AWL OR SEWING
    MACHINE FOR MAKING HOLES
MALLET
HARDWOOD BOARD
LACING

    OPTIONAL

PLIERS
LARGE-EYED EMBROIDERY NEEDLE
ROTARY PUNCH
AWL

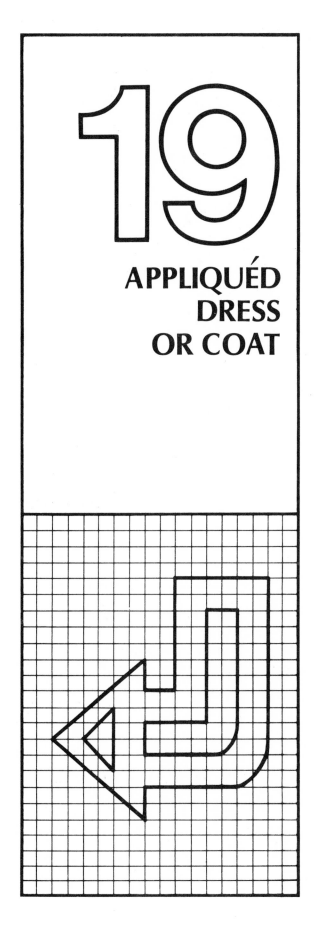

# 19

# APPLIQUÉD DRESS OR COAT

Another way to use appliqués is to put them on a dress or coat such as the one in the color photograph — a short-sleeved dress with a hidden zipper in the front. But it could easily have long sleeves and a large industrial zipper to make a coat.

To make a similar dress or coat, get a commercial pattern shaped like the one in the color photo. If you are going to use a special separating (jacket type) zipper — which will extend the length of the garment — make sure there is a seam line straight up the front of the dress. (Any pattern should have an opening up the front to allow you to lay it out flat and attach the appliqués easily.) For a coat get a pattern with long sleeves. The dress I made has kimono-type sleeves and would be ideal for full-length sleeves shaped to match the A shape of the dress. You can add a collar, following the directions given for their attachment in the section on jackets; and if you prefer to use fasteners such as snaps or ties, get a pattern with an overlap and fasteners. These can be adjusted to any type of fasteners you want, the pattern acting as a placement guide.

You can buy a commercial pattern for any style you want and attach the appliqués, but I like a casual, looser look, especially for a coat to be worn over other garments.

No matter what style pattern you buy, if the pieces are exceptionally large you may have to adjust them to fit the size skins you are using. I can't usually find leather hides large enough to accommodate the pattern pieces required for full-length or even ¾-length dresses or coats. You may have to divide the pattern pieces in two or even more sections in order to fit into the smaller skins. This is especially important if you have skins with very small surface areas such as chamois, which can be bought by the yard already sewn into patchwork squares, and is rather nice to work with that way.

To adjust the pattern pieces, draw a rough sketch of the garment to be made or trace the picture from the pattern envelope. Put in dividing lines where you think would be the most convenient (I divided my dress just below the hips). These dividing lines don't have to be straight across, but if you are using concealed seams as I did here or if you want to keep the background plain and let the decoration of the appliqués show through, it's a good idea to do it this way.

Once you decide where these dividing lines

**213**

are going to go, transfer these markings to the little sketches of the pattern pieces that come with commercial patterns, and then finally to the full-sized pattern itself. Remember that with a curved hem such as that usually found on dresses or coats, any new seams should follow the curve of the hem. Cut the pattern apart along these new lines and add seam allowances. To do this, tape strips of paper about 2 to 3 inches wide (depending on whether you are adding length and the type of seaming being done) along the cut edges (see Fig. N-1). Draw in the seam allowances for the type of seam you are planning. For traditional concealed seams add ⅝ inch to both sides, and for overlapped seams add ⅝ inch to whichever side you want to *underlap*.

You must adjust the other seam allowances on the pattern to correspond with the type of seaming you plan. If you are using traditional seams, leave as is. If you are using overlapped seams for either hand or machine sewing, eliminate the seam allowances from the side which you want to overlap. If you are hand-sewing and planning to edge-stitch, eliminate the seam allowance from the neckline unless you are going to add a collar.

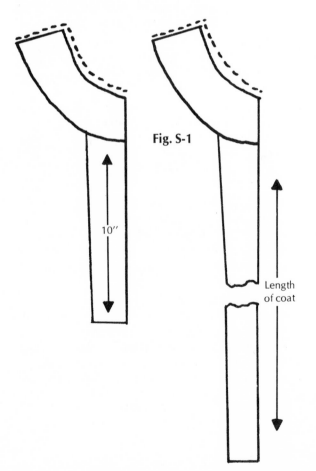

**Fig. S-1**

10''

Length of coat

If you are putting in a zipper, decide whether it will be an industrial or regular concealed type. For an industrial zipper, eliminate the seam allowance plus ¼ to ⅜ inch. If you are using a regular zipper with traditional concealed seams, leave the seam allowances. If you are using a regular zipper and overlapped seams, then eliminate the seam allowances on both edges.

You will need the neckline and top front facing to make the dress or coat (see Fig. S-1). Eliminate the center front seam allowances from both edges. If there is no front facing, only a neckline facing, eliminate the center front seam allowance from this. Then take your dressmaker's ruler and add a strip 2½ inches wide and 10 inches long onto the bottom of the center front of the neckline facing for a dress, and the entire length of the garment front for a coat.

If you are machine sewing, follow the directions given with the pattern. Sew up the dart, all the seams except the under-sleeve seam, and the center front. If you are putting in a regular zipper and left the seam allowances, sew up the seam with a long basting stitch. If you eliminated the seam allowances and are putting in a regular zipper, turn the garment inside out, abut the edges, and tape them together on the wrong side. If you are using an industrial zipper, leave open.

If you are sewing by hand, always do any darts first. Then overlap the seams and glue down, but do not sew yet. Treat the center front as you would for machine sewing.

Now glue the appliqués down any way you want. As you can see from the photo, I laid them right across the center front (see Step 1, Fig. S-2). Do the same if you are using a regular zipper with concealed or abutted seams. Later you can cut right through the center of these appliqués (see Step 2, Fig. S-2), sew them down, and insert the zipper, thus forming a continuous design across the center front. You cannot do this with an industrial zipper, however — you can line the edges right up with the appliqués, but can put nothing to extend beyond or actually across the front (unless, of course, you don't mind having the large teeth of a zipper cutting right through the design.)

If you placed appliqués over the center front, you must open up the front seam, slitting right through each appliqué that fell over the

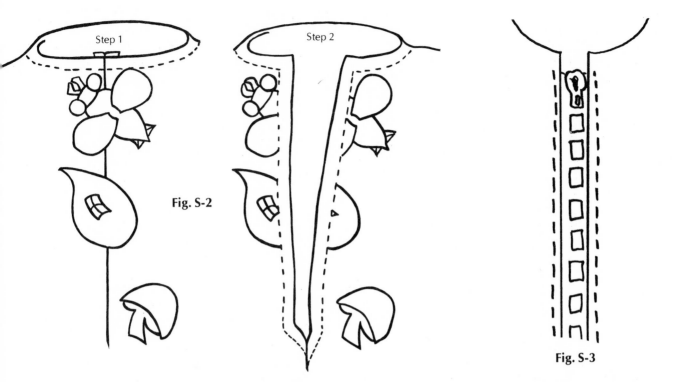

Step 1    Step 2    **Fig. S-2**

**Fig. S-3**

center front seam. Then lay your garment out flat. Be sure that the center front seam allowances, if there are any, extend beyond the seam line of the center (see Step 2, Fig. S-2). If you used traditional seams, glue the rest of the seams open flat. Then sew the appliqués down, either by hand or machine. With machine sewing, sew each section by topstitching ⅛ inch from the edge. With hand sewing, you will be sewing through both seams and appliqués at the same time, so as to avoid bulk and avoid punching through the lacing of a seam, thus pulling it apart. When hand-sewing appliqués of leather to leather, use a small puncher and fine lacing and punch on either side of the raw edges. In fact, different-colored lacings for different appliqués will further enhance the design.

After all are sewn down, put in the zipper. It will extend from ¾ to 1 inch from the neckline to 1½ to 2 inches above the hemline, and will open at the bottom, allowing the entire front to come apart. Therefore, you must either take up the hem before inserting the zipper, or at least mark the hemline so that you can be sure the zipper falls within the proper placement. If you are hand-sewing and want to edge-stitch the front, do so now.

The zipper can be inserted in several different ways, depending on whether you are using an industrial or a regular zipper.

With an industrial, simply take the raw

edges of the dress front, place them against the edge of the teeth (see Fig. S-3), and either topstitch by machine or hand-sew, using a close running stitch or a small careful, cross-stitch. For hand sewing, be sure to punch through both the zipper tape and the leather, but avoid punching holes where some have already been punched for attaching the appliqués. Make allowances for getting around these other stitches by sewing into the same holes. You won't have any of these holes in the zipper tape, however, so push an awl through each hole (push it to one side of the hole to avoid the lacing). Now punch with a hammer if necessary — with wood underneath, of course.

If you are using a regular-sized zipper as opposed to a large industrial zipper, abut the edges of the center front, forming a continuous layer of leather over the front and thus hiding the zipper. If you have eliminated the seam allowances, simply abut the raw edges over the center of the zipper teeth, glue the zipper tape to the wrong side of the leather, and topstitch by hand or machine. You can turn the dress inside out, abut the edges, tape together, and then place the zipper so that the center of the teeth are exactly over the abutted edges.

If you left the seam allowances and are sewing with traditional seams, then sew up the seams with a basting stitch, glue it open flat, and put the zipper down on the leather so that the

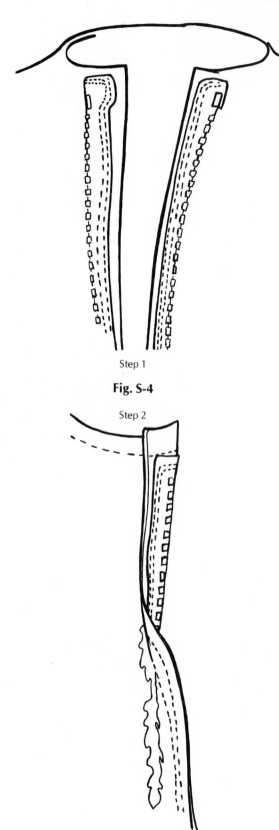

Step 1

**Fig. S-4**

Step 2

teeth are right over the seam. Glue the tape to the inside of the seam allowances and sew in place, either by machine or hand. If you don't want to sew up the seam, then glue the seam allowances down, put the edge of the teeth just on the edge of the opening, and topstitch.

There is another way to put in a zipper so that no stitching shows. Leave the seam allowance, and sew up the center front with a basting stitch. Then instead of gluing down the seam allowances, tape them down with masking tape. Now glue the zipper tape to the taped-down seam allowances, being sure that the teeth are over the center of the seam line. Open the zipper, then undo the seam, remove the tape, and lay the seams open flat with the front of the dress (see Step 1, Fig. S-4). Then machine sew the zipper to the seam allowance, first doing a row of stitching right next to the teeth and then another about ⅛ to ¼ inch away from the first, on the tape. Or you could simply tape the seam allowances down rather than sewing up the seams, glue the zipper down so that the teeth are just inside the edge, and sew. Once the zipper is sewn down, take the center seam allowance of the dress to which you have just added the zipper and glue it down against the inside of the garment with permanent cement, being sure that the zipper teeth never extend beyond the edge of the leather (see Step 2, Fig. S-4).

Once the zipper is done, put on the neckline and front facings. You should use a permanent cement, as it will be glued rather than sewn to the front. To attach the facing you must remove the seam allowances from the center front edge of the facing. Now take the neckline facing with the center front facing attached and sew it to the neckline of the dress only (see Fig. S-5). For hand sewing and edge-stitching, eliminate the seam allowance from the neckline: Simply align the edges wrong side to wrong side and glue together. For machine stitching and overlapped seams, you can also eliminate the seam allowances, glue together, and topstitch ⅛ inch from the edge. If you are using traditional concealed seams, sew the facing to the garment with the correct seam allowances and glue down. Before gluing, clip small notches in on the neckline seam allowances (see Fig. S-6) so that the neckline seam allowances can spread open and thus fit properly against the inside of the garment.

After the neckline facing is attached around

216

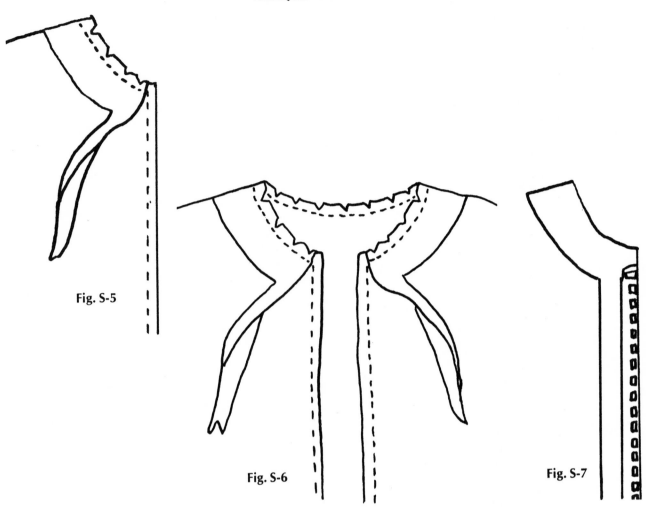

Fig. S-5

Fig. S-6

Fig. S-7

the neckline, you will see that even with the seam allowances removed the front facing extends over the zipper teeth. Therefore you will have to trim it so that it fits just beyond the first row of stitching on the zipper tape (see Fig. S-7). Eliminate about ½ inch on all parts of the facing that fall over the zipper. But do not eliminate anything above the top of the zipper — simply glue down so that it aligns with the front edge just below the neckline. Now glue down the neckline facing and the neckline seam allowances with permanent cement.

Sew up the sleeve seams. Turn up the bottom of the sleeve and add any required finishing touches such as edge-stitching around the neckline and sleeves. Your dress or coat should now be complete.

Of course, there is nothing to stop you from deciding on an overlap and fasteners instead of a zipper for your dress or coat. If you want to use ties, then lay out your garment and overlap the front as indicated on the pattern. Then place your appliqués on the front where you want them, basting the overlapped edges together. Glue the other appliqués to the garment, turn it inside out, fold the inner underlap back, and tape it flat against the inside of the garment. Take scissors and cut along the join line of the now-abutted edges of the overlap and the folded back underlap, cutting straight through the appliqués. Be very careful not to cut any of the leather on the main part of the coat or dress. Your appliqués will now be placed so that when the garment is closed, the design will fall correctly. You can now attach your snaps or ties, being sure to line up the two parts of the appliqué correctly.

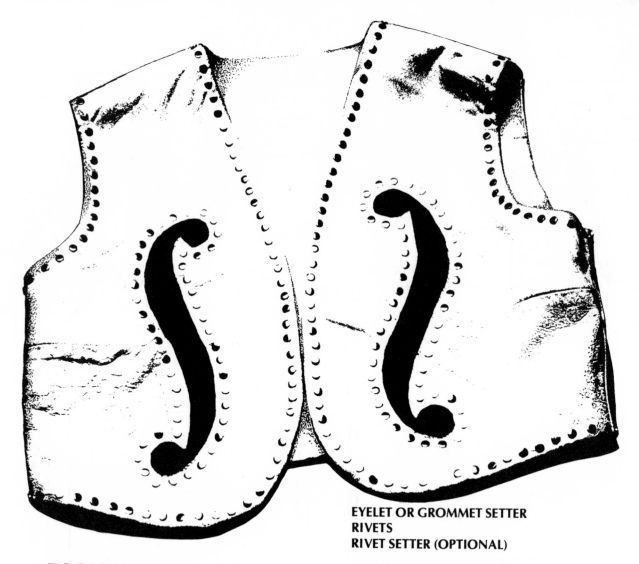

## TOOLS NEEDED

HEAVY BROWN PAPER
GRAPH PAPER, BOTH THE LARGE AND
   SMALL SIZES
DRESSMAKER'S RULER
SHEARS AND SMALL SCISSORS
STUD SETTER
FELT-TIPPED PEN
RUBBER OR LEATHER CEMENT

- **IF YOU DON'T USE THE STUD SETTER:**

AWL OR SMALL DRIVE PUNCH
MALLET
HARDWOOD BOARD
PLIERS

### OPTIONAL

PERMANENT CEMENT
MUSLIN
MASKING TAPE
FOR THE BELT
DRIVE PUNCH
X-ACTO OR UTILITY KNIFE
BUCKLE

EYELET OR GROMMET SETTER
RIVETS
RIVET SETTER (OPTIONAL)

- **FOR MACHINE SEWING**

EVEN-FEED OR WALKING FOOT
   (OPTIONAL BUT HIGHLY
   RECOMMENDED)
HEAVY MERCERIZED THREAD
TISSUE PAPER (OPTIONAL)
GLOVER'S NEEDLES FOR BOTH MACHINE
   AND HAND SEWING
NOTE:  I DON'T RECOMMEND HAND
     SEWING FOR THIS SUIT, BUT IT
     CAN BE USED ON THE VEST.
     FOR THE PANTS, USE THE
     TOOLS LISTED FOR WORKING
     ON DENIM.

- **FOR HAND SEWING (VEST ONLY)**

LACING
HARDWOOD BOARD
MALLET

### OPTIONAL

AWL
LARGE-EYED EMBROIDERY NEEDLE
PLIERS
ROTARY PUNCH

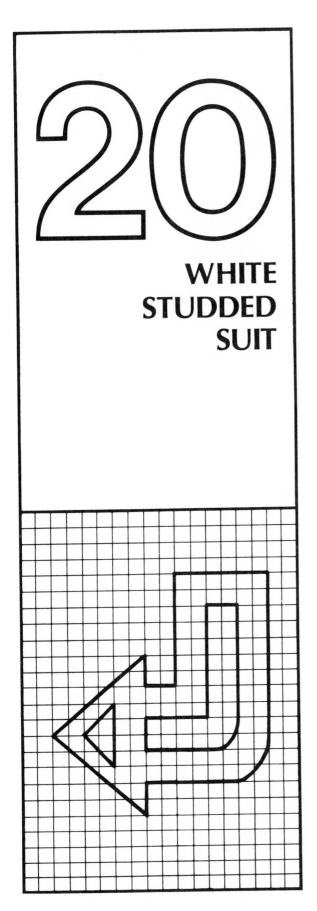

# 20
## WHITE STUDDED SUIT

For the white and red studded suit with the cut-out and underlaid pattern, you must make the entire vest from scratch, and apply leather appliqués to a finished pair of pants, either made by you or store-bought. The suit in the photo is rather spiffy, but it can be made more casual simply by changing the type and color of the leather and pants.

## THE VEST

The type of vest I recommend is a bolero type (see Fig. T-1) that reaches exactly to the waist or just above. It should have a V-shaped neck and should curve at the bottom front. It shouldn't have any front overlap, but should just meet at the center or be slightly apart. This vest can be lined or unlined. If the leather is finished on both sides you need not bother to line. If only one side is finished then it requires lining with a soft fabric. Whether you decide to line or not, you must use facings so that the edges are finished off nicely. You can use traditional concealed, overlapped machine-sewn, or hand-stitched seams, or you can even stud the overlapped seams together. For this vest you can buy a commercial pattern, make one from the pattern made for the fringed vest (Section 14), or make a pattern from a favorite vest in your wardrobe.

If you buy a vest pattern, buy one that fits the above-mentioned type. There should be a ⅝-inch seam allowance around all the outer edges of this vest including the neckline, center front, bottom, and armholes. If there is none, you will need to add a seam allowance. If you are planning on using overlapped seams, adjust the pattern accordingly; if you are going to use traditional concealed seams, leave as is.

If you are using the pattern for the fringed vest, trace around the vest back and front, and down the side seams just to the waistline (which should be marked if you made the other pattern properly). Now connect the two side seams with a straight line. Then draw another line parallel to it, so that you shorten the vest by 1 or 1½ inches. On the front, curve a new front vest bottom to meet the front edge (see Fig. T-2).

Allow a ⅝-inch seam allowance around all the outer edges of the vest. Add the correct allowances for the type of seaming you are planning — ⅝ inch to both edges of the shoulder and side seams for traditional concealed seams, and ⅝ inch on the back shoulder and side seams for overlapped.

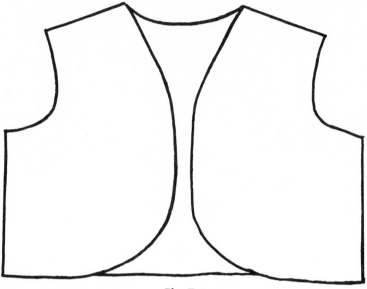

Fig. T-1

Fig. T-2

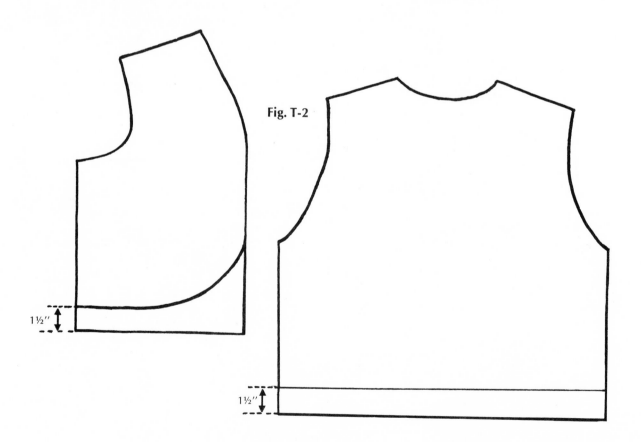

1½″

1½″

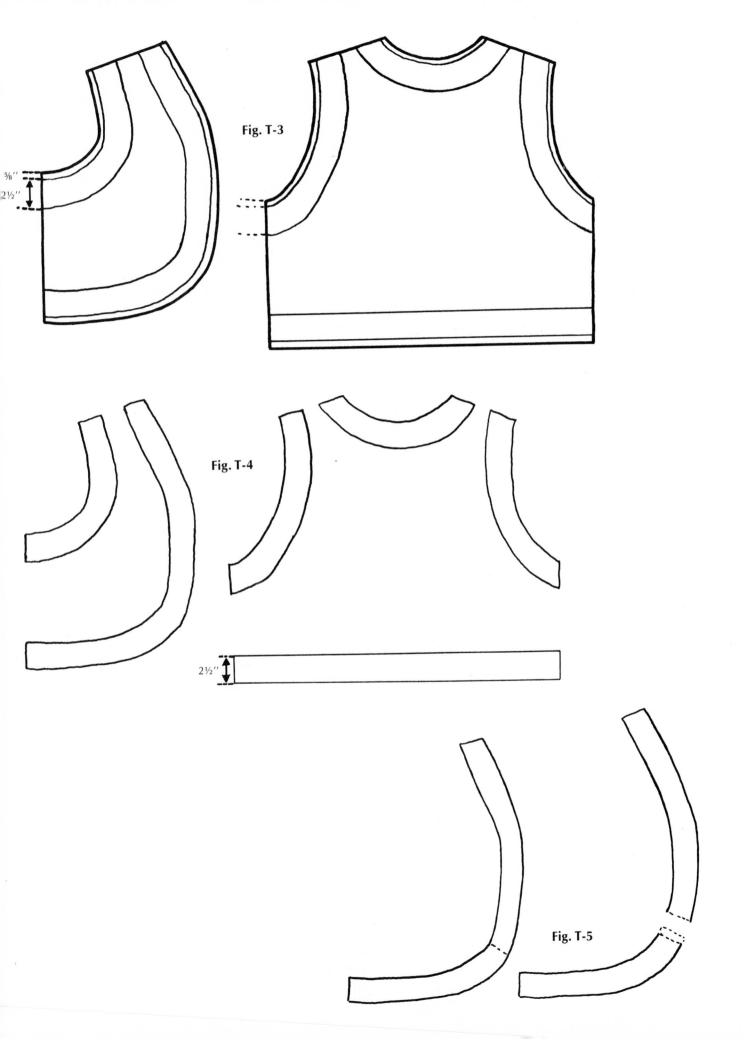

Fig. T-3

⅝″
2½″

Fig. T-4

2½″

Fig. T-5

If you want to make the vest up from a pattern obtained from your own favorite vest, you must make up a muslin copy first and then a regular brown paper pattern. Smooth and pin some muslin across the entire back of your vest as you did for the yoke on the denim jacket. Start from the bottom or on any long straight seam line and pin it to the side seams, bottom of the back, around the neckline, down the shoulders and around the armholes. With a felt-tipped pen, mark along the center of the shoulder seam line, around the neckline, the bottom, side seam line, and the outer armhole opening of the vest. For the front of the vest, start pinning at the center front, then across the shoulder and down the side seam.

You may have to adjust here to allow for a dart on the side if there is one. Working down the seam, smooth and flatten the muslin over the garment where you feel the dart. Pin the muslin along the dart-line seam, being sure it follows the underfabric perfectly.

Mark along this one side of the dart with a felt-tipped pen. Now make a fold in the muslin equivalent to the size of the dart beneath and pin it on top of the other pins. Mark the second side of the dart. Continue pinning the side seams, being sure the muslin is always flat against the original pattern. The muslin should be contouring itself in the same way as the garment beneath. Don't force the muslin by stretching or easing, or it will give the wrong shape to your finished piece.

You will find that darts and other easings and curves will fall automatically in place if you just keep smoothing and pinning and readjusting to fit any changes that occur. Once everything is pinned down, mark with your felt-tipped pen around the outer edges and darts, including the neckline, the side seams, center side front, armholes, and shoulder seams. All this may seem hard to follow, but just try it a few times and you'll soon have the knack of it.

Once this is done, remove the pins and lay out the pattern. Add seam allowances around the outer edges — including the armholes, bottom and center front. Then add seam allowances to the side and shoulder seams according to the type of seaming you are planning, traditional or overlapped.

Now tape these muslin pattern pieces to

brown paper and trace around them for the final draft. Check to make sure seam allowances have been added where necessary. Cut out duplicates for the front pieces, marking the top on each to be sure that you will get reverse duplicates when you cut out the leather. These are the pattern pieces to be used for the vest. Don't forget to transfer all relevant markings such as darts and seam allowances so you can easily transfer them again to the leather.

Whether you are lining or not, you will also need to make facings for the vest. A pattern piece for neckline and front facings comes with commercial patterns. Just eliminate the seam allowances from the outer edges, and they are ready for use. For the bottom facing you may have to construct a facing the same width as the front facing with the seam allowances removed, and long enough to fit around the bottom edge of the vest. Adjust the joining seams on all facing pattern pieces to suit the type of seaming you plan — concealed or overlapped.

If you are copying from a garment or the fringed vest pattern there may be no facings. If not, make up your pattern for the full vest as previously described. Lay it out on brown paper and trace around all the outer edges. Then mark in a ⅝-inch seam allowance around all outer edges. Mark in another 2½ inches measured from the seam allowances just marked. Do this around the neckline, armholes, bottom of the vest, and center front edges, but *not* on the side seams or shoulders (see Fig. T-3). Now cut out the newly made facing pattern pieces — namely the areas between the first inner line marking the ⅝-inch seam allowance to the second line measuring 2½ inches more (see Fig. T-4).

Since you are working from patterns with the inner seam allowances already adjusted for the type of seaming you want, these will be all set and you can just copy as is. Now cut out the appropriate pattern pieces. If you don't want to make a facing out of one piece of leather that extends around the entire front, then cut it at whatever points seem most convenient for saving leather, and add the appropriate seam allowance to this join (see Fig. T-5).

If you want to line the vest, take the part that remains after cutting out the facing patterns. Use this as the basis for a lining pattern. Take these center pieces left from the full pattern

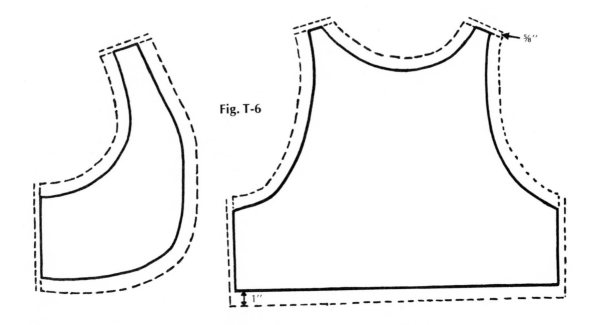

**Fig. T-6**

pieces and tape them down on another piece of brown paper. Trace around them, then remove. Add an extra 1-inch allowance around the outer edges. Do this for the back and both sides of the front (see Fig. T-6). In addition, if your original pattern was made for overlapped shoulder and side seams, readjust them for traditional concealed seams.

## THE PANTS

If you are using dress pants, make sure they are good ones with a certain amount of body, since they must hold leather on the bottom. For a suit like the one I made, use the soft kid-type leather. If you are using more casual pants, or even rougher jeans, take your choice of whatever type of leather you want. The pants, leather appliqués, and insets can be of whatever colors you like best. However, I like to make the insets match whatever shirt or sweater I intend to wear with the outfit. For example, if you are using bleached-out dungarees, use navy for the vest and the gussets, and make the underlays under the cutouts red, green, or orange.

To make the pattern for the V-shaped gusset inset of the bottom of the pants, use the same procedures as for the dungaree suit. You can use two different-sized gussets, one reaching only half to three-quarters of the way up the calf and the other higher up on the leg to just below the

knee where you can feel that spherical bone on the side of your leg when you bend it. Take a tape measure and measure from this point straight down the leg to the base of the foot. If you wear your pants shorter or longer, deduct or add accordingly. On brown paper, draw a straight line 14 or 10 inches lone — 14 inches for the high gusset and 10 inches for the low — and mark the ends of these measurements. Then mark the center of this line. Draw a line at right angles to the base from this point and mark the desired length — 14 inches high on the 10-inch base or the length to your knee on the 14-inch base. Then draw lines forming the sides of the triangle by connecting the two marks on the base to this point (see Fig. Q-1).

You could, of course, use this same principle to make it whatever height and width you want. A good rule to follow here is higher and wider for dress and show, and lower and narrower for casual or conservative. If you find your base is too wide for the pants bottom, then undo the seam or mark and slit the jeans as you would if you were using straight legs on the dungaree suit. Slit to about three-quarters the height of the center line and spread to the desired width (see Fig. Q-9).

**The Waistband Or Belt** — If you want to replace the waistband of the pants with a studded leather one, simply remove the existing band and put it aside. To make the new pattern, measure around the top of the pants along the

223

stitching line where the waistband was connected to them and add ⅝ inch to either end. (Don't use the waistband itself as the pattern, because it is the wrong length for the new leather one.) The width of the band will be 3¼ inches if you plan to use traditional concealed seams, and 2 inches if you are using overlapped seams for sewing or studding. To make this pattern, measure and construct a strip whose length is equal to the size of the waistline seam of the original pants, plus 1¼ inches. For the backing of this leather waistband you will be using grosgrain ribbon 2 to 2½ inches wide and the length of the waistband plus 4½ inches.

If you are using hip-huggers or don't have a waistband, you can make a new belt using your own favorite belt as the pattern. (It is a good idea to make a brown paper pattern from this belt, however, so that you can reuse it whenever a belt is needed.) Use a belt with a buckle such as that illustrated in Fig. T-7, and of the same color metal as the studs being used. Lay this belt out on brown paper and trace around it just to the buckle. Then measure the flap holding the buckle in place, and the small piece under the buckle that you missed. Extend the sides of the belt this much longer, and join the ends. Now transfer all relevant markings from the original belt, including such things as holes and the placement of the buckle. When marking the buckle placement, indicate the oblong hole for the tongue of the buckle, and also the placement of the rivets joining the flap that holds the buckle (see Fig. T-8). When you cut out this pattern be sure you cut on the inside of the lines, or else it will be the wrong width. From this pattern you will need to cut one piece of the soft leather used in the vest and pants, and a heavier piece for a backing. Transfer all relevant markings such as the placement of such hardware as required on the belt.

Now cut out your leather for the whole outfit. You should cut out a vest back, two reverse duplicates for the front of the vest, facings for the

armholes, neckline, front edges, and bottom of the vest frokt and back. You will also need to cut a waistband or a soft leather version of the belt and a heavier leather backing — a not-too-heavy pliable cowhide split will do, as it will be reinforced by a second layer. In addition, cut two V-shaped gussets for the outer edges of the pants bottom.

Once these leather pieces are cut, sew up the rough outline of the vest — namely the shoulder seams, side seams, and dart.

First sew the darts if there are any. Machine sew by folding along the center of the dart and sewing along the dart lines from the base to the point. If you are hand-sewing, cut out the dart completely to the sewing lines. Abut the edges, put a strip under these abutted edges, punch, and sew. Then do the shoulder and side seams with traditional concealed seams, overlap and topstitch with double machine stitching, hand-stitch with lacing the color of the underlay, or just overlap and stud through both layers, thus joining the vest back and front together. This overlap should be ⅝ inch and can be either from the front or the back, but should always be so that the side of the seam with the seam allowance added forms the underlap. Mark the overlap edge on the wrong side with a ⅝ inch seam, align the raw edge of the underlap to this mark, and glue. Then sew or stud.

**The Cutouts and Underlays** — Now cut out your designs on your leather pieces, and prepare your underlays. The diagrams show exactly how each piece is decorated. The first step in this process is to do the cutouts. These can be in any shape, colors, or position. (I have used a violin S-shaped cutout surrounded by studding, which gives a certain amount of traditional style.)

The pattern for the cutout on the vest is in Fig. T-9, and for the pants in Fig. T-10. The pattern part to be underlaid is in Fig. T-11 for the vest, and the pattern for the pants in Fig. T-12. Enlarge these patterns onto 1 inch graph paper as

**Fig. T-7**

**Fig. T-8**

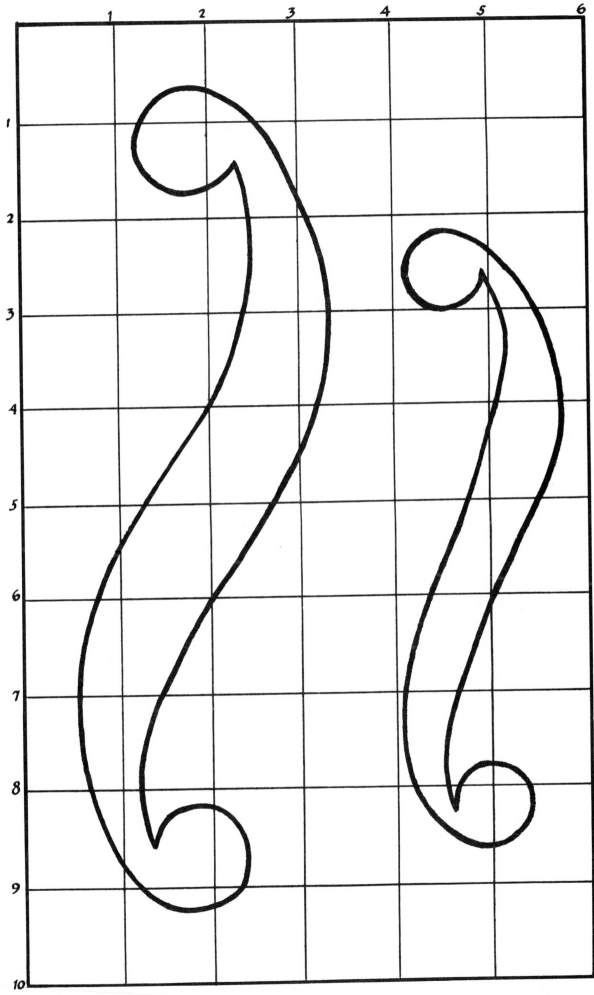

**Fig. T-9**

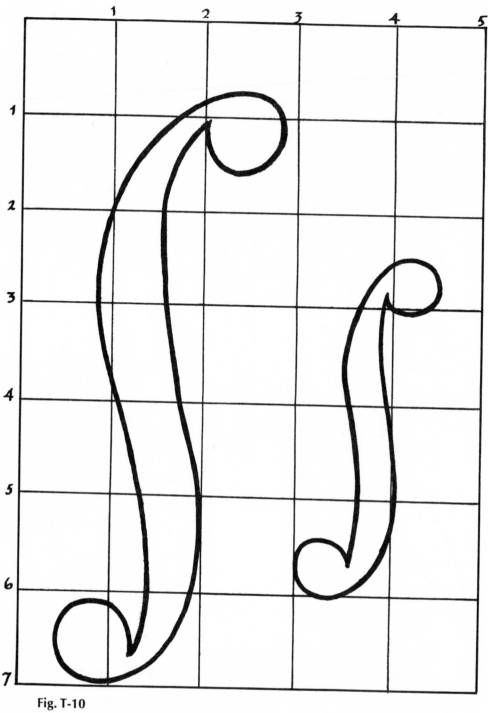

Fig. T-10

226

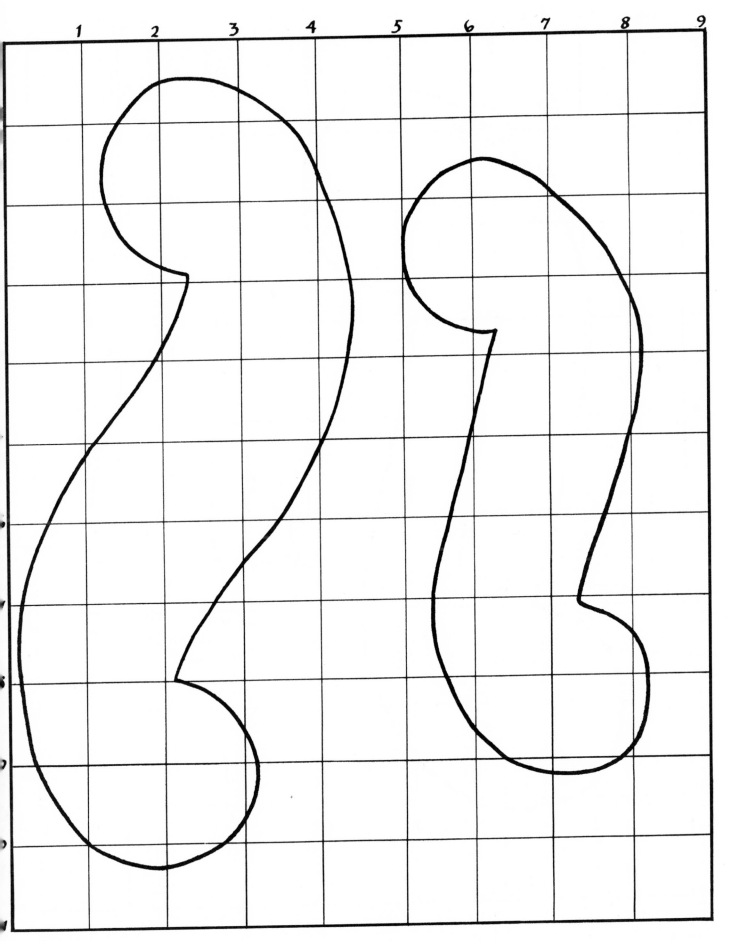

Fig. T-11

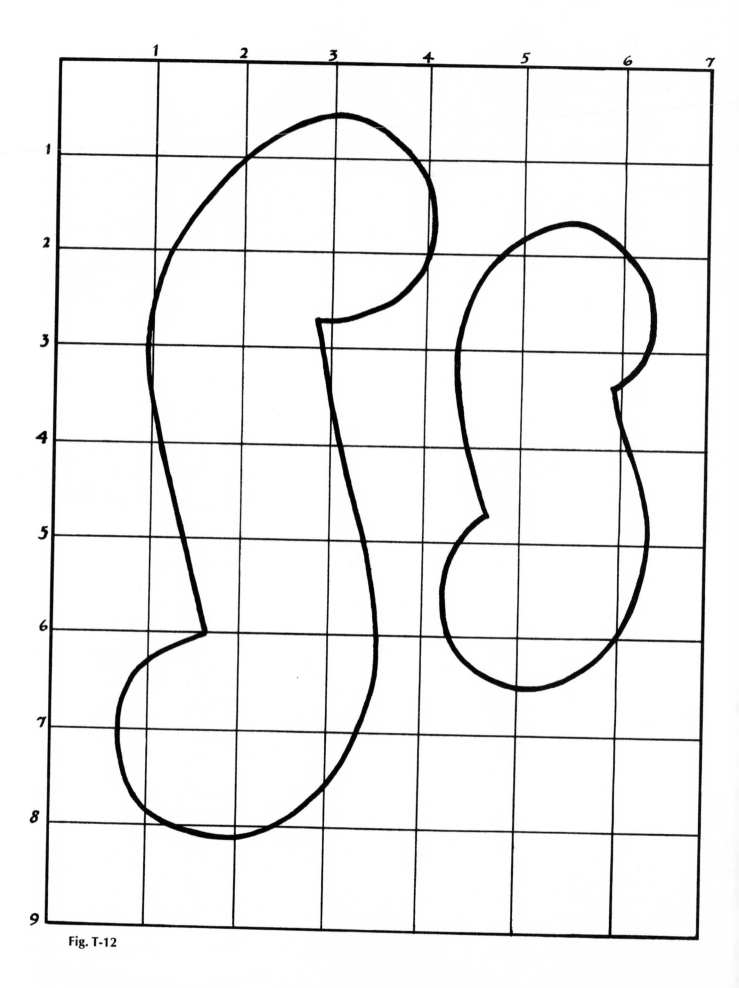

Fig. T-12

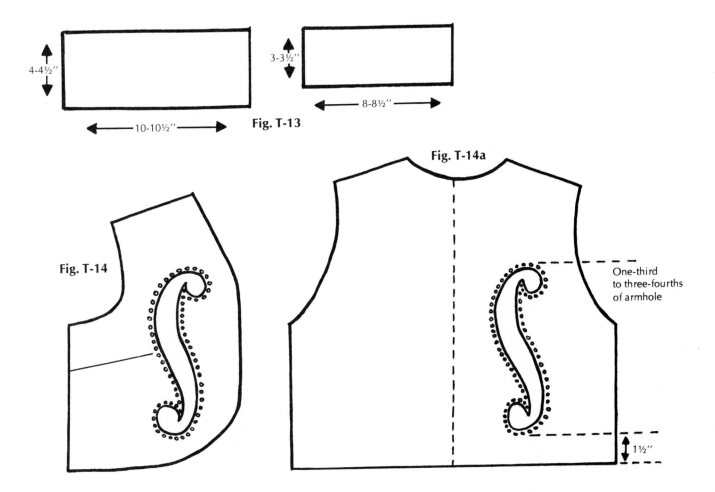

Fig. T-13

Fig. T-14

Fig. T-14a

One-third
to three-fourths
of armhole

1½''

4-4½''

10-10½''

3-3½''

8-8½''

you would with any other designs. Be very careful here to make sure the line shape within each square corresponds exactly with that in the smaller graph paper. You are dealing with a very exact pattern with small, precise curves. The underlay pattern is the exact same size as the cutout pattern, but with ⅝ to ¾ inch added all around the outer edges. Cut out a pattern to correspond to the desired shape, lay it down on another piece of brown paper, trace around it, and remove. Add a ⅝ to ¾ inch seam allowance all around this second piece, which becomes the pattern for the underlay. Mark which pattern piece is for the cutout and which for the underlay so there is no confusion.

Another — and perhaps easier — way to make underlays for this pattern is to cut out rectangular pieces of leather 4 to 4½ inches wide and 10 to 10½ inches long for the vest and 3 to 3½ inches wide and 8 to 8½ inches long for the V inset (see Fig. T-13). To find out the size of the square or rectangle required to underlay, measure the widest point of the design, adding 1½ inches. Then measure the longest point and add another 1½ inches.

The cutouts on my design are positioned so that they fall in the approximate center of either side of the front (see Fig. T-14). Be sure they don't interfere with the dart if you have one, and place them so that they fall just beyond the point of the dart. On the back mark the center back, and place one cutout on either side of this center back mark (see Fig. T-14a). This means that the cutouts will start anywhere from three-quarters to one-third up the armhole and extend to at least 1½ inches up from the bottom of the vest. These measurements will vary slightly according to your size. On the pants gussets, place the cutouts on either side of the center, and if necessary point the tops of the S shapes inward toward each other so they fit into the allotted area.

Be sure that the direction of the S shapes is reversed on either side of the back, the two sides of the front, and either side of the V-shaped gusset for the pants. Before cutting, be sure the leather is marked properly, with the cutouts correctly indicated. Once you are sure the cutout designs are laid out and marked properly, cut them out from the leather, keeping the edges as smooth as possible. (I like to use small, sharp scissors here.) Then mark a ⅝ inch seam allowance around the outer edges of each cutout design — on the wrong side of the leather, of course.

Now cut out the underlays from scraps. With a brush and rubber cement — or permanent cement if you are not going to sew and are very careful — brush glue over the ⅝ inch seam allowance area marked around each cutout. Do one at a time. Press the underlay into place carefully so that the overlay shape is not distorted. The cutout leather must keep its shape as it is pressed against the underlay. Once all is glued and dry, you can sew all around the raw edges of the cutout, reinforcing the glue.

For the studding you will need about 420 size 15 studs for the vest, 14 size 30 and 40 size 15 for the belt or waistband, and 296 size 15 for the bottom of the pants. (Size 15 is approximately ⅜ inch in diameter and size 30 approximately ⅝ inch.) Stud around the outer edges of these cutouts, spacing them so that the center of each stud is ¼ inch from the edge and ½ inch from the next stud. The size stud used here is a 15. Trim the underlays to a neat shape around the wrong side of the cutouts after they are studded, especially if you are not lining. Use the same small studs around the outer edges of the vest.

Remember there are ⅝ inch seam allowances around the entire vest. This seam allowance should already be marked, but if not, mark it now. Mark the placement of the studs ¼ inch in from this seam line and ½ inch apart — this is center stud to center stud and edge to center

stud (⅞ inch in from the raw edge and ½ inch apart) — on the wrong side around all the outer edges including the neckline, center fronts, bottom and armholes (see Fig. T-15).

Once the cutouts, underlays, and studding around them is done, then apply the gusset triangle to the pants, as on the denim suit. If you are sewing, finish the outer seams with a double row of stitching. Then stud between these rows as you did for the denim suit. Or if you prefer, just stud the gusset in place along the two long sides of the triangle. Space the studs ½ inch apart and ¼ inch in from the edge of the leather.

On the wrong side of the outer edge of the facings for the armholes, neckline, center front, and bottom, mark a ⅝ inch seam allowance (see Fig. T-16). Join the seams of the facings by traditional concealed, overlapped and topstitched, or overlapped and glued with a permanent or heavy rubber cement. If you used traditional seams, glue the seam allowances flat.

If you are not lining, then after joining the seams, overlap the vest facing over the vest just to the marked ⅝ inch seam allowance. Glue the right side of the vest just to the seam allowance line all around the outer edges, so that the facing overlaps the seam allowance of the vest body on the right side. Now machine stitch ⅛ to ¼ inch from the outer edge of the facing, thus connecting the facing to the garment around the armholes and other outer edges of the vest. Glue down the facing, folding along the line marking the ⅝ inch seam allowance on the vest body. This will give body to the edges of the vest so that it falls nicely and has a neat finish.

If you are lining the vest, use a soft fabric. Cut out a back and two reversed front pieces. Sew up traditional seams for the shoulders and sides and press them open. Then mark a ½ inch seam allowance on the *inner* edge of the facing (see Fig. T-17). Sew the lining to the facing with traditional concealed seams, placing the lining and facing right side to right side. Align the raw edges and stitching along the marked seam allowances. Or press down a ½ inch seam allowance around the entire outer edge of the lining. Topstitch the lining to the facing by aligning the raw edges and sewing through the leather and the two layers of lining. Attach the facing to the inside of the vest. First glue down the seam allowances around the outer edge. Then brush

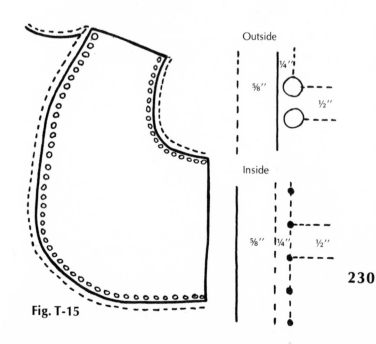

**Fig. T-15**

Outside

¼''

⅝''

½''

Inside

⅝''  1¼''  ½''

**230**

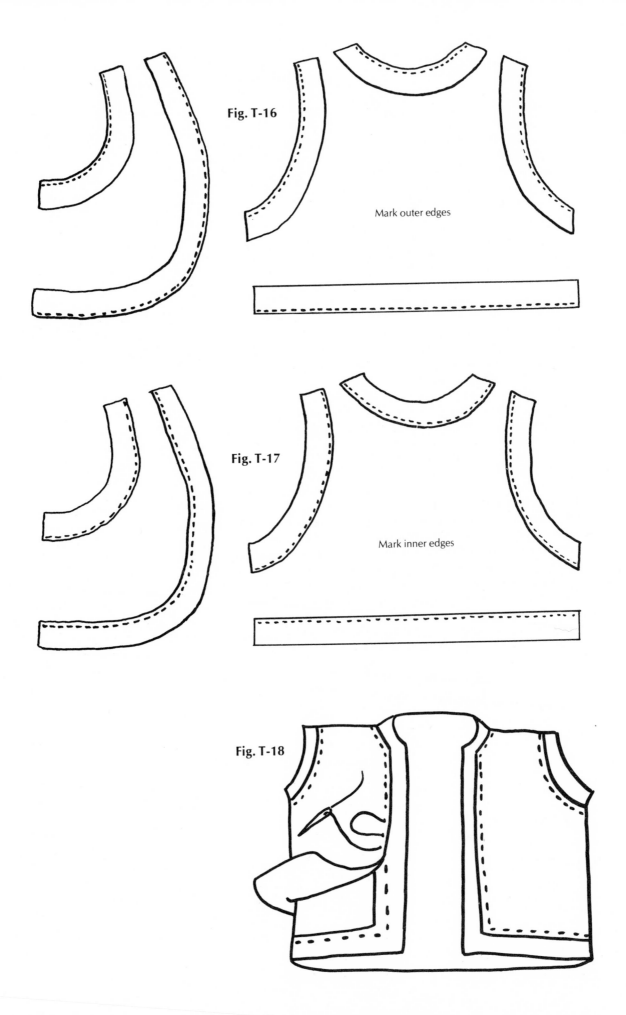

**Fig. T-16**

Mark outer edges

**Fig. T-17**

Mark inner edges

**Fig. T-18**

glue thickly, evenly, and smoothly, on the leather facing and press it carefully around the inside of the outer edges of the vest, being sure you align the edges or put the facing in ⅛ inch from the edge.

If you are not putting any studs near the edge, or if you can stitch very easily close to the edge, align the edges and topstitch around the entire outer edges and armholes by machine or hand. Or if you prefer, you can even wait to stud until after the lining and facing are done. This way, you will attach straight through both the vest and its facing.

Another way to secure the lining — the method I used — is to attach the facing as if it were an unlined vest. Iron down the seam allowances on the outer edges of the lining toward the inside, raw-edged side. Then machine stitch without thread, perforating the leather at ½ inch along the inner edge of the facing. Then hand-sew the lining to the leather facing through the already-made holes (see Fig. T-18).

If you are replacing the waistband with a studded leather one, stud only through the soft leather of the top, following the diagram in Fig. T-19. If you are using seam allowances, mark them around all outer edges. Now take a ruler and draw three parallel lines evenly spaced ½ inch apart and ½ inch from either edge along the length of the band. Draw vertical lines intersecting these three at right angles, 1 inch apart and ¼ inch from either end. (These measurements, of course, are exclusive of the already-marked seam allowances, if there are any.) Place the studs at the intersecting points of these lines, following the pattern. Once the design is completed, attach this new waistband to the pants with ½ to ⅝ inch extra on either end. Sew along these lines to join the band to the pants with traditional seams. If you have no seam allowances, align the band's edge along the actual seam line on the pants and machine stitch ⅛ inch from the edges to attach it to the pants. For the back of the band, you now need a piece of grosgrain ribbon the length of the band plus ½ inch on one end and 4 inches on the other.

If you are using seam allowances, overlap the ribbon to the seam allowance on the top of the band, aligning the edges of the front end. Topstitch ⅛ inch from the edge of the ribbon to attach it to the leather. Now take the ribbon and

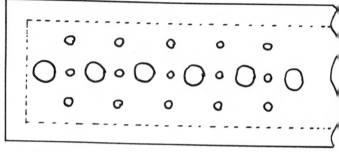

Fig. T-19

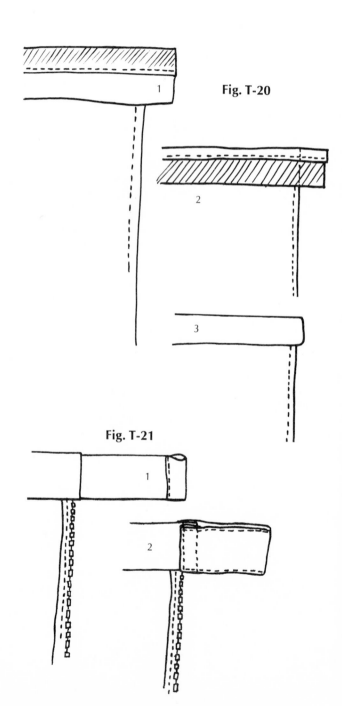

Fig. T-20

Fig. T-21

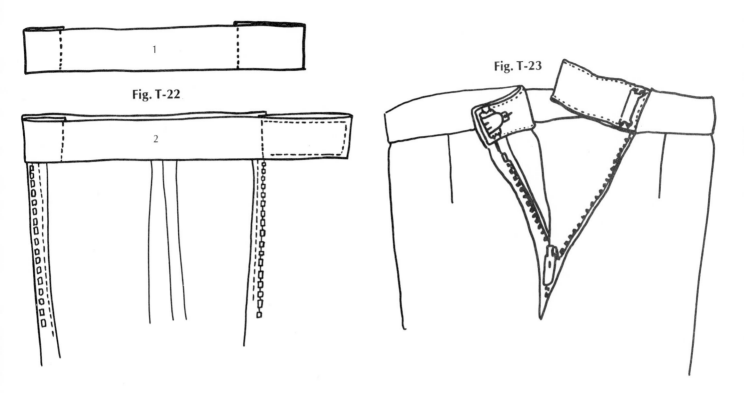

Fig. T-22

Fig. T-23

fold it over the right side of the band. Sew a ½-inch seam on the front end, then turn it back (see Fig. T-20). Turn under a ½-inch seam on the other end of the ribbon, overlap it over the top of the band, and topstitch through all the layers. Then edge-stitch along the ribbon underlap, thus joining the two layers there together (see Fig. T-21).

If you have no seam allowances, then turn the grosgrain ribbon under ½ inch on the front end of the ribbon and 2½ inches on the other end, and sew down. Align the ribbon's edges with the leather and topstitch ⅛ inch from the top edge (be sure to align the front end of the leather band with the end that has the ½ inch turned under). Topstitch across the ends joining the backing to the leather. Then glue the grosgrain against the back of the band and slip stitch it along the bottom to attach it to the material of the pants (see Fig. T-22). Use large industrial-type heavy-duty fasteners (see Fig. T-23) and sew them only to the grosgrain band. Then when you hook them together, the top layer of the leather will simply abut at the side, and an extra piece of grosgrain will form the underlap.

For all garments with waistbands, this is the neatest method and it prevents bulk around the waist. You will find that a good permanent

leather cement eliminates the need for much sewing and is a good work-saver if applied properly in spots like this.

**Belt** — To make a belt, use the same principles as for the waistband: Stud first, then overlap the thin leather to a heavier back leather with permanent cement. Mark and stud within an area starting 1½ inches after the last hole and 1½ inches from where the buckle will end (see Fig. T-24). Use the same patterns and measurements you would for the waistband, but confine it to the studding area. Once the studding design is complete, glue this soft leather to a base of heavier leather to act as a backing. The base should be made from the exact same pattern as the top. If you have room around the outer edges, stitch by machine or hand around the outer edges. Now punch holes where marked. If you copied the information from your original pattern correctly, this should all be marked on the leather.

To attach the buckle to the belt, mark a dot to indicate where the buckle tongue is to pass through the leather. If you do not have this marked, go back to the original belt from which you took your pattern and measure the distance from the buckle end of the belt to the hole hold-

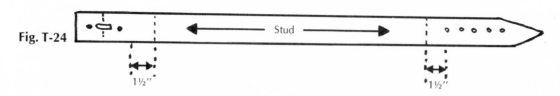

Fig. T-24     Stud

1½"                      1½"

ing the tongue. Mark this point on your belt. Punch an oblong punch here to make the hole, or with a round punch make two holes overlapping to form a single, longer hole. Then mark a dot (or two dots ½ inch apart) on either end of the hole at the distance of the placement of the rivets holding the flap, which holds the buckle in place. Punch holes the size of the rivets being used over these dots. Thread the straight end of the belt through the buckle, and place the tongue of the buckle into the large hole made for it. Pull the belt down through the other side of the buckle. Then fasten the flap formed here to the belt with a rivet or two. (If you have no rivets, the top half of a snap will do as well.)

**Rivets**    Rivets are what are found on dungarees to hold the corners of pockets together for added strength; they are commonly used as permanent fasteners in leather. They generally join the leather wrong side to wrong side, but can join wrong side to right side such as when at-

taching handles. A rivet setter is available, but is not a necessary tool.

A rivet comes in two parts (see Fig. T-25) and in various sizes. To apply it, you must punch a hole through the two or more layers of leather to be joined. Insert the part with the point (B) into the hole in the bottom piece of leather. Then place the second piece of leather on top of it, so that the rivet point sticks through the hole in the second layer. Place the other part (A) of the rivet over this point, and press down firmly. Then turn the work over on a flat metal surface — even a coin — so that the point of part B is now pointing down toward part A of the rivet. Then hammer the rivet in place with a metal hammer.

Once these rivets are set and the buckle thus secured, you can go back and put eyelets or grommets of the correct size through the holes made at the beginning of the belt to further enforce the join of the soft and heavier leather backing (they are going to get a lot of wear).

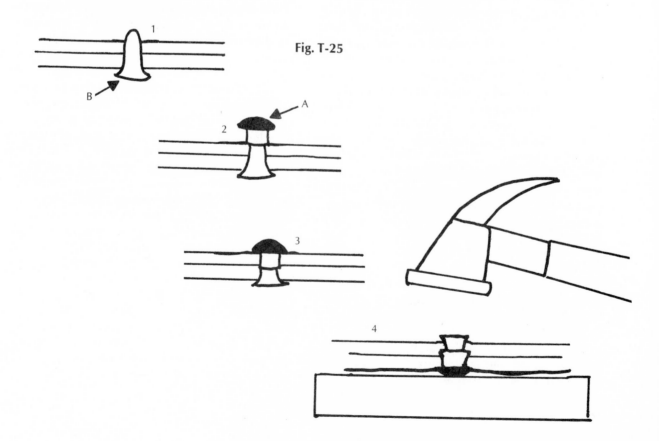

Fig. T-25

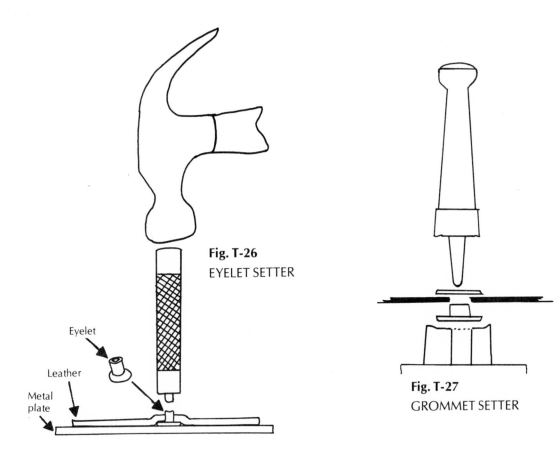

**Fig. T-26**
EYELET SETTER

Eyelet

Leather

Metal
plate

**Fig. T-27**
GROMMET SETTER

**Eyelets —** Eyelets or grommets are indispensable reinforcements for the holes punched in leather to prevent them from ripping or stretching out of shape. Eyelets consist of one piece and are for more lightweight purposes, whereas grommets are for more heavy-duty use.

You will need a tool to insert the eyelet — either of two types of pliers for lightweight leather, and a hammer and anvil type for all leathers, heavy or lightweight. They are both minimally priced and readily available; if you can't find them, send to a mail-order supplier listed in the Appendix.

To put in an eyelet, mark where you want it, and punch a hole as big as or a little smaller than the eyelet's inner hole. (Match this hole up with your puncher to be sure it is correct.) Push the eyelet through the leather from the right side. If the leather is not too thick, place the plier applicator over the eyelet as if you were using a rotary punch, and press to set.

If you are using a heavier leather or if you just prefer the hammer and anvil setter as I do (see Fig. T-26), then turn the leather over after the eyelet is put into the hole. Place it right side

down on a very hard surface such as metal. Place the eyelet setter into the eyelet from the wrong side of the leather. Hit it with your rawhide mallet and hammer down to set it.

**Grommets —** Grommets are like two-piece eyelets, but larger and used for heavier purposes. To insert them, you will need a grommet setter (see Fig. T-27). This tool is also minimally priced and well worth the investment.

To insert a grommet, punch a hole the size of the grommet hole in the leather. Place the larger half of the grommet into the base of the grommet setter. Place the leather right side down so the hole is right over the grommet. Now place the smaller half of the grommet into the hole. Place the top of the grommet setter over this smaller part and hit it sharply with a rawhide mallet, driving it into its larger mate.

Make sure the eyelets, grommets, buckle, and rivets match the metal color of your studs. Use this same technique of belt-making for all belts, but generally you will use only a thick single layer of leather.

235

# APPENDIX

## WHERE TO BUY SUPPLIES FOR WORKING WITH LEATHER

This is just a partial list of all the many fine suppliers throughout the country. They carry most of the supplies needed for making the items described in this book.

**Catalogs of leather and/or supplies** — First send for the catalogs suggested. Then call the tanners listed in your area in the catalog from the Tanner's Council. If they don't sell retail, ask them for a list of the retail outlets near you. Be persistent — they will tell you if you ask nicely. Also check your local directory for leather suppliers, and, if you don't find any, check the phone directory of the large city nearest to where you live. If you can't find any place to buy leather nearby, contact any of the mail-order suppliers listed below — if they provide a catalog, get it.

### Deerskin Products
Little Delaware Rte. 28,
Delhi, N. Y. 13753
This company deals exclusively in deerskin hides. They sell by the hide, but since hides here can run as small as 10 square feet to much larger, you have a wide range. Send a stamped self-addressed envelope with any queries so they can easily send pertinent information. Quality here is excellent.

### Leathercrafter's Supply Company
25 Great Jones Street
New York, N. Y. 10012
A catalog here costs one dollar, but it contains a listing of a complete selection of excellent quality tools, glues (including rubber and Barge's All-Purpose permanent cement), findings, other accessories, and such skins as deerskin splits, chamois and chamois patchwork, garment cowhides, and a limited amount of buffalo.

### MacPherson Brothers Leather Company
730 Polk Street
San Francisco, Calif. 94109
This company deals in numerous types of leather

and is a well-known and popular company. They sell garment cowhide, sheepskin, suede, lightweight kidskin, and kid suede and have a large mail-order business. Their catalog is a good reference and you can also go to their retail outlet at the same address (or another one at 200 South Los Angeles Street, Los Angeles, Calif. 90015). They also carry a complete line of tools, leathers, and other accessories.

### Minerva Leather Company, Inc.
78 Spring Street
New York, N. Y. 10012
This company deals in most of the leathers you will normally need — garment, cowhide, cabretta, splits, suedes, kid, lambskin and many more too numerous to name. Send for their catalog, which has a complete listing of all kinds of leathers. "Big Sam" Rubin is the man to contact here — he knows all about leather and is just the man who can really help you find the best leather for your projects.

### Tandy Leather Company, Inc.
P. O. Box 79
Fort Worth, Texas 76101
This catalog contains a listing of Tandy's over 100 retail outlets throughout the country plus a mail-order form for supplies. It has a complete selection of tools, leather, glues, snaps, rivets, and in fact just about everything needed for working leather.

### Tanners' Council of America
411 Fifth Avenue
New York, N. Y. 10016
This catalog has a list of all the tanneries throughout the U. S. and the types of leather they deal with. Some of them have retail outlets. Call the ones near you for information. These tanneries basically aren't retail outlets, but some of them have retail outlets attached and if they don't they can tell you where you can purchase leather in your area.

237

**Beads** — Large-hole beads (such as tubular squaw beads) and seed beads are generally available in sewing, notion, or hobby stores. If you can't find them, contact:

**Glori Bead Shoppe**
172 West 4th Street
New York, N.Y. 10014

**Plume Trading Corp.**
155 Lexington Avenue
New York, N.Y. 10016

**Plume Trading Corp.**
P. O. #585
Monroe, N. Y. 10950
Besides the real glass Indian beads, tubular squaw, and seed beads, this company also deals in all Indian artifacts. It is a fascinating little store, but if you are shopping in person, be advised that it is open only on Wednesday and Saturday, 10:00 A.M. to 5:30 P.M.

**Tandy Leather Company, Inc.** (see *Leather*)

(Or any of the over 100 retail outlets) They deal with plastic imitation-glass Indian beads, tubular squaw and seed beads.

**Cement** — Rubber and leather cements — permanent or otherwise — are generally available in hobby, hardware, stationery, or sewing stores. If you can't find any, send to:

**Barge Cement Division of National Starch & Chemical Co.**
100 Jacksonville Rd.
Towaco, New Jersey 07082
This is the manufacturer of Barge's All-Purpose Cement.

**Sobo Glue**
Slomon's Laboratories
Long Island City, N. Y. 11101

**Leathercrafter's Supply Co.** (see *Leather*)

**Tandy Leather Company** (see *Leather*)

**Director's chairs**    These chairs are usually available in most department stores. If you can't find them, contact:

**Neal Schwartzberg**
**Dallek Inc.**
534 Broadway
N.Y., N.Y. 10012

**Findings and fasteners**    (Eyelets, Grommets, Rivets, Snaps, and Buckles) These are available in most notion and sewing stores, but if you can't find them there, send to:

**Leathercrafter's Supply Co.** (see *Leather*)

**MacPherson Brothers Leather Co.** (see *Leather*)

**Sure Snap Corp.**
49 West 36th Street
New York, N.Y. 10018

**Tandy Leather Co.** (see *Leather*)

**Graph paper** — Small graph paper can be purchased in most stationery stores. Large graph paper comes in large pads called Lecture Pads which contain about fifty 27 by 34 inch sheets of 1 inch graph squares. These can be purchased in most large art supply stores or well-stocked stationery stores. (Specify 1 inch square graph Lecture Pads when you purchase it.) Another way you can get large graph paper is in large rolls from sewing stores. If you can't find it, ask the store to order it for you. Otherwise, contact:

**Grand Central Artist's Materials, Inc.**
18 East 40th Street
New York, N.Y. 10016
This store has the large 1 inch graph Lecture Pads and has assured me that they will mail them to anyone who can't get them in their area. Contact them for prices.

**Sewmaker's Inc.**
1614 Grand Avenue
Baldwin, N.Y. 11510
This company sells by the sheet rather than by the pad, but please write to them for exact details.

**Hand-sewing tools** — (Punches, Mallets, Glover's Needles, etc.) Consult your phone book for leather craft and hobby shops. Otherwise — for a very large selection — check your catalogs and contact:

**Leathercrafter's Supply Co.** (see *Leather*)

**MacPherson Brothers Company** (see *Leather*)

**Tandy Leather Co.** (see *Leather*)

**Sewing machine accessories** — (Needles, Special Sewing Feet, and Thread) These can be found in most sewing and notion stores, or can be ordered by them. Otherwise for information check the catalogs or contact:

**The Singer Co.**
30 Rockefeller Plaza
New York, N.Y. 10020
This company manufactures a walking foot, called an even-feed foot.

**Studs and Studding Machines** — First check the local sewing and hobby stores to see if they are available. If you can't find them, contact:

**Sheru**
49 West 38th Street
New York, N.Y. 10018
They carry a small machine, good as a second machine because it can get into tight spots such as pants legs. But it is not as stable or versatile as the one sold by:

**A.H. Standard Co., Inc.**
28 West 38th Street
New York, N. Y. 10018
This company manufactures the Brisk-set Nail Head Stapler. This machine accepts different-size heads for different-size studs and is convertible into a rhinestone setter. It is an excellent machine. I have used it and recommend it readily.

**Zippers**    Most sewing, notion, or hobby stores carry a supply of different types of zippers. If you can't find what you want consult your phone directory for a zipper manufacturer or contact:

**Talon, Inc.**
43 East 51st Street
New York, N.Y. 10022
This is a large manufacturer of zippers and may be able to direct you to a supplier.

# INDEX